NEXEN IS PLEASED
TO PRESENT YOU
WITH THIS 2010/2011
SHORTLISTED BOOK.

The DONNER Prize

Le Prix DONNER

Beyond the Indian Act

Beyond the Indian Act

RESTORING ABORIGINAL PROPERTY RIGHTS

Tom Flanagan
Christopher Alcantara
André Le Dressay

McGill-Queen's University Press
Montreal & Kingston | London | Ithaca

© McGill-Queen's University Press 2010
ISBN 978-0-7735-3686-9

Legal deposit first quarter 2010
Bibliothèque nationale du Québec

Reprinted 2011

Printed in Canada on acid-free paper that is 100% ancient forest free
(100% post-consumer recycled), processed chlorine free

This book has been published with the help of a grant from the Canadian
Federation for the Humanities and Social Sciences, through the Aid to
Scholarly Publications Programme, using funds provided by the Social
Sciences and Humanities Research Council of Canada.

McGill-Queen's University Press acknowledges the support of the Canada
Council for the Arts for our publishing program. We also acknowledge the
financial support of the Government of Canada through the Book Publishing
Industry Development Program (BPIDP) for our publishing activities.

LIBRARY AND ARCHIVES CANADA CATALOGUING IN PUBLICATION

Flanagan, Tom
Beyond the Indian Act : restoring aboriginal property rights / Tom Flanagan,
Christopher Alcantara, André Le Dressay.

Includes bibliographical references and index.
ISBN 978-0-7735-3686-9

1. Aboriginal title – Canada.   2. Indians of North America – Land tenure –
Canada.   3. Indians of North America – Legal status, laws, etc. – Canada.
4. Native peoples – Land tenure – Canada.   5. Native peoples – Legal status,
laws, etc. – Canada.   I. Alcantara, Christopher, 1978–   II. Le Dressay,
André, 1964–   III. Title.

KE7739.L3F53 2010   346.7104'3208997   C2009-907268-8

Set in 10.5/13.5 Sabon with Scala Sans
Book design & typesetting by Garet Markvoort, zijn digital

CONTENTS

Foreword   vii
Manny Jules

Acknowledgments   xv

Introduction   3

PART ONE | PEOPLES AND PROPERTY

1 Property Rights in General   13

2 The Panorama of Indian Property Rights   30

3 A Failed Experiment: The Dawes Act   42

PART TWO | LIMITED PROPERTY RIGHTS
UNDER THE INDIAN ACT

4 The Legal Framework of the Indian Act   57

5 Customary Land Rights on Canadian Indian Reserves   73

6 Certificates of Possession and Leases: The Indian Act
   Individual Property Regimes   91

7 The First Nations Land Management Act: An Alternative
   to the Indian Act   108

PART THREE | BEYOND THE INDIAN ACT

8 Why Markets Fail on First Nations Lands   123

9 Escaping the Indian Act   137

10 Back to the Future: Restoring First Nations
    Property-Rights Systems   160

    Appendix: Announcement of the Nisga'a Landholding
    Transition Act   183

    Notes   185
    Index   215

Manny Jules

Let me be a free man, free to travel, free to stop, free to work, free to trade where I choose, free to choose my own teachers, free to follow the religion of my fathers, free to talk, think and act for myself – and I will obey every law or submit to the penalty.[1]

Contrary to popular belief, Chief Joseph was not a war chief. He was a community chief. This statement reminds us that he understood that a community is a combination of innovative individuals and their willing commitment to community responsibilities. I use this quote often when I speak because our quest for individual freedom from the Indian Act and the Department of Indian Affairs will only be realized when we are able to look after our collective responsibility.

This book is part of an agenda I have been pursuing all my adult life. We are trying to build a system of First Nations government that allows our individuals to have the freedom to pursue their creativity, have access to capital, and be entrepreneurial. This system also has to generate sufficient revenues for us to be self-reliant.

I see a system where our local governments are supported by First Nations national institutions. Our institutions, much like provincial governments, will provide our governments with the expertise and support they need to exercise their responsibilities in a manner that frees our people to be as successful as other Canadians.

For the last thirty years, I have worked on establishing our tax jurisdictions over property, sales, business activities, and development. I have helped to ensure that we have access to long-term infrastructure financing and that we build an institutional framework that creates investor confidence. For me, a book about establishing a system of property ownership that protects our underlying title and unleashes our creativity is just the next part of this agenda.

However, my real interest in a book like this started in autumn 1997, when I travelled with a close friend, Bud Smith, the former attorney general of BC, to eastern Mexico. It was the first time I had been there. The reason we had gone was so that I could visit Chichen Itza, where every year during the spring and autumn equinoxes the sun casts a shadow that resembles a snake descending to the ground. The shadow joins up perfectly with the carved stone snake's head at the base of the pyramid. The pyramids, monuments, and other public infrastructure at Chichen Itza were built around 600 AD, or 1,400 years ago.

As I stared, I had an epiphany. Our people built this without the aid of federal government funding. We had governments that financed themselves. Our governments were able to provide the infrastructure and institutions to build a thriving economy that supported millions of us. In 1542, Barolomé de Las Casas, the first Spaniard to try to estimate the population of the Americas, said, "It looked as if God had placed all of or the greater part of humanity in these countries."[2]

Our people created some of the greatest civilizations of the last five thousand years. In Peru, archeologists have found seven technically sophisticated cities that have large-scale public buildings. These cities date back to 3200–2500 BC – i.e., contemporaneous with the first cities of Sumer, which almost all history books consider the birthplace of civilization.

Wheat, barley, and other grains grow wild throughout the world. Their discovery was aided by nature. Corn does not grow wild anywhere in the world. Our people genetically engineered corn and gave this gift to the world. We also domesticated tomatoes, peppers, and beans. Experts estimate that we developed 60 percent of all crops currently in global production.[3]

We independently came up with the mathematical concept of zero. The Olmec invented zero in about 32 BC. It appeared in Mayan script about 400 AD, well before it appeared in Europe during the twelfth century. Mathematicians call the discovery of zero a turning point in mathematics, science, and technology.

We discovered medicines that are still in use today. The Mayan Long Calendar begins on what is estimated as 13 August 3114 BC. The Mayan calendar is considered much more complex and accurate than the European calendars.

Market economies were not foreign to us. We created them ourselves. We traded goods over hundreds of miles. The Maya had a complex trade network. How could pipestone, dating back to before contact, end up in my territory in south-central British Columbia when it only comes from a few places in the world, such as Pipestone, Minnesota, if we did not trade? How could corn be used all throughout the Americas before contact, if we did not trade?

Trade cannot be financed without capital. We had to build transportation methods such as boats. We had to build public buildings and maintain armies to provide order. These required community investments based on a future return to the community and to individuals.

Markets need institutions to facilitate trade. From Alaska to California we agreed to a common trade language, Chinook. We recorded transactions relating to labour and goods. We built roads and trails that are still used today. We used money such as dentalium shells and wampum strings.

We had individual property rights. Our clothes and shoes were not made to fit everyone. Our winter homes belonged to certain families. According to our written history, my community had individual property rights dating back to the early 1800s to specify where our potato crops were. As is made clear in this book, many of us had individual property rights.

Do you think this was all achieved through divine intervention from the gods? Or was it because we somehow evolved into a "natural" socialist system that lasted thousands of years? Both of these ideas are nonsense. We achieved success because we created balance between our individual creativity and our collective responsibility. We created systems that supported and encouraged individual initiative and ensured we generated public resources to sustain our communities and advance our cultures.

Among my people, the Secwepemc, we had a tradition that clarified how we achieved balance. When a young man was fourteen, he was sent off to live on his own for a period of time. By that age, he would have all the requisite skills for survival. If after a specified time, he returned to the community, he was obliged to live by the rules of the community and support us with his particular skills. Very few chose a solitary existence.

The creative energy of our people, however, was halted in 1492. As Jared Diamond so concisely states, our civilizations were mowed down by guns and steel and especially germs.[4] Almost 90 percent of our populations were wiped out. Religious zeal and prejudice tried to destroy what few of us remained. It is a testament to our strength and determination that we have survived.

We became the poorest of the poor because after contact the governments of Canada and the United States passed legislation that removed us from the economy. We had been prosperous even after contact as an integral part of the fur trade. But in the 1800s they began to destroy our economic institutions, which had always supported our trade. And then they prohibited us from participating in the new economy and new trading relationships that they established. And finally they saddled us with a property-rights system that prevented trade and created a 100-year credit crisis from which we have yet to recover.

Since then, my life and that of every other First Nations leader has been dedicated to rebuilding our communities and economies. The path I chose was to legislate our way back into the economy and build institutions that implement our collective rights and release our individual creative energy.

I was there in November 1969, as a seventeen-year-old, to attend a meeting where all but four First Nations communities in BC came to Kamloops to reject the proposed federal assimilation policy known as the White Paper. I listened as leaders such as Phillip Joe, Forrest Walkem, and my dad spoke of a vision to restore our nations, build our economies, generate our own revenues, and become self-reliant governments within Canada.

In 1974, I left my training to be a draftsman at Boeing to serve on the Kamloops Indian Band council. I was in Chilliwack in 1975 when all First Nations in BC rejected government funds. I have learned the hard way how hard it has been to achieve the vision of my father and his contemporaries. I watched our attempt at freedom in 1975 fail. I have watched us lose court cases. I have participated in negotiation processes that never end. I have watched us fail to change the Constitution.

I served as a councillor in my community from 1974 until 1984 and as chief from 1984 until 2000. Through experience, I have learned that change requires a pragmatic approach that reconciles diverse interests. Change must be incremental. It must be supported by legislation and institutions. Most of all it must be optional, so that our communities can exercise their freedom of choice.

I have participated in successful changes. I helped with the first Indian-led amendment to the Indian Act in Canada's history to give us authority over property taxes. In 1990 and again in 1995, we created provincial legislation in BC and Quebec to allow a seamless transition to our tax authority in those provinces. In 1998, with the backing of my community, we implemented authority over the GST on our lands for fuel, alcohol, and tobacco. We helped to expand this authority to all GST-eligible products and services in 2003. In 2005, I helped lead the First Nations Fiscal and Statistical Management Act, which created four national First Nations institutions to help our governments implement their powers in a manner that created a positive environment for markets.

For me, the First Nations Property Ownership Act discussed in this book is the next step. To fully realize the full value of our land we need a secure property-rights system. To restore our property rights we need to first protect our underlying or collective title. The little bit of land we currently have can never be lost. The reversionary and expropriation rights must always be held by us. Once our collective title is secure, we can issue the type of individual title that we choose. Some of us may choose to issue fee simple and others may choose to implement leasehold. This title must be registered in a Torrens title system – the best system in the world. This will ensure our lands will be worth as much as any other lands in Canada, should we so choose.

This book explains how to achieve this vision, which I believe was first articulated by Chief Joseph and later by my father. At its most basic level, this book represents the long journey of our leaders. It begins with our proud history of markets and property ownership, explains how our property rights were rendered virtually worthless, discusses some of our second-best attempts to compete, and presents a proposal to restore our property ownership. This book, however, is much more than that.

This is a book about pragmatism. In order to advance we need to find common cause with those who disagree that our governments need to be part of the Canadian federation to reduce our poverty. Hopefully, as a result of this book these doubters will appreciate that keeping us out of Canada through past legislation and inappropriate institutions is the root cause of our higher levels of poverty and reliance on public funding. It is in all our interests to make change. Our poverty costs taxpayers an additional $4 billion every year in higher social, health, and education costs. Moreover, because of our younger populations, in ten years time up to one in ten retirees will be replaced by a young First Nations worker. We have to contribute to this country. This book demonstrates that, when our governments are supported by our national institutions, we can and do contribute to Canada. It illustrates that the current system of property rights has failed, and it proposes a solution that most Canadians take for granted.

This book is about the freedom to choose. Throughout our history we have had the ability to choose successful innovations and reject poor ones. Our most successful innovators were the Maya, Aztecs, and Incas, but each of our cultures built on our competitive advantage and created sustainable economies. After contact, a system of central planning was imposed on us. This did not work in Eastern Europe, and it does not work for us. It meant that we lost our ability to choose and became mired in poverty. We have now begun to re-establish our institutions, and First Nations will determine which ones are successful by their choices. This book demonstrates what happened when our freedom to choose was taken away, and it speaks of our efforts to create new choices that free us from dependency and the Indian Act.

Most importantly this book is about hope. We have prospered in the past. We have been decimated by disease, warfare, and most recently the good intentions that created our dependency. We have begun to rebuild the legal and administrative foundation to support markets on our lands. Once we restore our property rights to our lands, I believe we will unleash a wave of First Nations creative and entrepreneurial spirit.

In 1910, the Secwepemc people issued a statement to Prime Minister Wilfred Laurier. We call it the Shuswap Memorial because it has guided every one of our leaders since then. In the statement we speak about how we find ourselves "without any real home in this our own country." We reminded the prime minister that "we expect much of you as the head of this great Canadian Nation, and feel confident you will see that we receive fair and honorable treatment."

It has been one hundred years since we have made our case to Canada, but I believe, with the passage of the First Nations Property Ownership Act, that, in the words of my ancestors, "We will make each other good and great."[5]

We are grateful to the Aboriginal and non-Aboriginal interviewees who generously shared their time and expertise with Chris Alcantara. The names are too numerous to mention, but we are truly appreciative of the willingness of Aboriginal officials from Six Nations, Cowichan Tribes, Westbank First Nation, Piikani, Siksika, Blood Tribe, and Sandy Lake First Nation to speak about their property and housing regimes. This book would not have been possible without their knowledge, patience, and guidance.

We also thank the First Nations Tax Commission, the successor institution to the Indian Tax Advisory Board (ITAB), for allowing us to draw on several consulting reports completed by Fiscal Realities for ITAB. In particular, we thank Manny Jules, chief commissioner, and Ken Scopick, chief operating officer for the First Nations Tax Commission, as well as Bob Kingsbury of Indian and Northern Affairs Canada for their support and guidance in the development of a ten-year research agenda into the multiple sources of higher transaction costs on First Nations lands. Significant contributions were also made by André Le Dressay's colleagues at Fiscal Realities, including Greg Richard, Jason Calla, Tylor Kroad, Jason Reeves, Kate McCue, Norman Lavallee, and Katherine Livingstone.

We acknowledge Springer Science+Business Media, University of Toronto Press, *Alberta Law Review*, Bearpaw Publications, *Queen's Law Journal*, and Stanford University Press for granting us permission to draw on the following publications: Christopher Alcantara, "Reduce Transaction Costs? Yes. Strengthen Property Rights? Maybe: The First Nations Land Management Act and Economic Development on Canadian Indian Reserves," *Public Choice* 132 (2007), 421–32; idem, "Certificates of Possession and First

Nations Housing: A Case Study of the Six Nations Housing Program," *Canadian Journal of Law and Society* 20 (2005) 183–205; idem, "Individual Property Rights on Canadian Indian Reserves: The Historical Emergence and Jurisprudence of Certificates of Possession," *Canadian Journal of Native Studies* 23 (2003), 391–424; Tom Flanagan and Christopher Alcantara, "Individual Property Rights on Canadian Indian Reserves: A Review of the Jurisprudence," *Alberta Law Review* 42 (2005), 1019–46; idem, "Individual Property Rights on Canadian Indian Reserves," *Queen's Law Journal* 29 (2004), 489–532; idem, "Customary Land Rights on Canadian Indian Reserves," in Terry Anderson, Bruce Benson, and Thomas Flanagan, eds, *Self-Determination: The Other Path for Native Americans* (Stanford, CA: Stanford University Press, 2006), 134–58.

Thanks to Mike Zekulin for compiling the index. Finally, we thank all our loved ones who sacrificed so much family time so we could finish this book: Kerry Lee Hunt and Kees Rafael Alcantara; Christine Beaton and Cameron Le Dressay; and Marianne Flanagan.

Beyond the Indian Act

Aboriginal people are the least prosperous demographic group in Canada. In life expectancy, income, unemployment, welfare dependency, educational attainment, and quality of housing, the pattern is the same: aboriginal people trail other Canadians. And within the category of aboriginal people, another pattern also stands out: First Nations (status Indians) do worse than Métis and non-status Indians; while among First Nations those living on-reserve do worse than those living off-reserve. These patterns have been more or less stable for decades. Aboriginal people and First Nations are progressing on most indicators compared to other Canadians, but the progress is painfully slow, and it will take centuries to achieve parity at these rates of change.[1]

Ironically, although First Nations are at the bottom of socioeconomic rankings, they are potentially wealthy landlords, with land reserves totalling 6.5 million acres (2.7 million hectares).[2] To be sure, some reserves are of modest economic value, because they have no natural resources and are located far from population centres. But others have arable land as well as commercial timber and valuable deposits of oil, natural gas, and minerals. Also, as Canadian cities continue their inexorable expansion, more and more reserves are finding that their location makes them valuable. Dozens of reserves are now situated within or on the edge of major cities such as Vancouver, Edmonton, Calgary, and Montreal, as well as rapidly growing smaller towns such as Kamloops, Kelowna, and Courtenay-Comox. All this land represents an enormous economic asset that could and should make a major contribution to raising First Nations' standard of living.

Indeed, some of that is now taking place. We are seeing almost an explosion of aboriginal entrepreneurship in the age of "red capitalism."[3] Across Canada, First Nations are opening casinos, shopping centres, industrial parks, golf courses, and residential developments; they own trust companies, airlines, trucking firms, sawmills, and oil wells. But these developments, impressive as they are, are handicapped by an inadequate framework of property rights. Investors are deterred by uncertainty; legal work and litigation multiply; projects take longer than they should, and many potentially profitable developments never happen because all these factors raise the cost structure.

A recent study of aboriginal business ventures by the Conference Board of Canada highlighted part of the property rights issue:

> Prohibited land ownership under the *Indian Act* and limits on alienation of municipal lands that arose out of the referendum that followed the *Nunavut Land Claims Agreement* make it difficult for Aboriginal entrepreneurs to access funding for businesses, since they are unable to leverage land as collateral for a business loan.[4]

Lack of collateral is indeed a well-known and serious obstacle to aboriginal business ventures, but it is only the tip of the iceberg of property-rights issues. Our book will lay out the difficulties in detail and then make constructive proposals for dealing with them through federal legislation and administrative innovations.

Defects in the property rights of First Nations exist at two levels. The first level of difficulty is that, with a few exceptions created by recent treaties, First Nations do not own their lands; the federal Crown has legislative jurisdiction over and manages these reserves for the use and benefit of their residents. In practice, this means that many economic transactions involving reserve land have to be reviewed by the Department of Indian Affairs, adding layers of legal work and delay to an already cumbersome approval process. We believe that Indians should own their own lands and are capable of managing them, and that those First Nations who wish to take over that responsibility should be able to acquire the title to their reserves from the Crown.

Collective ownership by First Nations of their reserve land will also make possible ownership in fee simple by individuals. A standard reference work explains that fee-simple ownership is the "most extensive [land tenure] and allows the tenant to sell or to convey by will or transfer to the tenant's heir upon death intestate. In modern law, almost all land is held in fee simple. This is as close as one can get to absolute ownership in common law. Legal fiction, indeed, because the owner in fee simple can do what he or she pleases with the land including sale to another and the ability to pass it on to next-of-kin *ad infinitum*."[5]

Most First Nations do not have fee-simple title, either collectively or individually. Most bands do not own their reserve lands in fee simple, nor do individuals living on reserves have fee-simple title to portions of those reserves. Most reserves are at least partially subdivided through some combination of certificates of possession and leases (both provided for in the Indian Act) as well as customary landholdings (not mentioned in the Act). These existing individual rights are certainly useful up to a point, but they are all seriously deficient for economic purposes, as we will show in the second part of this book. We believe that those First Nations people who wish to take on the responsibility of owning land in fee simple should have that opportunity, as do other Canadians; and we will show how that can happen without jeopardizing the integrity of the First Nations land base. The key to that is for First Nations to possess the underlying or reversionary title, which is now held in most cases by the provincial Crown. Once they have the reversionary title, First Nations can create fee-simple title for individuals on their own lands, confident, like other Canadians, that their own governments will protect their land base while also protecting individual rights created upon it.

This is a voluntary, First Nations–led initiative, inspired by the work of the Nisga'a people and advocated by Manny Jules. First Nations who want to go down the path of reversionary title and fee-simple ownership should be emancipated from the Indian Act and allowed, but not forced, to do so. This proposal differs from what was tried in the United States under the aegis of the Dawes Act (1887), when Indian reservations were subdivided and privatized in an attempt to break up tribal communities. In contrast, this proposal is meant to strengthen the economies of First Nations by giving them access to modern, effective property rights. Unlike the Dawes Act, we do not propose breaking up First Nations lands and abolishing institutions of aboriginal self-government.

By facilitating economic development on reserves, property rights reform will doubtless create more Indian millionaires. We don't apologize for that; every community should have successful entrepreneurs, whose economic leadership creates jobs and opportunities for others. But property rights reform is not only, or even primarily, for the well-to-do. Its greatest benefits will fall upon ordinary First Nations people, especially through the improvement of housing on reserves.

Reserve housing in Canada is a national disgrace. In the 2006 census, Statistics Canada found that 26 percent of reserve housing was "crowded" (compared to 3 percent off-reserve) and 44 percent needed "major repairs" (compared to 7 percent off-reserve).[6] Most reserves have long lists of people waiting to be assigned to houses for which, on many reserves, they will pay little or no rent once they are installed. Aboriginal Policy Analyst Don Sandberg of the Frontier Centre (Winnipeg) notes that

> at least one band, the Opasquiak Cree Nation (OCN) situated next to The Pas, Manitoba, is challenging this culture of entitlement and dependency by informing its people that there will be no more "free homes." In fact, band members are now required to arrange financing for their new homes and, in contrast to most reserves, are now responsible for repairs to their homes as well as the cost of water and garbage services.[7]

Unfortunately, however, such initiatives are more the exception than the rule.

Governments have repeatedly tried to alleviate problems of quantity and quality by spending more money to build more houses, but the fix never lasts. There will never be adequate housing on Indian reserves as long as most homes are built and owned by government. Only a housing market, based on a combination of rental and home ownership as exists in the rest of Canada, can balance supply and demand and keep the housing stock in good repair. In short, it is a question of property rights – there must be owners who take pride in their own homes and see them as a savings vehicle, as well as landlords for whom housing is an investment to yield a profitable return.

Our approach follows in the footsteps of Peruvian economist Hernando de Soto, who has argued in two bestselling books that defective property rights make life miserable for the poor in the Third World.[8] Tens of millions of people squat on poorly controlled government land in metropolitan areas such as Lima, Rio de Janeiro, and Cairo. Unable to get title to the land on which they live, they cannot use it as security for loans to improve their homes or start a business. Often, absence of ownership rights and of a legal address means they cannot even get utility hookups or police protection. The problems of First Nations in Canada, though not identical in detail to what de Soto describes, are similar in principle.

One of the co-authors has taken primary responsibility for each of the three parts in this book. Tom Flanagan wrote the first part, on property rights in general and aboriginal property rights in particular. It is an expansion of topics that he treated all too briefly in *First Nations? Second Thoughts.* Anyone who has read that book will realize that his views on aboriginal property have evolved since then. Mainly through discussions with Manny Jules and André Le Dressay as well as by studying the Dawes Act experience in the United States, he has come to realize that making property rights functional for First Nations requires recognition of their underlying title to their lands. Although Flanagan didn't address the point clearly when he wrote *First Nations? Second Thoughts,* he would have thought at that time that the Crown must hold the underlying title on Indian reserves and that any reform of property rights on reserves must come from Parliament through top-down legislation. Flanagan is grateful to Jules and Le Dressay for convincing him of the superiority of the voluntary, bottom-up approach outlined here.

Flanagan hopes that the legislation proposed in this book has the potential to break the aboriginal policy stalemate that he recently described in the second edition of *First Nations? Second Thoughts.* Broadly speaking, the political left in Canada believes in aboriginal self-government, while the political right emphasizes the integration of native peoples into the mainstream of Canadian life. Each side seems to have political veto power over major innovations, so that nothing big seems to get done. But our proposals should appeal to both left and right: First Nations will get underlying title to their land, which is an important part of self-government; but they will also find it easier to adopt individual property rights for their land-holdings, which will facilitate their participation in the Canadian economy. Is it too much to hope that left and right can put a little water in their wine and come together on a proposal like this, which gives each of them something corresponding to their worldview?

Chris Alcantara wrote the second part, which deals with individual property rights on Indian reserves (certificates of possession, leases, customary holdings) as well as the First Nations Land Management Act. This is an outgrowth of the work that he first undertook in a political science Master's thesis under Flanagan's direction in 2002 and continued thereafter in several publications.

André Le Dressay is the author of the third part, which explains in detail the legislative and administrative changes required to restore the property rights of First Nations and make them fully functional. Many of these proposals are derived from studies that his consulting firm, Fiscal Realities Economists, carried out for Manny Jules and the First Nations Tax Commission (previously the Indian Taxation Advisory Board).

Although each of the co-authors has taken responsibility for a particular section based on his previous research, we have all participated in discussing the drafts of all the chapters, so the book is a genuine collaboration. We collectively endorse the line of thought and the practical recommendations contained in all three parts of *Beyond the Indian Act*.

Of course, we don't claim that improvement of property rights is a magic wand that will make everything right for First Nations. There are no magic wands in the real world of public policy. What we do claim is that getting "beyond the Indian Act" to restore aboriginal property rights will enhance economic activity on reserves, create more jobs and business opportunities for First Nations people, and improve both the quantity and the quality of housing on reserves. Recognizing First Nations' ownership of their lands is the single most useful reform of the aboriginal condition that is constitutionally and politically possible at the present time.

Finally, a note about vocabulary: in this book, we use the terms "First Nations" and "Indians" interchangeably. "First Nations" has become the politically correct term to refer to the people who used to be called "Indians," but the word "Indian" is still found in the Canadian Constitution as well as in much legislation. It was also universally used, not least by Canadian native people themselves, up to the 1980s and is still in use in the United States. Because our book ranges widely across legal topics as well as Canadian and US history, we could hardly avoid using the older terminology, at least part of the time. In the end, we decided to speak both of "Indians" and "First Nations" without intending any difference thereby.

PART ONE

Peoples and Property

In part 1, we take a theoretical and historical look at property rights. Chapter 1 explains why property rights are important, and why they always have a collective as well as an individual aspect. Chapter 2 debunks the myth that native Americans were natural communists with no conception of property. In fact, their societies evolved elaborate collective and individual institutions of property, suited to the circumstances in which they lived and the types of technology at their disposal. They also modified their institutions of property as European contact introduced new technologies and created new economic opportunities. Finally, chapter 3 analyzes the failed experiment of the 1887 Dawes Act, in which the United States government tried to impose individual ownership rights on American Indians while breaking up their reservations. The experience of the Dawes Act lies behind the First Nations–led proposal for a bottom-up, voluntary approach to property rights for First Nations rather than a coercive, top-down imposition.

Property Rights in General

God cannot create a tribe without locating it. We are not birds. We have to walk on the ground ...

　　　　　Louis Riel, Address to the Court, Regina, 1 August 1885.[1]

We are writing about the specific property rights issues of First Nations in Canada; but First Nations people are human beings, and the principles of biology and economics apply to them as much as they do to any other group of people. Hence we build a platform for understanding First Nations issues by providing a short, non-technical introduction to property rights as understood in contemporary economics and evolutionary biology.

THE LEGEND OF BLACK BEAR CROSSING

We wish the following story were a legend, but unfortunately it's true. After the end of World War II, the Department of National Defence built the Harvey Barracks as part of the Canadian Forces Base (CFB) in Calgary. Harvey Barracks included, in addition to other military buildings, 204 apartments for married soldiers. Like all military housing, it was on the Spartan side, but for decades it was good enough for Canada's fighting men and their families.

Part of CFB Calgary, including Harvey Barracks, was located on land purchased in 1952 from the Tsuu T'ina Nation, then known as the Sarcee Indian Band. After the band threatened litigation, the purchase was converted to a lease in 1991. When the federal government decided in 1994 to close CFB Calgary and transfer its troops to Edmonton, the plan was to return the land to the Tsuu T'ina, who had the choice under the lease to keep the buildings or ask them to be demolished at government expense.[2] Because of Calgary's rapid growth, the leased land was now almost in the inner city and had extraordinary economic potential. The Tsuu T'ina were busy making plans for a casino and other revenue-producing projects.

Initially, the Tsuu T'ina had thought of renovating Harvey Barracks and leasing the apartments in the Calgary rental market as a money-making venture,[3] but they were already cooling toward that idea when in August 1998 approximately one hundred band members occupied the now-empty Barracks, claiming they had nowhere else to live. It was estimated at the time that the Tsuu T'ina Nation had a shortage of approximately one hundred houses for an on-reserve population of approximately one thousand. After a few days of ignoring orders to leave, the squatters, whose numbers were increasing daily, received permission to stay. The DND gave the keys to Harvey Barracks to the band council, which decided to tolerate the presence of the squatters.[4] A few reportedly started paying rent to the band, which converted them from squatters to tenants.[5]

By early 1999, more than eight hundred people were living in the Barracks, now dubbed "Black Bear Crossing," and tensions with neighbouring communities started to emerge.[6] According to a Tsuu T'ina spokesman, more than half the squatters were not members of the Tsuu T'ina Nation.[7] Some were status Indians from other bands, some were non-status Indians with Tsuu T'ina relatives, some were not Indians in any sense of the term. The opportunity to live without paying rent had drawn a motley crowd.

Fast forward to 2006. In September the Tsuu T'ina Nation broke ground on its long-awaited casino project. Since 2004, the band had been promising to use profits from the casino to build new housing to replace Black Bear Crossing.[8] Also in September 2006, the band invited Health Canada to test the barracks for asbestos after a fire in one of the units exposed the old-style insulation. Health Canada put out an advisory, and in October the band asked all residents to leave because of the health hazard.[9]

Then ensued a period of jawboning about what to do with the displaced people. Indian Affairs Minister Jim Prentice said his department would pay to house them in Calgary hotels for thirty days while repairs were made, then send them back to Black Bear Crossing until a long-term solution could be found. But the band council didn't want them back. "Indian Affairs is not the decision-maker. Tsuu T'ina is not the decision-maker. Health Canada is the decision-maker," said their spokesman.[10]

A deal was finally reached in December 2006. Approximately one hundred non-Tsuu T'ina were turned over to provincial welfare authorities. Thirty-four units at Black Bear Crossing were declared safe and people moved back in. To house the remainder, the federal government pledged a special $2.2 million grant to the Tsuu Ti'na Nation to rent apartments in Calgary for the next eighteen months. This $2.2 million was in addition to $2.9 million that the federal government had paid ($65,000 a day) since October to put evacuees up in Calgary hotels.[11]

When the federal commitment ended in June 2008, the Tsuu T'ina Nation pledged to continue paying rent in Calgary for Black Bear evacuees. In the meantime, said the band council, it was nearing completion of twenty-five new homes and starting twenty-five more. The plan was ultimately to build three hundred new homes, using federal subsidies along with casino revenues.[12] In theory, this should be enough to house a band membership now totalling approximately 1,500 people, but we wonder about the outcome if the band persists in building and owning homes and assigning them administratively to residents. It is difficult to maintain the quality of housing stock without the pride and incentives of homeownership.

It is the big picture that is interesting in the context of this book. The Tsuu T'ina Nation, which had a chronic housing shortage, suddenly had the opportunity to acquire at no cost 204 apartments in good condition. But with neither the Band Council nor the Department of National Defence able to exercise normal property rights as a landlord during the transitional period, squatters invaded the complex and in less than ten years turned it into a derelict health-hazard. Everyone lost: Canadian taxpayers had to shoulder the bill for housing evacuees and tearing down the buildings, Tsuu T'ina has to assume the shelter costs for evacuees in Calgary going forward, and there is still a housing shortage.

Ironically, the Tsuu T'ina leadership has demonstrated in another context that it understands property rights and housing markets. In the 1970s, the band entered into a leasing agreement to build 351 houses sited around a golf course. The leases, which expire in 2048, can be bought and sold in the market. The result is a thriving community of more than one thousand people, living in a beautiful setting on the reserve near the hamlet of Bragg Creek.[13] The essential fact is that private property rights in the form of leases transformed a small part of the reserve into high-quality housing for a population roughly the size of the Tsuu T'ina Nation. Contrast that to the never-ending housing shortage that afflicts Tsuu T'ina members.

We do not contend that the Redwood Meadows approach could be applied directly to solve the housing problems of the Tsuu T'ina; Redwood Meadows is a community designed for upper middle-class incomes, and most members of the Tsuu T'ina Nation cannot afford that type of housing. But property rights and markets are not just for the well-off; they can work at any level of income. For example, Tsuu T'ina members with modest incomes could begin by renting houses or apartments under a "right to buy" program of the type that Margaret Thatcher's government employed to transfer British council housing to private ownership.[14] All or part of the rent can be treated as mortgage payments, building up equity in the form of eventual ownership.

A LITTLE BACKGROUND

Let's examine property rights more systematically. Our approach to property is not rooted in the Lockean idea of natural rights. We do not think it is possible to deduce complex legal institutions from philosophical abstractions about human nature. Rather, we draw inspiration from philosophers such as David Hume, John Stuart Mill, and Friedrich Hayek, who saw property rights in a historical context, evolving through time along with other social institutions. As such, the test of property rights is not the logical criterion of whether they conform to someone's idea of human nature but the practical criterion of whether they contribute to human welfare in a specific social context. As the legal theorist Richard Epstein has written, "From the beginning, private property always rested on its productive advantage, and not merely on an obscure natural law claim that property rights are necessarily 'immutable' across all times and places."[15]

However, institutions of private property, while not directly deducible from human nature, are consistent with what modern biology teaches us about that nature. It is important to make that point because the social sciences are beginning to acknowledge that human beings are not blank slates and that human behaviour, while always culturally mediated, has genetic roots.[16] According to the famous metaphors of Richard Dawkins, all organisms are "survival vehicles" for the "selfish genes" within.[17] That is, in a competitive world of scarce resources, the heritable characteristics (i.e., nature) of all species are determined by the prevalence of specific genes, as determined by which individuals leave more progeny. In their competitive struggle for survival and reproductive success, organisms make use of the world around them for foraging, protection, and breeding. Hence Dawkins' idea of the "extended phenotype,"[18] according to which beavers are not just the animals themselves but also the dam that they build and the pool that the dam creates. Likewise, property is part of the extended phenotype of human beings.

But human beings, like all other primates, are a social species. That means that the society is a survival vehicle for the individual, just as the individual is a survival vehicle for the interior genome. Hence, Jane Goodall's discovery that chimpanzees, our closest relatives, wage low-intensity war with neighbouring bands is not surprising.[19] Collectively, chimps, especially adult males in small groups, patrol the boundaries of their group territory and kill chimpanzees from other bands when they can achieve numerical advantage. In their struggle for *Lebensraum,* they drive away or even exterminate other bands and incorporate their territory into their own. Individually, chimps also seek control over resources; they take possession of and defend the food they collect, the places they choose to sleep, and objects they use as tools and playthings.

Of course, human territoriality is not reducible to chimpanzee behaviour. As Robert Sack insisted in his often-cited work *Human Territoriality,* human behaviour is consciously thought out and mediated through culture; it is not just the mechanical expression of instincts.[20] But we are still a primate species with a characteristic combination of individuality and sociality. Thus we would expect human possession of land to assume both individual and collective dimensions. We will see that to be true as we examine the concepts of property and territory.

WHAT IS PROPERTY?

The nineteenth-century French anarchist P.-J. Proudhon memorably answered that question by saying, "Property is theft."[21] A more mainstream answer is that property is a bundle of rights governing the use of things. At first glance, property rights seem to apply to lands or things that are owned, but it is more precise to say that they apply to human conduct. They set out the prerogatives of owners that non-owners must respect, under threat of retaliation from owners or enforcement by a third party such as government. Richard Epstein says that the three big sticks in the bundle known as property are the right to exclude others, the right to use what is owned, and the right to dispose of it.[22] Of course, each of these three can itself be broken down into smaller, separable rights.

Exclusion. If I own a home, I can decide whether to let someone in the door or not, but I can't exclude a policeman carrying a search warrant. Or, if I own a farm, I can exclude other farmers who would like to plow my land; but I can't stop a utility company from running a power line across my land if it has a right-of-way on my property, which it can get through a court order if necessary. So the right to exclude is never absolute; it is always qualified by considerations of the state's police power and the larger needs of the community.

Use. Use can mean simply the right to be present, as in the case of a condo owner who has the right to swim in the recreation centre. It can also mean the right to extract resource units, as in the case of fishing-club members at the lake owned by their club.[23] Or it could mean the right to receive a share of the profits, as in owning shares of a joint-stock corporation. Another dimension of use is the right to manage or share in the management of the property.[24] Common-stock owners have the right to vote for directors of a corporation, whereas owners of preferred shares do not, having traded their management rights for greater security of investment.

Disposition. Permanent disposition can take place by sale, gift, or inheritance, while temporary disposition involves leasing or occupation by permission. The owner of land in fee simple can exercise all these rights within certain limits (e.g., your spouse has certain rights to your estate, and you can't knowingly rent your property for criminal purposes); but other forms of ownership may have more restrictions. For example, under the old English system of entail, landed estates were a sort of family property that could not be sold but had to be willed to family members.

WHO CAN BE OWNERS, AND WHY DOES IT MATTER?

Individuals

Individual people can own land, houses, and all sorts of objects. They can also own shares in joint activities, such as stock in a corporation or membership in a club. As long as individuals can sell their portion without getting permission from other owners, these cases are best regarded as individual property, even though they obviously have a collective aspect.

Individual ownership tends to put property to its highest economic use because it unites knowledge and motive to creative incentive. As Friedrich Hayek has shown, we live in a world of imperfect information in which coordination is best achieved through "spontaneous order," i.e., allowing actors to make decisions on the basis of knowledge that only they have.[25] Individuals are in the best position to know their own desires and abilities and to figure out how to advance their interests by using those parts of the world they own and control. Transaction costs are minimized because individuals can make their own decisions, or they can hire a specialist to decide for them; they do not have to negotiate with other owners to reach a consensus on action. Individuals reap the benefits and suffer the losses from whatever they decide, giving them incentives to learn from the experience of bad decisions and to do better in the future.

Groups

Husbands and wives, or other groups of family or friends, sometimes own property jointly, so that disposition requires the consent of all owners. Going beyond such partnerships with a definite number of members are indefinite groups. Ownership of land in most civilizations before the modern age was usually based on families rather than individuals, and families vary in size depending on who is being born and who is dying. In such family ownership systems, someone will have the power to manage the property and distribute its benefits, but within limits that preserve the property for the family.

Ownership involving larger, non-kin groups is usually referred to as community property. Examples would be the grazing commons often found in agricultural communities. Farmers who own land individually for growing crops or pasturing their livestock may also have a right to turn their livestock loose in a commonly owned area. Such community ownership requires effective group management to ensure it does not deteriorate into the infamous "tragedy of the commons," in which the value of the land is destroyed through overgrazing. There have to be mechanisms to limit the number of participants and the size of the herds turned out to graze. The upshot of hundreds of recent studies is that common property arrangements are most effective when there is a limited number of owners who know each other and can monitor each other's behaviour on a face-to-face basis – e.g., ranchers watching how many cattle their neighbours bring to the summer grazing reserve, or lobster fishermen counting how many traps their competitors put in the water.[26]

Common property can be superior to individual property where the costs of creating individual ownership are high relative to the benefits. A well-known example is that ranchers in the western United States and Canada originally treated the prairies as a commons. Before the invention of barbed wire, there was no effective and affordable way of enclosing portions of the prairie. Barbed wire made individual, enclosed ranching economically feasible, and the days of the great cattle drives were soon over.[27] In general, the choice between individual and common property is greatly influenced by the state of the technology required to demarcate assets into bundles that can be individually owned.

A special form of common property is government property, which at the federal and provincial levels in Canada we call Crown property. Governments typically claim to own property in the name of the entire community, but members of the community have no role in the enjoyment, use, and disposition of this so-called community property except through the government. The Government of Canada owns national parks, supposedly for the benefit of all Canadians; but I as a citizen cannot visit a park except by paying a fee set by government officials. Nor do I have any say in selecting lands for park status, except indirectly by voting for members of Parliament.

The defining characteristic of government is legitimate coercion, which allows governments to acquire property by command rather than consensual agreement. If I am a businessman who wants to open a store, I have to persuade someone to sell me land or rent me space; but if I am a government wanting to build a road I can expropriate the land. Governments in Canada are bound by legislation to pay compensation for expropriation, but that does not change the coercive nature of the transaction.

Government ownership is at odds with economic efficiency, for two reasons. One is that genuine economies producing Pareto-optimal results emerge out of voluntary agreement, not coercion. Voluntary agreement is essential for individuals participating in transactions to make use of knowledge about their own preferences and abilities that only they possess. Another reason is that government officials have few incentives for economic efficiency. Since they don't own the property themselves, they do not reap any direct rewards if they manage it efficiently; any surplus will revert to the government's treasury. Indeed, officials are more likely to be punished for mistakes than rewarded for achievement (particularly for mistakes that embarrass their political masters), making them notoriously risk-averse, yet a market economy is built on taking risks.

Despite these fundamental problems, there is a role for government property in situations where other values trump economic efficiency. In a dangerous world, governments need to own land for military purposes and national defence; we wouldn't want a military base to be subject to closure and sale because its private owner wanted to develop a shopping centre on the site. Certainly, ordinary government office space can be leased in the real-estate market, but would we want the Parliament buildings to be owned by private investors who might decide that the location was just right for a condominium complex?

Finally, in opposition to all these forms of property in which someone or something – a person, a group, or an organization – exercises rights of exclusion, use, and disposition, we have regimes of open access. All the Earth's land except Antarctica is now owned by someone, at least in the collective form of state sovereignty over territory, but no one owns the atmosphere or the oceans. All of us help ourselves to the air we breathe or use in industrial processes, and all of us put our bodily exhalations as well as industrial emissions in the atmosphere. Similarly, the high seas are open to ships of all nations for travel, fishing, and military exercises.

Stemming perhaps from Garrett Hardin's famous essay, "The Tragedy of the Commons,"[28] open-access regimes are often confusingly referred to as commons.[29] But Hardin's parable referred not to common property but to an open-access regime, where no one could exercise control over the number of livestock turned out to pasture. Real-world grazing arrangements are usually not open access but common property, in which the collectivity of owners engages in exclusion of outsiders, monitors the behaviour of insiders, and manages the land.

The non-property regime of open access makes sense where something is so abundant relative to demand that is not worth investing anything at all in creating property rights. All regimes of property, whether collective or individual, cost something to create, maintain, and enforce. The Neolithic hunter who made a flint scraper and regarded it as his tool had to be willing to retrieve it if someone took it (risky if the thief was large and violent) or else persuade friends to help him get it back (costly in terms of time, and risky if the thief also had friends). If flint scrapers were just lying around everywhere waiting to be picked up, there would be no point in treating them as property; but flint is relatively rare, and it requires skillful workmanship to turn a flint stone into a scraper. At any given time in history, human beings assert ownership over scarce resources but leave in open access those resources that seem virtually infinite in their abundance. As Locke put it, "Nobody could think himself injured by the drinking of another man, though he took a good draught, who had a whole river of the same water left to him to quench his thirst."[30]

THE DUALITY OF PROPERTY

Contemporary thinking about property rights is largely derived from an influential article, "Toward a Theory of Property Rights," published in 1968 by the economist Harold Demsetz. He described property as a "bundle of rights"[31] that "develop to internalize externalities when the gains of internalization become larger than the cost of internalization."[32] In less jargon-laden language, the historian Richard Pipes wrote that "for property to arise, two conditions have to be met: an object has to be desirable and available in limited quantities."[33] Like everything else in economics, property involves trade-offs of costs and benefits, dependent upon environmental conditions as well as the state of technological development.

A full-fledged system of private property in land is expensive to operate. It requires techniques of measuring land and marking boundaries; administrative methods, usually involving writing, for recording titles and transfers; a legal code to define property rights with some precision; and a judicial system to settle disputes. No society will develop such elaborate and expensive institutions unless the value of land is great enough to make it worthwhile. At a minimum, this means the society must have arrived at the stage of intensive agriculture, so that the same piece of land can be farmed indefinitely without destroying its productivity. The population must also be dense enough that good agricultural land is in short supply. Otherwise the costs would far outweigh the benefits of a system of real property.

Demsetz's insight that property rights depend on the costs and benefits of creating a system of rights under given conditions of technology is absolutely fundamental, but also subject to further qualification. Some economists have labelled his theory as "naïve," because it portrayed property rights as emerging from voluntary market transactions and did not take adequate account of the role of government in creating, enforcing, and sometimes abusing these rights.[34] A related point is that Demsetz wrote only about the individual level of property rights, whereas human societies have a two-level understanding of property, combining community control of a broad territory with family or individual control of specific tracts of land or other resources. With these considerations in mind, we can now tell a simple story about the evolution of property rights.

Before the invention of agriculture, human beings survived by hunting and gathering. In exceptional circumstances, such as the rich fisheries of the Pacific coast of northern North America, societies could become sedentary and establish property rights to productive fishing spots; but hunting-gathering societies normally have to be mobile, to take advantage of fish and game migrations as well as seasonal patterns of plant growth. Under such conditions, societies claim areas of land as "their" hunting and foraging grounds, but the lines are fluid and always subject to contestation from neighbouring societies. There is neither a clearly defined territorial boundary around the community nor an organized government that could enforce such a boundary. Internally, individuals or families may establish customary rights to particular berry patches, groves of trees, fishing spots, etc.

The introduction of agriculture led inexorably to a new order of property rights because it made land much more valuable. With sufficient water through rainfall or irrigation, cultivation of land could produce many times more calories than use of the same land for hunting and picking berries, nuts, and wild grasses. As Demsetz explained, the new value of land under a regime of sedentary agriculture made it worthwhile to elaborate systems of property rights at both the collective and individual levels. Collectively, organized government – the state – emerged to define the boundaries of community territory, defend it from outsiders, and expand it through warfare with other societies.[35] Internally, individual and family ownership of agricultural land became imperative to create incentives for productivity. Individual title to land depended on collective title, as the state became the enforcer of individual and family property rights.

In effect, there developed a bifurcation in property rights between the collective title, held by the state in the name of the community, and family or individual ownership. The collective title of the community became identified with the *territory* of the state under the jurisdiction of sovereign authority. Ownership became identified with *property,* held by individuals, families, or corporations under laws created and enforced by the state.

The modern industrial age is associated with the further individualization of property rights, as family and community aspects of ownership have been diminished. Landmarks in the English-speaking world were the enclosure of the commons and the abolition of institutions such as entail and primogeniture. On the European continent, the abolition of feudalism in the French Revolution undercut ownership of land by aristocratic families as well as religious corporations. By the end of the eighteenth century, progressive thinkers regarded individual property as a fundamental human right and enshrined it in such documents as the French Declaration of the Rights of Man and of the Citizen ("The right to property being inviolable and sacred, no one ought to be deprived of it, except in cases of evident public necessity, legally ascertained, and on condition of a previous just indemnity")[36] and the Fifth Amendment to the US Constitution ("Nor shall private property be taken for public use without just compensation").[37] The nineteenth century saw the proliferation of new forms of individual property, such as patents, copyrights, and shares in limited-liability corporations.

This flowering of individual property rights was an integral part of the spread of the market economy around the world. Secure and enforced property rights in land, resources, enterprises, and ideas created incentives for innovation and risk-taking. At this point, it is difficult to conceive how a modern economy could function without institutions such as real-estate agencies, corporations, stock exchanges, markets in futures and derivatives, and patent registries, all of which depend upon individual property rights for their very existence.[38] Yet this efflorescence of individual property rights was accompanied by an equally striking expansion of government. The state created armies and police forces to protect property rights, court systems to settle disputes, and infrastructure such as roads, canals, and harbours to make property more valuable. Also important were legal innovations such as land registries and the Torrens system of land titles to make real-estate markets more efficient. (In the Torrens system, described at greater length in chapter 10, the government not only records the deeds of real-estate transactions but also guarantees the validity of title.) As a nineteenth-century Canadian legal authority wrote, the Torrens system, by guaranteeing land titles and thus facilitating sales, leases, and mortgages, struck "a death blow to the old doctrine which depended on the theory that land was not to be dealt with freely, and render[ed] real estate as negotiable as any other property."[39]

But the nineteenth century also brought forward a challenge to the duality of property in the form of monistic socialism. Theorists of socialism, above all Karl Marx and Friedrich Engels, evoked a future world in which the collective and individual aspects of property would be collapsed into ownership by the community or the society – hence the terms communism and socialism. Socialization of the means of production became the watchword of the international socialist movement and was actually carried out after the Communist revolutions in Russia and China. In practice, community ownership became state ownership, as large communities are incapable of acting except through some form of organization. In the heyday of the Soviet Union and Communist China, the state owned all land and factories; railways and airlines; print media and electronic broadcasters; hospitals and schools; wholesale suppliers and retail outlets; and of course housing.

These state-owned and managed economies proved able to do almost anything their masters wanted (build a hydrogen bomb, put a man on the moon, win the most medals at the Olympics) but incapable of providing a decent standard of living to people at large, because that requires balancing many objectives simultaneously, which, as Hayek explained, is only possible through the flexibility of a market order based on the incentives of private ownership. Ultimately, in the Soviet Union, the state-owned command economy collapsed of its own weight, and in the People's Republic of China it was transformed into a form of authoritarian capitalism.

The end of the twentieth century saw not only the collapse of full-fledged totalitarian communism but also a massive sell-off of government-owned assets in the mixed economies of the Western world. Governments divested themselves of land, corporations, railways, mines, and other economic assets. Canadian examples include the sale of Air Canada, Canadian National Railways, and Petro-Canada, to cite only the best-known cases.

State-owned assets nevertheless remain in every market economy. In the confusion surrounding the worldwide recession that began in 2008, some governments acquired ownership interests in financial institutions and other industries such as automobile manufacturing; but these were also generally presented as temporary, emergency measures, not long-term acquisitions.

PROPERTY RIGHTS OF FIRST NATIONS

Canadian sovereignty, which carries with it the underlying title to Canadian land, can be traced back to the seventeenth century, when the European powers came to North America and asserted their right to rule under the international-law doctrines of discovery and (sometimes) conquest. French sovereignty in what is now Eastern Canada passed to Great Britain through the Treaties of Utrecht (1713) and Paris (1763). Canada inherited these rights when the Dominion was formed in 1867 and added to them by purchasing Rupert's Land from the Hudson's Bay Company in 1870, thereby acquiring a title stretching back to the British assertion of sovereignty in the Hudson's Bay Company charter of 1670.

That all of this happened without any consultation with the native people of North America may be cause for regret and may ultimately lead to profound constitutional changes in Canada as the rights of indigenous peoples become more prominent in international law. For the present, however, Canadian sovereignty over the whole of Canada is recognized both internationally and by Canadian courts. Even the far-reaching *Delgamuukw* decision (1997), which held that aboriginal title had not yet been extinguished in British Columbia, did not challenge Canadian sovereignty.[40]

Within the Canadian federal system of divided sovereignty, the constitution gives the national Parliament legislative jurisdiction over "Indians, and lands reserved for the Indians."[41] In contrast, the constitution gives the provinces legislative jurisdiction over the lands and natural resources within their own boundaries.[42] Indian reserves, therefore, are islands of federal jurisdiction within seas of provincial jurisdiction.

In most of Canada, however, except for British Columbia and the three Territories, the provinces hold the underlying or reversionary title to Indian reserves, even though they do not have legislative jurisdiction. That is, if a First Nation became extinct through demographic decline or decided to surrender its reserve for economic reasons, its land would revert to the provincial Crown, not the federal Crown. This rather odd situation was established by the Judicial Committee of the Privy Council in the famous *St Catherine's Milling* case.[43]

Although the provincial Crown holds the underlying title to provincial land, the provinces allow individuals, corporations, and other organizations to acquire fee-simple title to particular pieces of land. Subject to legislative restrictions such as zoning and land-use regulations, and subject also to the Crown's power of eminent domain, holders of fee-simple title exercise all the rights of ownership; they can exclude others, use and manage their property, and dispose of it through gift, sale, or inheritance. These individual property rights make possible the market system in which Canadians can own their own homes, farms, and business premises.

Of course, a province may also hold other lands as Crown land; that is, the government exercises all the rights of exclusion, use, and disposition that are exercised by individuals in the context of fee-simple ownership. Typically, provincial governments bring Crown lands into the economic marketplace by granting leases, licenses, and tenures for the exploitation of natural resources such as grass, timber, and minerals. Such lesser forms of property rights are important but not nearly as robust as fee-simple ownership because they are usually in force only for a limited time and are subject to contractual or legislative limitations.

Most First Nations lands, or Indian reserves, are provincial Crown lands put under federal control and dedicated to a specific purpose. According to s. 18 of the Indian Act,

> reserves are held by Her Majesty for the use and benefit of the
> respective bands for which they were set apart, and subject
> to this Act and to the terms of any treaty or surrender, the
> Governor in Council may determine whether any purpose for
> which lands in a reserve are used or are to be used is for the
> use and benefit of the band.

The Act goes on to spell out in considerable detail who has decision-making authority over Indian reserves. For major decisions, authority is generally vested in "the minister," which in practice means the bureaucracy of the federal Department of Indian Affairs. Band councils are empowered to make some decisions, such as allowing members to take possession of tracts on land on the reserve, but even that local decision is subject to override by the minister.[44]

In short, the basic reality of Indian reserves in Canada is government ownership of land. The reversionary title rests with the provinces in most cases, while decision-making authority is divided between two other levels of government, the band council on the reserve and the Indian Affairs bureaucracy in Ottawa. Indian Affairs is by far the senior partner in this arrangement, with the right to overrule almost everything that local authorities in the band might wish to do with land on the reserve.

Whether or not this system ever had any historical justification for the protection of Indian lands, it is anachronistic in the modern world because it is neither politically democratic nor economically efficient. It is undemocratic because "the minister" who controls First Nations lands is accountable not to the First Nations but to the House of Commons, which is elected by voters of whom only a tiny proportion are members of First Nations. It is economically inefficient in the same way that all government ownership tends to be inefficient, because it does not create incentives for managers to put resources to their most profitable use. This particular scheme of management is also administratively inefficient because power is divided between band councils and Indian Affairs officials in Ottawa, which leads to misunderstandings, delays, and buck-passing.

The scheme is mitigated somewhat by the quasi-property rights that individuals can exercise on Indian reserves under certain conditions – customary land rights, certificates of possession, and leases. However, later chapters will show in detail that these rights are limited, insecure, and subject to various administrative problems. They fall far short of the rights of exclusion, use, and disposition that Canadians receive with fee-simple ownership.

Our line of argument points toward Parliamentary adoption of a First Nations Property Ownership Act, as mentioned in the foreword by Manny Jules, to recognize First Nations' reversionary title to their lands while also creating the machinery for a system of individual title on those lands. A key component of the system will be a Torrens Land Title Registry System, which will make First Nations' land titles as secure as those guaranteed by any of the Canadian provinces. The intended result is to enable First Nations to use their land and natural resources effectively in the modern economy. As they benefit from capitalizing on their assets, so will other Canadians; for a market economy is a wealth-creating, positive-sum game in which call can benefit from the progress of others.

The Panorama of Indian Property Rights

An old and recurrent fantasy about American aboriginal peoples is that they had no conception of property. Christopher Columbus got the impression that "in that which one had, all took a share, especially of eatable things."[1] The Baron de La Hontan, who had served as a soldier and explorer in the New World, wrote in 1703 in *New Voyages to North America:* "The *Savages* are utter Strangers to distinctions of property, for what belongs to one is equally another's."[2]

The same misconception cropped up in our own day in the speech allegedly given by Chief Seattle in 1854 but actually composed by a Texas writer in 1971, popularized in a made-for-TV movie the following year, and quoted with approval by US Vice-President Albert Gore in his environmentalist book *Earth in the Balance.*[3] Seattle is made to say, "The earth does not belong to man; man belongs to the earth,"[4] and "the President in Washington sends word that he wishes to buy our land. Buy our land! But how can you buy or sell the sky? The land?"[5] It's all a modern invention; none of it is the words of Chief Seattle.

Aboriginal advocates often portray Indians as natural collectivists, indeed proto-communists. According to Vine Deloria, Jr, Indians have a "tribal-communal way of life, devoid of economic competition ... While the rest of America is devoted to private property, Indians prefer to hold their lands in tribal estate, sharing the resources in common."[6] Ward Churchill writes that "the nature of the indigenist impulse is essentially socialist, insofar as socialism – or what Karl Marx described as 'primitive communism' – was and remains the primary mode of indigenous social organization in the Americas."[7]

Though frequently expressed, such conceptions of American Indians as lacking institutions of private property are simply wrong. The historical and ethnographic literature shows that Indians were abundantly familiar with property, albeit in forms unfamiliar to European explorers and conquerors, for whom rejection of the reality of Indian property was often a prelude to expropriation with little or no compensation. It is both ironic and tragic that this originally European conception of Indians as natural communists has now been accepted by many aboriginal leaders and thinkers and become a barrier to native participation in the modern economy. The reality is that the original inhabitants of the Americas had institutions of property before European contact. Of course, they modified those institutions as European contact changed the circumstances in which they lived, but they were never without their own conceptions of property rights.

Let us look at some of the evidence, as it has been summarized in recent works of scholarship. It is necessary to look separately at different cultural areas, for the natives of the Americas had vastly different cultures correlated with their type of technology and way of making a living. As modern property-rights theory deriving from Harold Demsetz would predict, their property institutions depended on the relative scarcity of land, fish, game, and other valuable resources.

FARMERS

The Aztecs of the central Mexican plateau had a large-scale society that combined intensive agriculture and urbanization. Contrary to what has been written in some earlier literature, scholars of the Aztecs now realize that their institutions of private property were highly developed. Unfortunately, Aztec legal codes have not survived, so what we know comes from early Spanish observers.

Reminiscent of European feudalism, the Aztecs had several categories of landownership, all ultimately dependent on the emperor. Some land was deeded to individuals, such as noblemen, warriors, judges, and priests. Other tracts were tied to institutions, such as palaces, courts, and temples. Land could be transferred by the emperor, who, like the British king, possessed an underlying title to all land; but some types of land could also be bought and sold, given and willed, by others. In any case, the land was actually worked at the ground level by a variety of tenant farmers, serfs, slaves, and communal villages *(calpullati)*. Commoners were supposed to own land only as part of these local communes, but in practice there were wealthy commoners with large holdings, who "probably bought, sold, and passed on land in many areas of the empire with minimal or no government interference."[8] Clearly this was a society with robust property rights – not the ownership in fee simple that sustains a capitalist economy but a feudal network of rights suitable for supporting a regime of divine kingship.

Prior to contact with Europeans, agriculture based on the cultivation of maize and beans existed across the southwestern and southeastern United States as well as the northeast, including what is now New England, New York, and southern Ontario and Quebec. It had also been practiced in the river valleys of the Great Plains but was largely given up there after the introduction of horses in the eighteenth century made buffalo hunting more profitable. According to Galbraith, Rodriguez, and Stiles, "among almost all North American farming tribes, land was considered private and either individually or family owned as long as improvements were made and the land used."[9]

Relying on the seminal work of Ralph Linton,[10] Leonard Carlson writes that "tribes in those areas that practiced farming had some elements of land tenure and agriculture in common. By and large, farming was done by women. Land generally belonged to the tribe, with a usufructuary right being held by individual family or kinship groups."[11] Anthropologist Bruce Trigger gives a more detailed portrait of Huron farming in what is now Canada:

> The planting, care, and harvesting of crops were women's tasks ... One of the most arduous horticultural tasks was the clearing of the fields. The transformation of forest into clearing was men's work ... Armed with stone axes, the men cut down the smaller trees ... then girdled the larger ones and stripped off some of their branches [which] were burned at the base of the larger trees to kill them. The women then planted their crops between the stumps ... Huron horticultural

practices forced them to relocate their settlements at intervals which varied between ten and thirty years ... the pressure on land does not appear to have been great enough to induce particular communities to occupy a number of specified sites in rotation.

Teams of men working together could clear as much land as they wanted or were able, and this land remained in the possession of their extended families as long as the women of these families wished to cultivate it. Once abandoned, however, a field could be used by anyone who wished to do so. It is unclear to what degree each woman regarded the corn, beans, and squash she planted as her property, or the women living in a single longhouse considered all the food they produced to be their collective possession.[12]

Although time has obscured the details, the general picture is that of temporary ownership of agricultural land by extended families. Absence of machinery and draft animals meant that farming had to be a collective enterprise involving human muscle power, and lack of animal manure for fertilizer meant that fields had to be abandoned periodically. Under the circumstances, permanent ownership of specified lots would have been senseless.

In the US southeast, the four main nations (Cherokee, Choctaw, Chickasaw, and Creek) had an agricultural economy and institutions of property similar to those of Indians in the northeast, only more productive because of the warmer climate. Through contact and intermarriage with British settlers, they quickly adopted more intensive forms of agriculture. Most became yeoman farmers, cultivating around five to seven acres, but a wealthy planter and slaveholding class also emerged among these Indian tribes.[13] Even after deportation to Oklahoma in the 1830s, the wealthy elite continued to own slaves and supported the Confederacy in the Civil War.

In the US southwest, where irrigation was required to grow crops in the arid landscape, forms of private property also existed. After surveying Pima, Yuma, Pueblo, Hopi, and Navaho agriculture, Carlson concludes:

In summary, land tenure arrangements found among native peoples in the southwest were consistent with the relative

scarcity of resources and the costs of enforcing property rights
… Economic activities were largely conducted by individuals or families with individual rights to land and animals
that were recognized by the tribe. Centralized management
of group activities, which meant monitoring individuals who
might shirk, were [sic] common only for the construction and
maintenance of public goods such as irrigation systems.[14]

Indians in the southwest and California also exercised individual
ownership of fruit and nut trees, such as the pinyon, and looked
after them to ensure their continued productivity.[15]

FISHERS

The greatest proliferation of property rights in North America
occurred in the fishing societies of the Pacific Coast. According to
the anthropologist Leland Donald,

ideas of property and ownership were highly developed
throughout the culture area. Almost everything could be and
often was owned. From the indigenous point of view this
included not only resource loci and material goods but also
noncorporeal property such as songs, myths, and knowledge
of various types.[16]

There was no farming, except occasional growing of tobacco, but
the predictability of the salmon runs generated landownership at
specific sites. Salmon were abundant and easy to catch at certain
places; and those places, along with weirs, traps, platforms, and
smokehouses, belonged to families. These rights could be transferred through lease, sale, or inheritance, often witnessed publicly at
potlatch celebrations.[17] A certain egalitarian mythology has grown
up around the potlatch because property was given away at these
ritual celebrations, but such festivals of lavish gift-giving could exist
only because people owned things in the first place – i.e., had strong
property rights.

Salmon-fishing was central to survival for the Pacific Coast people,
but they also exploited many other natural resources and thus cre-

ated property rights over broad expanses of land. Land administrator Diane Cragg describes the Nisga'a situation as follows:

> From time immemorial the Nisga'a owned the valley of the Nass River from mountaintop to mountaintop and from the headwaters to the sea. The Nass Valley covers an area of approximately 24,000 square kilometers, and every inch belonged to someone.
> At the risk of gross over-simplification of the way that Nisga'a people owned land:
>
> - Property, and the resources on it, belonged to the Wilp, or extended family, through the auspices of a Simoo'git or Chief, who had the responsibility of managing and allocating both land and resources for the use of his Wilp.
> - Property could be, and was, transferred from one Wilp to another for commercial or cultural reasons.[18]

If the West Coast Indians had harvested salmon on the high seas, they probably would have treated the resource as a commons, as the prairie Indians treated the buffalo herds. However, the coastal Indians did not have the technology necessary for blue-water fishing, so they harvested salmon in tidal waters and rivers, which created a favourable milieu for the establishment of private property rights. According to legal theorist Bruce Johnsen,

> local group leaders appear to have operated along the lines of franchisees to their clan leader, who had a similar relationship with the broader tribal leader. As local resource manager, the leader directed the harvesting and preservation of salmon and allocated a customary share of the output to each member of the house in return for the family's labor services ... Almost uniformly up and down the coast, wealthier titleholders were known by a name that translated roughly into "river owner."[19]

Johnsen argues that the West Coast Indians engaged in "husbandry" of the streams that they owned, protecting the banks, improving spawning beds, and transferring eggs from one site to another. Beyond that, they even engaged in "purposeful selection of salmon stocks to develop populations with preferred biological characteristics."[20] For example, the average size of fish can be increased by taking smaller specimens for food consumption and allowing the larger ones to spawn, a Darwinian principle that is increasingly recognized in modern fisheries management.[21]

The Yurok and some of their neighbours in northern California seem to have had particularly precise conceptions of property. According to economist Bruce Benson,

> the owner of a fishing spot on the banks of the Klamath had exclusive use of the site. However, he could sell a temporary right of use to a second party if he wished ... The owner was responsible for seeing that the user was not injured while fishing. If a user slipped on a rock, for example, and suffered an injury, the owner had to pay damages. Ownership rights for a fishing location could also be permanently shared in the sense that several individuals could possess limited ownership rights to the same spot, with each having exclusive rights (including liability) to its use during certain specified times.[22]

Rare among hunting-gathering peoples, the natives of the Pacific Coast also practiced slavery on a large scale.[23] Hunter-foragers seldom hold slaves because it is uneconomic in their way of life. You can't send slaves out to track a deer or trap a beaver because they might escape, and there is not much for slaves to do in camp. But in the sedentary fishing culture of the West Coast, slaves could be put to work processing fish and cutting timber. As an economic asset, slaves were eagerly sought in war and were afterward subject to inheritance, gift, and sale. They were totally reduced to the status of property and deprived of all human rights and dignity. They were sometimes even put to death in a demonstration of the owner's power. Although Governor John Graves Simcoe had prohibited the importation of slaves into Canada in 1793, and slavery was legally abolished throughout the British Empire in 1834, it continued to exist in fact among the Indians of British Columbia until the late nineteenth century. One does not have to endorse slavery to note that its existence as an institution in any society shows a highly developed sense of property rights.

HUNTERS

After obtaining horses from the Spanish in the eighteenth century, the natives of the Great Plains began to exploit the buffalo as their main food resource. Because buffalo ranged so widely, laying claim to small areas of land would have been pointless. Moreover, buffalo-hunting was best carried out by large groups to chase the herd, slaughter the animals, and preserve the meat as pemmican. Under these conditions, tribes or nations had large but overlapping hunting territories. Perhaps more than anything else, the fluidity of the prairie situation has given rise to the stereotype that Indians had no conception of owning the land.

But even if the Plains Indians did not have individual property in land, they had institutions of personal property, as anthropologists have found to be true of all societies.[24] What Bruce Benson writes of the Comanche is generally applicable to all the buffalo-hunting tribes:

> private ownership was firmly established for such things as horses, tools for hunting and gathering, food, weapons, materials used in the construction of mobile shelters, clothing, and various kinds of body ornaments that were used for religious ceremonies and other activities. Cooperative production (group raids to take horses from enemy tribes or group hunts) did not imply communal ownership. The product of such cooperative activities was divided among participants according to their contributed effort. Individuals might share such things as food at times, but they did so out of generosity. Food could be given but not taken because it was private property not communal property.[25]

In addition to their individual ownership of objects, the prairie Indian nations also aspired to exercise collective control of hunting grounds, to exploit the buffalo for their own benefit, and to exclude other tribes. However, small populations and large expanses of territory meant that such control was seldom perfect. Unable to patrol boundaries all the time, tribes concentrated on strategies that would deter outsiders from entering – raids to steal their horses and, when advantage of surprise or numbers could be achieved, massacre of opponents, accompanied by terrorist tactics such as scalping.[26]

The prairie Indians had switched from river-valley agriculture to buffalo-hunting in the eighteenth century, after they started to get horses from the Spanish. When the buffalo disappeared as a commercial resource in the 1870s, the natives then started to switch back to agriculture. In the years from 1875 to 1896, acreage cultivated by reservation Indians in the United States (not including the Five Civilized Tribes in Oklahoma) more than tripled, from 117,267 to 369,974 acres.[27] The same thing happened north of the border, although progress in Indian agriculture was slowed down in the 1890s by the Canadian Government's misguided "peasant policy," which tried to force prairie Indians to farm only with hand implements and to produce enough only for personal consumption, not for sale on local markets.[28] On both sides of the border, this early transition of prairie hunters to agriculture relied mainly on "custom" or "use" landholdings, which families appropriated for themselves within reserved territories.[29]

The forest hunters of North America also practiced private property in personal possessions, but they faced a different situation in hunting and land use. Hunting in a forest usually means stalking or trapping animals one by one rather than exploiting a herd, as on the prairies. Hence forest hunters tend to work individually or in small groups rather than in large tribal aggregations, except for some kinds of fishing, when spawning runs produce herd-like density of prey.

There has been much scholarly debate over the extent to which eastern forest hunters developed institutions of collective and individual control over land in response to the incentives of the fur trade. European fashions for beaver and other pelts raised their value and certainly encouraged Indians in the direction of exercising control over trapping grounds. A modern author describes how the Montaignais of Labrador and Quebec assigned trapping rights in the eighteenth century: "It was a highly sophisticated system.

The Montaignais blazed trees with their family crests to delineate their hunting grounds, practiced retaliation against poachers and trespassers, developed a seasonal allotment system, and marked beaver houses."[30]

There is also evidence of both collective and individual forms of landownership in the seventeenth century before there had been much contact with Europeans. The Jesuit missionary Paul LeJeune wrote of the Montaignais in 1637: "These Barbarians have a very remarkable custom. When other nations arrive in their country, they would not dare pass beyond without permission from the Captain of the place; if they did, their canoes would be broken to pieces."[31] The Franciscan missionary Chrestien Leclerq wrote of the Attikamek (Cree of the St Maurice region of Quebec) later in the century:

> It is the right of the head the nation ... to distribute the places of hunting to each individual. It is not permitted to any Indian to overstep the bounds and limits of the region, which shall have been assigned to him in the assemblies of the elders. These are held in the autumn and in spring expressly to make this assignment.[32]

According to the anthropologist Peter Usher, the Inuit of the Arctic also had "definite concepts about the territorial rights and limits of the tribe and band, as well as systems of tenure and allocation within these groups. Rights in land and resources rested with the group, which maintained the right to use its territory through occupancy."[33] There was considerable overlapping use, based on peaceful agreements between groups to share. Within the band, individuals and families subdivided the territory for hunting and trapping based on usage.

> Even in the case of individual activities such as trapping, there were not individual property rights in land. Individuals or partners were recognized as having preeminent rights to a trapline or a fishing spot so long as they used it; when they stopped doing so, whoever sought to use it in their place

would ask their permission. Individuals or families were also recognized as having preeminent rights to dwelling sites, but again only for as long as they occupied them.[34]

Though not the same as ownership in fee simple in the British tradition, these are definitely institutions of property involving control of land and the right to exclude others, but with the emphasis on the collective rather than the individual side.

CONCLUSION

This brief survey of North American Indian property institutions allows us to make several generalizations. Aboriginal people everywhere in North America practiced personal ownership of possessions such as clothing, tools, weapons, animals, and housing. With respect to land, there was always a collective sense of territory based on the tribe or nation, combined to varying degrees with specific use rights of families and individuals.

Property institutions were related to the economy and culture of the particular society. Prairie hunters pursuing the buffalo over vast territories put great emphasis on tribal hunting grounds but did not try to develop individual property rights in land. Forest hunters had tribal hunting grounds but also developed family and individual rights to particularly valuable spots. The fishing societies of the Pacific Coast developed family and individual rights to valuable fishing stations, weirs, and spawning streams, as well as claims to broader expanses of surrounding land. Farmers had customary family and individual rights to cultivated fields. The society of the Aztecs, with its intensive agriculture and urbanization, had a fully developed system of private property rights in land comparable to that of feudal Europe. The sedentary societies of Mexico and the Pacific Coast developed the ultimate form of private property – slavery, that is, the ownership of other human beings.

This panorama of native American property rights is consistent with Demsetz's theory that property rights evolve as needed. They become more elaborate as land becomes scarcer relative to population and more valuable because of technological advances. Indeed, Indian property rights were never static. The prairie hunters abandoned ownership of land in river valleys when the acquisition of horses made buffalo hunting more profitable. When the buffalo were exterminated, they returned to agriculture and created customary landholdings on their reserved lands. The forest hunters intensified their familial and individual control of trapping grounds when the fur trade made pelts more valuable. The agricultural tribes of the American southeast adopted European practices of agriculture and institutions of ownership, including large plantations and slavery. The fishers of the Pacific Coast entered the commercial salmon fishery and even today make up a significant portion of boat owners in that industry.

In short, the historical evidence shows that the aboriginal peoples of North America are like all other human beings. They claim territories as collectivities but have no particular aversion to private property in the hands of families and individuals. Unless they are prevented by the *force majeure* of government, they change with the times and are willing to adopt whatever institutions of property are most economically efficient for the world in which they live. Say goodbye to the primitive communist of Marxist fantasy and hello to the worker, owner, and investor of the modern global economy!

A Failed Experiment: The Dawes Act

Beginning with passage of the General Allocation Act (Dawes Act) in 1887, the United States experimented on a large scale with introducing private landownership onto Indian reservations. The experiment was concluded in 1934 with the passage of the Indian Reorganization Act (IRA) amid a general feeling, which still prevails today, that the experiment was a failure. Indeed, the reaction has been so intense that the Dawes Act is often held up as conclusive proof that any interest in individual property rights for aboriginal people is a token of sinister motives. We have to look more closely at that period of US history to see what lessons it holds for helping Canadian First Nations obtain better access to the institutions of private property. Without trying to defend the Dawes Act, it is essential to find out exactly why things went so badly awry when it was implemented.

THE DAWES ACT

The idea of introducing Western conceptions of private property into Indian life has deep roots in US history. Many nineteenth-century treaties contained some provision for private allotments of land, often, though not exclusively, for people of mixed white and Indian ancestry. By 1885, the US Government had issued over 11,000 patents and 1,290 certificates of allotment to Indians under various treaties and statutes.[1] Meanwhile uncounted thousands of Indians had taken up customary land holdings on their reservations and were farming them virtually as private property, though without the right to sell them.[2] With the benefit of hindsight, we can now see that it would probably have been better to let this gradual evolution proceed, but it did not look that way to many political decision-makers of that era. Several factors came together to produce the "big bang" of the 1887 Dawes Act.

The geographical expansion of the United States on the North American continent was now complete and the Indian wars were over. To many Americans, it seemed like the logical time to fulfill the old dream of civilizing Indians, assimilating them into the body politic. Indian rights associations sprang up in the eastern United States, agitating to improve the Indians' condition by introducing private property, Christianity, and other institutions of Western civilization. Beginning in 1883, the annual Lake Mohonk Conference of Friends of the Indian became an influential forum for these social reformers.

Another factor was the ongoing decline in the Indian population, combined with the large size of their reservations. There were about 280,000 Indians in 1875 and only 260,000 in 1885,[3] and it was widely expected that their race might die out altogether. The US pattern of dealing with the Indians had always been to grant very large reservations, which would be whittled away in subsequent decades.[4] Thus 260,000 Indians in the mid-1880s had land reservations totalling more than 136 million acres[5] – more than 500 acres apiece at a time when the standard size of a homestead was 160 acres. Compare that to the formula used in the Numbered Treaties in the prairie provinces of Canada for computing the size of reserves – one section of land (640 acres) for a family of five, or 128 acres apiece. In the eyes of white observers, US Indians possessed far more land than they needed or could ever use, given that their population was on a downward trend.

This geodemographic situation created two kinds of pressures for privatizing the reservations. On the one side, land-hungry farmers, ranchers, lumbermen, miners, and railway companies wanted the reservations broken up so they could buy the lands and use them for their own purposes. On the other side, some Indians thought that private property might be the best way of retaining at least part of their reservations in their own hands.[6]

Economic historian Lawrence Carlson summarizes the multiple goals that found expression in the Dawes Act:

- Break up the tribe as a social unit;
- Encourage individual initiative;
- Further progress of Indian farmers;
- Reduce the cost of Indian administration;
- Secure at least part of the reservation as Indian land;
- Open unused lands to white settlers.[7]

In 1880 the Commissioner of Indian Affairs said that allotment "is a measure corresponding with the progressive age in which we live, and is indorsed by all true friends of the Indian."[8] Director John Wesley Powell of the Bureau of American Ethnology wrote in 1881, "No measure could be devised more efficient for the ultimate civilization of the Indians of this country than one by which they could successfully and rapidly obtain lands in severalty."[9] From 1879 onward, allotment legislation was always on the agenda in either the House of Representatives or the Senate. The best known of these bills was the "Coke Bill," sponsored by Democratic Senator Richard Coke from Texas. Passage of a different bill was finally secured in 1887 through the efforts of Republican Senator Henry Dawes from Massachusetts, a frequent speaker at the Lake Mohonk conferences.

Support for the Dawes Act crossed lines of party and region. Interestingly, however, the main opponent was Republican Senator Henry Teller from Colorado, who claimed far more personal familiarity with the Indian situation than could Senator Dawes or the other eastern reformers. Teller said presciently in 1881:

> If I stand alone in the Senate, I want to put upon the record
> my prophecy in this matter, that when thirty or forty years
> shall have passed and these Indians shall have parted with
> their title, they will curse the hand that was professedly
> in their defense to secure this kind of legislation and if the
> people who are clamoring for it understood Indian character,
> and Indian laws, and Indian morals, and Indian religion, they
> would not be here clamoring for this at all.[10]

The Dawes Act authorized the president to allot agricultural lands on reservations according to the formula of 160 acres for (male) heads of families, 80 acres for single persons over eighteen or orphans under eighteen, and 40 acres for children under eighteen. These allotments could be doubled if the reservation was suitable only for grazing livestock but not for growing crops. If the reservation did not have enough land to accommodate these grants, the land would be subdivided in the same proportion; there was no provision for acquiring additional acreage. The president would appoint special agents to carry out the allotment of the reserves, acting in consultation with the residents. Indians would become citizens of the United States upon receiving their allotments, but they could not sell them for twenty-five years, until a patent had been issued for the land. This was meant to provide a transitional period for them to become self-supporting family farmers rather than make a quick dollar by selling the allotment.

After the allotment was finalized and a patent in fee granted, the land would become like any other privately owned land. It could be bought or sold, given or willed, to anyone. The title would be documented in the state land registry; there was to be no special federal registry of allotments.[11] All this was consistent with the larger aim of the Dawes Act of assimilating Indians into the citizenry of the United States.

Reduction of reservations was also part of the plan. The tribe could cede any land left over after allotment to the president, who could sell it and deposit the proceeds in a trust fund for the benefit of the Indians. The courts held in 1903 that surplus lands could be disposed of even without the approval of the tribe.[12]

Most significantly, the new regime was to be mandatory, even though earlier versions of the Coke Bill would have given Indians the choice of opting into private property or remaining with communal ownership. Choice was taken out of the bill in the final conference to reconcile different versions passed in the Senate and House of Representatives; it is not clear who pushed for the mandatory approach. No matter where compulsion came from, it was a fateful decision. According to economist Terry Anderson, who is a strong proponent of private property rights,

the problem with allotment and subsequent policies lies in the top down nature of institutional design and not necessarily privatization itself. Prior to allotment, Indians were figuring out how to organize agricultural production on reservations ... They were adapting, although they were not necessarily doing so with formal private property rights to individual land parcels. When allotment was imposed on the reservations, it made no consideration for traditional management schemes that may have embodied abundant knowledge and experience; it assumed that rectangularly surveyed property rights were the only way to get the incentives right.[13]

Or, as Jennifer Roback says more concisely: "The allotment policy did not institute private property among the Indians; instead it overturned a functioning property rights system that was already in place."[14]

An equally important observation is that the Dawes Act failed to recognize the collective dimension of Indian property. It assumed that the United States held the underlying title to Indian reservations and could dispose of them as it chose, as was in fact done through the sale of "surplus" lands. The scheme of private property rights introduced by the Dawes Act was meant to incorporate Indians and their lands in the US polity, not to recognize them as separate communities capable of making governmental decisions about their own lands. The introduction of individual rights was in itself not the fatal flaw of the Dawes Act; the great error was the imposition of a property rights scheme while recognizing neither the collective title of native communities nor the private property rights that they had already evolved for themselves.

IMPLEMENTATION OF THE DAWES ACT

As with all sweeping legislation, the implementation of the Dawes Act was far from simple, with many subsequent amendments and variations in policy until the ultimate repeal in 1934. Without trying to chart all these twists and turns, let us indicate the main areas where changes took place.

Application. The Dawes Act was intended for universal application, but allotment proceeded irregularly. The allotment process entailed federal expenditures for surveying and administration, so the timing of allotment was influenced by the state of the federal budget. On the demand side, Leonard Carlson has shown that reservations that were more attractive to white settlers because of higher rainfall or greater population density in the surrounding area tended to be allotted first.[15] Hence it is not surprising that very little allotment took place in the arid southwest. When the IRA was passed in 1934, 118 of 213 reservations had been dealt with. Slightly more than 40 million acres were eventually allotted, out of approximately 136 million acres in Indian Country at the time the Dawes Act was passed.[16]

Eligibility for allotment and size of allotments. Wives were not mentioned in the original plan but were included in 1891. The basic grant for a family was kept at 160 acres but divided into 80-acre allotments for husband and wife.[17] There was, however, much variation in practice from the standard plan. Some reservations were too small to give every family a normal grant, while in dry country allotments were sometimes much larger.[18] Also, allotments were sometimes divided among two or more locations to take account of land quality, water supply, topography, and other local variables.

Leasing. The theory behind the Dawes Act was that Indians would work their own allotments and become self-supporting family farmers. Some did, but many others had little taste for farming or did not have the money for seed grain, equipment, fencing, and livestock. The government provided little assistance to would-be Indian farmers in the early years of the Dawes Act regime. Therefore, many allottees who would not or could not farm their allotments wished to earn some money from them by renting them out, which was legalized by amendments to the Act passed in 1891.[19] By 1900, there were 7,574 leases, compared to 10,835 families cultivating their own allotments.[20] Leasing reportedly often led to sales in the long term, as the lessors got used to receiving money without working and the lessees became virtual proprietors through years of residence.

Heirship. The vexing problem of heirship arose out the Dawes Act prohibition on sales for twenty-five years from the date of allotment. If the allottee died before sale, the allotment had to be divided among the heirs.[21] This policy quickly led to sizable amounts of land being divided and subdivided into parcels too small to be worked

Table 3.1 | Alienation of American Indian Land, 1887–1934

		Acres
1	All Indian lands, 1887	136,394,895
2	All Indian lands, 1933	69,588,441
	a Tribal lands, 1933	29,481,685
	b Individual trust (heirs), 1933	7,023,237
	c Individual trust (living), 1933	10,806,177
	d Allotments no longer in trust, 1933	22,277,342
3	Surplus lands surrendered, 1933	66,806,454
	a Surrendered lands sold to settlers	22,694,658
	b Surrendered lands retained by government	44,111,796

SOURCE: Carlson, *Indians, Bureaucrats, and Land*, 204.

economically. Indeed, this problem of fractionation continued to be-devil individual trust land in following decades. In 1981 there were

> over 200,000 surface tracts of individually owned trust land with an average tract ownership of 10 undivided interest owners. This means there are over 2,000,000 separate un-divided interests to keep track of. Ownership in some tracts is so complicated that owners own an undivided interest in which the common denominator is in the quintillionths.[22]

One expedient was to lease such parcels, which provided a little income for the owner but worked against the intent of the Dawes Act to create self-supporting Indian farmers working their own land. Also, sale of subdivided heirship lands became legally pos-sible after 1902, leading to the alienation of about 2.4 million acres, much of it to non-Indian purchasers.[23]

The interplay of all these processes produced a considerable dimi-nution of Indian Country during the sixty-seven years between pas-sage of the Dawes Act in 1887 and replacement by the IRA in 1934. Table 3.1 shows the size of the loss over that period of time.[24]

Let us round off the numbers for ease of explanation. Indian res-ervations had been reduced by almost half (67 million acres) from 1887 to 1933 through the surrender of so-called surplus lands. Of those ceded lands, about one third were sold to white settlers and the rest retained as public land under the control of the federal government, which managed it through grazing, mining, and timber leases. Beyond that an unknown proportion (Carlson estimates as high as 80 percent)[25] of the 22 million acres in patented allotments had been sold to non-Indians. Patented allotments were still considered part of the reservations but were in the hands of individual owners, whether Indian or other.

In 1933, there were still almost 18 million acres of unpatented individual allotments held as individual trusts. Over the next fifty years, that total declined to slightly more than 10 million acres as some of these (often highly subdivided) lands were allowed to be sold and others were returned to tribal ownership. By 1983, tribal trust lands had grown to about 42 million acres through recovery of individual trust lands plus purchase of additional land for tribes by the federal government.[26] Thus the size of Indian Country has rebounded slightly from the low point it reached in 1933, but many reservations are still "checkerboarded," consisting of three categories of land described as follows by economist Terry Anderson:

- *Fee simple,* under which individual Indians and non-Indians own the land, can determine its use, and can transfer it to new owners without BIA [Bureau of Indian Affairs] supervision;
- *Individual trust,* under which land has been allotted to individual Indians but remains held in trust by the BIA as a check on individual decisions; and
- *Tribal trust,* under which land is owned by the tribe but held in trust by the BIA as a check on tribal decisions.[27]

In an econometric study, Terry Anderson and Dean Lueck have shown that fee-simple land on American Indian reservations is farmed far more productively than either individual trust or tribal trust land.[28] This finding confirms the greater economic utility of fee-simple ownership as compared to more encumbered forms of property rights, but it doesn't reveal anything about the welfare of American Indians because the authors did not know whether these fee-simple lands are now owned by Indians or non-Indians.

The person most responsible for ending the allotment process was John Collier, commissioner of Indian Affairs from 1933 to 1945. Collier grew up in Atlanta, studied at Columbia University, and became a social worker in New York City. His early thinking was influenced by an eclectic variety of sources, including Prince Peter Kropotkin's anarchist theory of "mutual aid"; William Morris's nostalgic socialism; Friedrich Nietzsche's heroic individualism; and Lester Frank Ward's theory of "sociocracy," which called for the guidance of society by the new science of sociology.[29] Collier discovered Indians in 1919 almost by accident, when he went to visit a white friend living at the Taos Pueblo in New Mexico. The Indians' communitarian spirit inspired him with "a new, even wildly new, hope for the Race of Man," and he began to write about the Taos Pueblo as a "Red Atlantis."[30]

Invoking the lost civilization of Atlantis was a complex piece of symbolism. At one level, it emphasized that the Indians were being submerged in the sea of white America. But was that a good or a bad thing? Plato, the only source of the Atlantis story in classical literature, had depicted Atlantis as a militaristic threat to Athens. But Francis Bacon revalued the lost continent in his seventeenth-century essay *The New Atlantis,* making it a symbol of a utopian society that transcends the human condition.

Collier clearly saw Indians in this millenarian light. He wrote in 1947:

They [Indians] had what the world has lost. They have it now.
What the world has lost, the world must have again, lest it die ...
What, in our human world, is this power to live? It is the ancient, lost reverence and passion for human personality, joined with the ancient, lost reverence and passion for the earth and its web of life ...
If our modern world should be able to recapture this power, the earth's natural resources and web of life would not be irrevocably wasted within the twentieth century, which is the prospect now. True democracy, founded in neighborhoods

and reaching over the world, would become the realized heaven on earth.[31]

After his Taos experience, Collier became a prominent political advocate for Indians. When President Franklin Roosevelt appointed him commissioner of Indian Affairs 1933, Collier moved quickly to draft legislation – the Wheeler-Howard Act – to repeal the Dawes Act and introduce a new era of tribal self-government. He wanted to prevent any further allotment of land and recover for collective tribal ownership the almost 18 million acres of restricted land that had been allotted but for which a fee patent had not yet been issued. According to his original plan, these lands would be confiscated by the secretary of the Interior, with compensation not in money but with an "equivalent interest in tribal lands."[32] Collier, however, found that his proposal for collectivizing allotted land was unpopular with some Indians. One Comanche said at a consultative congress, "We love our allotments ... and we don't want to be segregated."[33] Opposition to this feature of the Wheeler-Howard Act was so intense that it was withdrawn, and the IRA as finally passed did not provide for the collectivization of the 18 million acres of restricted allotments. In other respects, however, it did break decisively with the land policies of the Dawes Act. In the words of Collier's biographer,

the IRA established a turning point in Indian history by abandoning future land allotment. It extended the trust period on restricted land [the 18 million acres], allowed for the voluntary exchange of allotments to consolidate checkerboard reservations, continued existing practices of inheritance, and restored to tribal ownership remaining surplus lands created by the Dawes General Allotment Act.[34]

The sixty-seven-year-long implementation of the Dawes Act did not achieve its overall objectives of breaking up all Indian reservations. It may have converted a minority of Indians into self-supporting landowners and assimilated them into US society, but it did not reach those goals for the majority. Its main real-world effects were to reduce the size of Indian reservations by half, create a new category of landless Indians as their population increased, and introduce the threefold system of reservation landownership described above by Terry Anderson.

CONCLUSION

The historiography of the Dawes Act is generally negative, emphasizing the alienation of land from tribal ownership and the checkerboarding of reservations.[35] In the most careful study to date, Leonard Carlson concluded that the Dawes Act allotment process hampered rather than hindered the progress of Indian agriculture. He found that there was substantial growth in Indian farming in the years 1870–1900, with Indians relying on informal and customary allocations of land. On most reservations, there was enough land available that any Indian who wanted to farm could simply choose a tract and start to work it. According to government statistics on numbers of farms, acreage cultivated, and value of production, Indian farming actually went backward in the years 1900–30 as Dawes Act allotments became more common.[36]

Carlson argues that the property rights imposed by the top-down approach of the Dawes Act were inappropriate to the situation of Indian farmers and thus fraught with unintended consequences. Most Indian farmers were working considerably less than a quarter-section before the Dawes Act. Hence, when they received an allotment for 160 acres or more, they often leased the extra land and used the rental income to reduce their work effort on the land they had previously farmed. Cession of surplus reservation land and sale to outsiders made it more difficult for Indian farmers to acquire free land, as they had done previously. In Carlson's view, it would have been better to continue with informal customary rights, which were actually working in practice, rather than impose the theoretically appealing system of 160-acre allotments.

Fred McChesney additionally points out that the rights of Indians as private owners were often damaged by the top-down process of the Dawes Act:

> Many of the features of land allotment had nothing with privatization but rather with the *lack* of it (i.e., with the retention of trustee rights in the government). Trusteeship made

it almost impossible for Indians to transfer small parcels or to combine holdings fractionated by death ... Taking of land after the *Lone Wolf* case [1903 decision authorizing compulsory taking of "surplus" Indian land by the federal government] was harmful to Indians but was hardly part of private ownership; indeed, taking was the very antithesis of allotment under the Dawes Act.[37]

Whatever the merits or demerits of the Dawes Act and its implementation, what we are putting forward for consideration in this book is very different from that piece of legislation. In the proposed First Nations Property Ownership Act, First Nations will retain control of their land, including the power to regulate and the exercise of eminent domain. This will apply even to lands whose title is granted in fee simple. We are not proposing to transfer First Nations' lands to the federal or provincial governments.

We support legislating a regime of fee-simple ownership that First Nations can opt into *voluntarily*. The Nisga'a are doing this now.[38] Some First Nations are interested in following soon, while others may want to wait longer or indeed may never wish to go down this path. This is not a top-down, Dawes-style privatization of land imposed upon all First Nations with or without their consent. In fact, the process we propose is meant to be led by First Nations themselves.

Along with the optional approach, we advocate a two-step methodology, in which First Nations can collectively acquire ownership of their reserve lands in fee simple and can later decide for themselves whether to introduce individual ownership. The Dawes Act provided for some consultation with individuals but did not leave any role for aboriginal governments to make decisions about the allotment process.

Consistent with this approach, a Torrens-style land registry should be created for collectively and individually held First Nations properties. Moreover, First Nations should control their own land registry; this is not a proposal to transfer their titles into provincial registries.

The Dawes Act led to loss of land not so much because it authorized individual allotments in fee-simple ownership but because unallotted land – indeed half the acreage of existing reservations –

was ceded to the federal government and much of it sold to white settlers. We do not believe that Canadian First Nations have any surplus lands, and we do not advocate the reduction in size of their reserves.

We do not see property-rights legislation as a means of effecting a grand transformation in the lives of native people, neither to "civilize" them nor to re-create a "Red Atlantis." We support making available, to those First Nations who are interested, the same property-rights tools that have made economic advancement possible for other Canadians.

The time from the Dawes Act to the IRA is an instructive period of American history, full of lessons about the difficulty of changing people's lives through top-down legislation. Scholars of all viewpoints would probably agree that neither piece of legislation came close to achieving its objectives, and that both were bedevilled with unintended consequences. But the lesson is not that improvement in the legal framework is never possible; it is that reform must proceed incrementally and voluntarily if it is to achieve its objectives. That is the spirit of the proposals laid out in the final section of this book.

PART TWO

Limited Property Rights
under the Indian Act

Several types of private property rights already exist on Canadian Indian reserves, including customary rights, certificates of possession, and leases. These rights are all based directly or indirectly upon the Indian Act. They are certainly better than nothing, and they enable quite a bit of economic activity to take place on reserves; but they all have intrinsic difficulties that limit their usefulness. Customary rights are often undocumented and in any case cannot be enforced in Canadian courts. Certificates of possession are closer to ownership in fee simple, but they can be transferred only to other band members, which prevents a market for them from emerging. Leases are enforceable and transferable, but they are temporary by their very nature, which limits their market value in comparison to freehold ownership.

Part 2 begins by reviewing the legal framework of the Indian Act, the source of all these rights. We then provide a detailed analysis of each type of right, including both strengths and weaknesses. Finally, we take a quick look at the First Nations Land Management Act (FNLMA), which allows First Nations to create property rights regimes outside the Indian Act. We find that the FNLMA, because it has the potential to reduce transaction costs, is an improvement over the other forms of property rights, but it throws First Nations on their own resources to create their own property-rights regimes. Without advisory institutions and legal templates to follow, the proliferation of First Nations property rights may become a new obstacle to doing business on reserves.

The Legal Framework of the Indian Act

Property rights on Canadian Indian reserves are governed by the Indian Act, an archaic piece of federal legislation passed in 1876 and still in operation today. This chapter examines the origins of individual property rights on Canadian Indian reserves by focusing on the historical evolution of the Indian Act. We begin by outlining British and Canadian Indian policy and the related colonial laws that preceded the Indian Act before discussing the regimes developed in the Indian Act of 1876 and beyond.

EARLY INDIAN POLICY IN NORTH AMERICA

Pre-Confederation: Protectionism

Formal Indian administration in North America originated in the late seventeenth century when the British colonies appointed Indian commissioners to regulate the fur trade and suppress liquor traffic among Indian peoples.[1] British and French Indian policies at this time and up until the late eighteenth and early nineteenth centuries were based on two interdependent precepts: fostering friendly relations with indigenous nations, and protecting Indian peoples and their land from European encroachment. Nonetheless, there were some important and subtle differences between British and French policies. For the British, the Iroquois and other Indian nations were crucial allies against the French. As such, the British colonial office conducted relations with Indians on a nation-to-nation basis, regularly giving them gifts, entering into formal alliances with them, and preventing European settlers from encroaching upon their lands.[2] The French, on the other hand, believed strongly in Christianizing Indian peoples, forging military alliances, and fostering the fur trade.[3] However, the Seven Years War brought the end of French power and the establishment of British hegemony in North America. The formalization of this hegemony occurred with the Treaty of Paris, signed in 1763.[4]

British policy after the defeat of the French continued to focus on maintaining friendly relations and military alliances with Indian nations, as well as protecting them and their lands from European encroachment. In the 1760 Articles of Capitulation signed by both the British and French after the fall of Montreal, article 40 stated that "[t]he Savages or Indian allies of his most Christian Majesty, shall be maintained in the Lands they inhabit; if they choose to remain there."[5] To quell aboriginal concerns and fears regarding European squatters and land sharks, the British Government included Indian issues in the Royal Proclamation of 1763.[6] According to the Proclamation, aboriginal lands could only be acquired if aboriginal peoples voluntarily ceded them to the Crown,[7] and the Crown was the only party that could negotiate treaties and land surrenders.

Although it did in a sense protect Indian lands by recognizing the existence of aboriginal property rights, the Royal Proclamation of 1763 also diminished Indian property rights in a number of ways. Above all, it was a unilateral document, issued by King George III after being drawn up by his advisors. There was no attempt at negotiation or even consultation with the natives of North America regarding the property rights which the Proclamation attributed to them. Without such consultation, the agents of the Crown failed to appreciate the complexity of property rights already in existence among North American Indians.

The provision that Indians could sell their lands only to representatives of the British Crown after discussion at a public meeting was a further infringement on their property rights. Imposition of a single purchaser always restricts the choices that sellers can make. At the time of writing, the political right in Canada is incensed about the fact that producers of wheat and barley in the prairie provinces are required to sell their grain to the Canadian Wheat Board; yet conservatives, who ought to be most vigilant guardians of property rights, have never condemned the diminution of Indian liberty wrought by the Royal Proclamation of 1763.

Another problem was that the term "possession" in the Proclamation meant "occupation" rather than "ownership." The designation of lands as Indian "hunting grounds" was legally questionable because, as we have already seen, many Indians in the area covered by the Proclamation practiced agriculture and had developed forms of family ownership of agricultural land. Many had also created forms of individual or family ownership of specific areas for hunting, trapping, and fishing. Rather than recognize the full spectrum of existing Indian property rights, the Proclamation reduced them all to the single category of occupation of "hunting grounds." At one stroke, the Proclamation merged individual and collective property rights while reducing the status of both from ownership to occupation.

This fateful wording led directly to the Judicial Committee of the Privy Council's later characterization of Indian title as "a personal and usufructuary right, dependent upon the good will of the Sovereign," in the *St Catherine's Milling* case (1888).[8] "Usufruct" is a Roman law concept implying the right to enjoy the benefits of property without being able to sell it or give it to someone else, i.e., without really owning it. Roman landowners could leave an estate in usufruct as a way of supporting a widow or other family members for the rest of their lives. The closest equivalent in British law would be a life estate. Further, for the JCPC to label aboriginal usufruct a "personal" right implied that it was not really a right to property, since the common law of the time distinguished categorically between personal and property rights.

In truth, the Royal Proclamation of 1763 is a profoundly ambiguous document. It has achieved iconic status in the discussion of aboriginal rights and for decades has been called the "Charter of Indian Rights."[9] But while it attempted to protect the existence of Indian property rights, it diminished their substance in major ways, with repercussions that continue to be felt in the present.

A Shift in Policy: Protectionism, Civilization, and Individual Property Rights

British policy toward the new world changed dramatically as a result of the War of 1812. After this war, the British Crown no longer saw the need for formal military alliances with its Indian allies.[10] The British had defeated the French in New France and repelled cross-border attacks from the Americans. Thus, with its borders relatively secure in the New World, the British Government allowed its military alliances with its Indian allies to lapse and began to discontinue providing annual gifts. After 1812, British policy gradually moved from protection and nation-to-nation relations to protection and civilization.[11]

The policy of civilization meant reconstructing Indian property rights in a Lockean mode. John Locke's conception of private property was very influential among government officials, both in Europe and in the New World. For Locke, "every man has a property in his person," and thus everyone has a property in their labour. Therefore, everyone has a right to property in what they mix their labour with.[12] Locke eventually used these premises to justify a capitalist market economy of unequal possession of the Earth.[13] Scholars such as Alice Kehoe believe that Locke's ideas laid the foundation for notions of Western superiority and private property rights for Indians in Canada.[14]

Locke's theory was capacious enough to recognize the property rights of hunting-and-gathering people; indeed, Locke started his train of thought about property with a foraging example – gathering acorns.[15] However, Locke emphasized property in land as the basis of agriculture:

> God gave the world to men in common; but since he gave it
> them for their benefit and the greatest conveniences of life
> they were capable to draw from it, it cannot be supposed he
> meant it should always remain common and uncultivated. He
> gave it to the use of the industrious and rational – and labor
> was to be his title to it – not to the fancy or covetousness of
> the quarrelsome and contentious.[16]

Later writers in the Lockean tradition, such as the Swiss publicist Emer de Vattel, postulated an actual right of agriculturalists to take land from hunter-gatherers, because they (the farmers) would make better use of it.[17]

In practice, the Lockean views of British, Canadian, and US officials led to a dualistic view of Indian property rights. Ignorant of the complex array of property rights that Indians had evolved for themselves in the New World, they tended to see Indians as hunting and gathering on the land but not otherwise owning it – in short, people without property. They saw property rights not as an outgrowth of the Indians' own culture but as something wholly new that would have to be introduced to them as part of the civilizing process. The official view was almost schizophrenic – Indians had no property rights in the present, but they would have to adopt them in the future to become civilized. It was also completely individualistic; Indians would have to adopt individual ownership in fee simple as that concept had developed in British law. There was little appreciation of the complex web of communal, family, and individual rights that were already part of Indian hunting and farming cultures.

As historian Sarah Carter put it, some colonists believed that private property would help indigenous people better focus "their hopes, interests and ambitions. Lacking a fixed abode, they could have no notion of a proper family life."[18] The introduction of private property would also quell the violent tendencies that colonials believed to be inherent in Indian peoples. "Most Canadians believed that private ownership of property and possession would put an end to Indian warfare, which was viewed as an irrational, bloodthirsty sport, perpetuated endlessly because the Indians had little property to lose."[19] Government officials, therefore, saw agriculture and private property as necessary elements for Indian peoples to climb out of savagery toward civilization. Government encouraged Christian missionaries to bring religion, education, and Western concepts of farming and property to the "backward" Indians.[20]

After 1812, Indian nations became an obstacle to British colonial expansion in the new world. Now that they were no longer useful as military allies, government officials had to wrestle with what to do with Indian British subjects who happened to occupy most of the available land. This desire to get control of Indian land joined with the civilizing mission to give birth to the modern reserve system in the 1830s. Part of the civilizing process was to move Indian groups off their resource-rich lands and onto isolated reserves away from British settlements, where missionaries and government officials could teach them the European way of life.[21]

British policy with respect to Indian civilization and property rights would become much more focused and comprehensive as a result of the Bagot Commission (1842–44).[22] This commission, established by Sir Charles Bagot, governor-general of North America from 1841 to 1843, had a powerful effect on British assimilationist policy in North America.[23] The commission reaffirmed the Royal Proclamation's protection of Indian lands, called for the centralization of Indian administration, and recommended their education and conversation to Christianity. More importantly, the commission "recommended that Indians be encouraged to adopt individual ownership of plots of land under a special Indian land registry system."[24] The commissioners believed that the government should encourage Indians to buy and sell land among themselves. They hoped that this type of market interaction would promote the spirit of free enterprise and help Indians learn about the European land-tenure system. The commission also recommended that Indians adopt a Western-style individual title system to discourage white squatters.[25] According to historian Olive Dickason, Indians appeared to Canadians as "an untaught, unwary race among a population ready and able to take every advantage of them."[26] Therefore, it was necessary to protect them by granting them Western-style property rights.

Although the commission's recommendations regarding aboriginal individual property rights were for the most part ignored until much later, they had an effect on Indian policy. After the publication of the commission's report, the colonial government's reserve-creation policy greatly accelerated. As Indian lands were acquired, the former Indian residents were moved onto isolated reserves far away from white settlements, where they would be educated, Christianized, and taught how to farm. The Indian residents, however, did not adapt to farming or learn English at the speed that government officials desired. Moreover, most of the Indian peoples did not convert to Christianity nor did they abandon their traditions in favour of European ones. Thus, in 1850, the British Government decided to move reserves closer to white settlements. They hoped that closer proximity to colonial villages might encourage the Indians to achieve civilization in a more reasonable amount of time.[27]

One unanticipated result of this decision was an increase in white settler encroachment and squatting on Indian reserve lands. In response to these developments, both the Upper and Lower Canada legislatures passed new Indian land legislation in 1850. There were four main provisions in this legislation. First, it reaffirmed the terms of the Royal Proclamation by making it an offense for non-Indians to enter into land transactions with Indians without government approval. Second, it made trespassing on Indian land illegal. Third, it exempted Indian land from both taxation and legal seizure for debts. Lastly, it introduced race as a determining factor in the classification of an individual as an "Indian."[28]

The 1850 Act was important to the development of individual property rights on Canadian Indian reserves in two ways. First, because settlers were not obeying the Royal Proclamation, the colonial governments felt it necessary to reaffirm the status of Indian peoples as subjects of the state with the right of protection by the Crown. Second, the exemption from taxation and legal seizure for debts, which was meant to protect Indians from potential abuse by colonial settlers, would become an entrenched feature of subsequent Indian legislation relating to individual property rights on Canadian Indian reserves.

Another Shift in Policy: Protection, Civilization, and Assimilation

The next major shift in colonial policy regarding Indian peoples and their property rights occurred in 1857. In that year, the legislature of Canada passed the Gradual Civilization Act, which made the practice of moving reserves closer to white settlements official government policy and created a process for enfranchisement (the voluntary revocation of Indian status) tied to the acquisition of private property. In the past, Indian settlements close to colonial settlements had adopted the European lifestyle more readily than isolated Indian communities.[29] In terms of enfranchisement, any Indian who was judged to be of good moral character, free of debt, and could read and write English would be granted enfranchisement.[30] Enfranchised Indians, having passed a three-year probationary period, would receive a life estate allotment of up to fifty acres of tribal land; after the individual's death, the land would pass to their heirs in fee-simple ownership. Enfranchised Indians would lose any title to the tribe's communal property, and the enfranchised individual's land would now be subject to taxation and legal seizure. Enfranchised Indians, moreover, could sell their land to anyone, including non-Indians.[31] In other words, Crown-recognized individual property rights were supposed to help enfranchise individual Indians. Note, however, that enfranchisement would have removed individual plots of land from reserve status, thus "breaking up the reserves."

The Indian response in the 1860s was to reject the enfranchisement process. According to some observers, what irked them the most was that enfranchised Indians were to be given tribal lands. Indigenous peoples were not opposed to civilization per se, which they defined as a revitalization of their traditional culture within an agricultural context, but they were opposed to losing their lands and any laws that attacked their notions of communal property and culture.[32] From 1857 until the passing of the 1876 Indian Act, only one Indian, Elias Hill, applied for and was granted enfranchisement. Due to community opposition to Hill's enfranchisement, however, he was not granted any land; rather, he was given a cash settlement six times less than the actual value of the land.[33]

Aboriginal Peoples and British Indian Policy: A Summary

Overall, British policy had three important effects, each of which had both a positive and a negative side. First, it strengthened the idea that aboriginal peoples should have occupancy rights to their Indian lands, and no more. In so doing, it ignored the Indians' own conceptions of property rights that had evolved within their cultures over the preceding centuries. Second, it promoted the idea that individual property rights were an important step for protecting aboriginal peoples and facilitating their integration into Canadian society and the economy. Unfortunately, this ignored the community and family aspects of indigenous conceptions of property. Third, British policy recognized that Indian lands were special and should be exempt from taxation and legal seizure. Moreover, they should be protected from unlawful white exploitation by ensuring that Indian land transactions could only be completed with the approval of the Crown. These measures may have protected Indian lands from sale, but they also radically curtailed Indians' economic opportunities by preventing them from mortgaging or selling their lands in private-sector transactions.

CANADIAN INDIAN POLICY: INDIVIDUAL PROPERTY RIGHTS ON CANADIAN INDIAN RESERVES

In 1867, the British Parliament passed the British North America Act (BNA Act), uniting Lower Canada, Upper Canada, and the Maritime provinces into the Dominion of Canada. The BNA Act was Canada's Constitution, setting out the division of powers between the federal government and the provinces, as well as setting up the institutions of governance for Canada. With respect to Indian peoples, section 91(24) granted the Parliament of Canada legislative authority over "Indians, and Lands reserved for the Indians." The federal government through section 91(24) had exclusive and extensive control over aboriginal rights and, up until the Supreme Court's *Delgamuukw* ruling in 1997, also had the unilateral power to extinguish those rights.[34]

In 1869, Parliament made its first foray into Indian policy with the passage of the Gradual Enfranchisement Act (GEA). Under the GEA, the amount of land that an enfranchised Indian received was left undefined, as opposed to the maximum fifty acres under the British Government's Gradual Civilization Act. Also, lawful possession of individual tracts of land on reserves was only recognized if the governor-in-council granted a location ticket. A location ticket gave the individual Indian lawful possession of the land as well as exemption from taxes/legal seizure, limited the transferability to non-Indians, and allowed the ticket to pass to heirs upon death.[35] Superintendent-General of Indian Affairs Hector Langevin called upon Parliament to pass the GEA because Indians could now be entrusted with "white man's privileges."[36] The GEA would further the goal of educating Indians in good conduct and in the white man's ways with the eventual goal of the enfranchisement of all indigenous peoples with fee-simple property rights.[37] The location ticket scheme became the direct ancestor of the certificate of possession system introduced in the 1951 Indian Act.

The most important piece of Indian legislation in Canada is the 1876 Indian Act. It was a consolidation of previous colonial Indian legislation into one act, with power over Indians centred in the superintendent-general of Indian Affairs. During the House of Commons debates over the Indian Act, members of Parliament said that its purpose was to raise the Indians "to the place of manhood"[38] and to "lift the red man ... out of his condition of tutelage and dependency."[39] According to another member of Parliament, the government should move the Indians onto resource-depleted reserves to give them a sense of ownership of the reserve land but keep them under the plenary power of Parliament. "As soon as they [Indians] knew exactly what they possessed, they would look for enfranchisement."[40] In 1873, Minister of Interior David Laird had stated that "the great aim of the Government should be to give each Indian his individual property as soon as possible."[41] Laird also saw private property as a means of ending Indian dependence on relief, which he believed was rooted in their communal lifestyle. "The Indian who makes a laudable effort to provide for the support of his family, seeing that his stores often have to go to feed his starving brethren, then loses heart himself, and drops down to the level of the precarious hand-to-mouth system of the Band generally."[42] With these purposes in mind, Laird introduced in 1876 the location-ticket system for Indians living on reserves after he had become minister of Interior and superintendent-general of Indian Affairs.

The location ticket system found in sections 5–10 of the 1876 *Indian Act* was a relatively weak system of property rights for indigenous peoples on reserves. Section 5 allowed the superintendent-general to subdivide reserve land into individual lots. Section 6 stated that an individual Indian could only gain lawful possession of land if both the band and the superintendent-general consented. Section 7 stated that, after an allotment was approved, the applicant should be issued a location ticket granting title of the land to the individual. Section 8 protected lands held under a location ticket from legal seizure and restricted the ability to transfer title to land to another Indian of the same band, subject to band approval. Section 9 allowed for land to be transferred to a widow and children. If no heirs nearer than a cousin were eligible, then the property became Crown land to be managed for the benefit of the band. Section 10 provided for any non-treaty Indians in the west and north who made improvements on their lands prior to the lands becoming reserve lands to enjoy location ticket rights and privileges.[43] Indians could gain fee-simple interest in land by enfranchising. Under section 86, individual Indians could apply for enfranchisement by demonstrating to the superintendent-general that they had "attained a character for integrity, morality, and sobriety."[44] After a three-year probationary period in which applicants had to demonstrate that they would use the land as a European would, they would be enfranchised and gain fee-simple interest in the allotted land.

In essence, the 1876 Indian Act created two systems of landholding. Under the first, non-enfranchised Indians could hold lawful possession (life estate) of reserve lands allotted to them by the band council with a location ticket issued by the superintendent-general. Under the second system, Indians enfranchised under sections 86 and 88 could gain a fee-simple interest to reserve lands; and upon their death the lands would go to their children in fee simple.[45]

Between 1876 and 1951, Canadian legislation relating to individual property rights on Canadian Indian reserves remained relatively unchanged. In 1890, the Canadian Government introduced certificates of occupation (COs) for the western Indian tribes, who had less experience with agriculture than eastern Indians. Under a CO, lawful possession of up to 160 acres could be granted to each family head. The CO, however, could be cancelled at any time by the superintendent-general of Indian Affairs.[46] In 1919, the deputy superintendent-general gained the power to grant location tickets to returning Indian war veterans without band consent.[47] In 1927, Parliament passed legislation stating that, if individual Indians made permanent improvements on reserve land, they must receive compensation if they were lawfully removed from the reserve.

In 1951, the Department of Indian Affairs introduced certificates of possession to replace location tickets. According to Superintendent-General of Indian Affairs W.E. Harris, the location-ticket system was unsatisfactory. Amendments to the Indian Act were necessary because the Indian population was growing rapidly, getting wealthier, had "pulled [their] weight in two world wars," and were now an indispensable part of the community.[48] The minister of Indian Affairs at the time agreed, stating that "[t]he Indian is our brother" and Canada's relationship with them had to be modified for their betterment.[49] One of the main goals in introducing the 1951 Indian Act was to create a more comprehensive and expanded system of private property that would eventually allow for the permanent integration of Indians into Canadian society. During debate the minister stated:

> The underlying purpose of Indian administration has been
> to prepare the Indian for full citizenship with the same rights
> and responsibilities as those enjoyed and accepted by other
> members of the community ... The ultimate goal of our
> Indian policy is the integration of the Indian into the general
> life and economy of the country.[50]

The certificate-of-possession system in the 1951 Indian Act was a major step toward fulfilling that goal because it provided band members with statutory property rights to individual tracts of reserve land. As will be described in more detail in chapter 6, under this system, individual band members could apply to get possession of an individual tract of reserve land. Once granted, members had significant security of tenure to use the property as they wished, including building a house or business on it. Yet the CP did not grant its holder fee-simple ownership rights. The key difference is that the member could only transfer or sell CP-held land to a fellow band member, and even then the transaction had to be approved by the minister of Indian Affairs. Nonetheless, the introduction of the system was important since it marked the transition from a relatively primitive form of property right (the location ticket) to one that was more akin to fee-simple ownership (the CP). Although the CP system was meant to be the final step before the introduction of fee-simple ownership, it has never been replaced and remains in effect today.

The CP is not the only form of property right available to band members living on Canadian Indian reserves. According to the Indian Act, all lands reserved for Indians are held by the Crown to be used by Indian bands. In practice, however, band councils exercise primary usage and occupancy rights over all reserve lands.[51] Band members can gain individual possession of reserve lands through three mechanisms: customary rights, certificates of possession (CPs), and leases. As discussed above, CPs are formal property rights that have a statutory basis in the Indian Act. The same is true of Indian leases, which are similar to leases off-reserve. The third type of property regime, customary rights, allows band members to take possession of a tract of land either through a band council resolution recognizing their ownership or through informal recognition by community members. As with CPs, band members can use those custom-held lands to build a house or business. However, customary rights are not legally enforceable in Canadian courts, meaning that their use is at the discretion of the band council.[52] All of these forms of property are discussed in greater detail in subsequent chapters.

There are a number of other provisions in the Indian Act that deserve special mention. Section 29 states that "[r]eserve lands are not subject to seizure under legal process," while section 89(1) adds that "[s]ubject to this Act, the real and personal property of an Indian or band situated on reserves is not subject to charge, pledge, mortgage, attachment, levy, seizure, distress, and execution in favour or at the instance of any person other than an Indian or band." In essence, these two sections prevent non-Indian individuals, organizations, and institutions from seizing or disposing of Indian land.[53] The one exception is leasehold interests, which are mortgageable and seizable as a result of 1985 amendments to the Indian Act. Nonetheless, the effect of these two sections has been to stifle economic development on Canadian Indian reserves. By preventing band members from using their individual property rights as collateral for loans to build homes or businesses, these provisions have created a major economic obstacle for many residents of Indian reserves in Canada.

The First Nations Land Management Act

From 1951 until 1999, band members living on Canadian Indian reserves had access only to the above-listed individual property rights. In 1994, a number of chiefs, led by Robert Louie (Westbank First Nation), Austin Bear (Muskoday First Nation), and Strater Crowfoot (Siksika First Nation), approached Indian Affairs Minister Ron Irwin about the possibility of fourteen First Nations opting out of the land-management provisions of the Indian Act to develop their own administrative regimes under a new legislative framework. The result was the First Nations Land Management Act, which allowed signatory First Nations to develop land codes that addressed the following issues:

(a) the use and occupancy of First Nation's land, including licences, leases, and allotments under s. 20(1) of the Indian Act; (b) the transfer of land interests and the revenues from natural resources obtained from reserve land; (c) requirements for accountability to First Nation members for land management and moneys derived from reserve land; (d) community consultation processes for the development of rules respecting matrimonial property issues, use, occupation and possession of First Nation land and the division of interests in First Nation land; (e) publication of First Nation laws; (f) conflicts of interest in the management of First Nation land; (g) the establishment of a forum for the resolution of disputes in relation to interests in First Nation land; (h) granting or expropriating interests in First Nation land; (i) delegation by the council of its authority to manage land; (j) approvals of an exchange of First Nation land; and (k) amending the land code.[54]

Once a land code was drafted, approved, and ratified, the First Nation would no longer be subject to the land-management provisions of the Indian Act. Instead, it could develop its own laws for governing its land, in accordance with its land code.

Since 1999, forty-one bands have opted into the FNLMA, ninety have inquired about doing so, and eighteen have their land codes in operation. The land codes that have been produced out of the FNLMA have been universally hailed as a success story of aboriginal/government cooperation. Observers praise the fact that the FNLMA enhances aboriginal capacity and respects aboriginal self-government by reducing federal involvement in local band affairs. They also laud the FNLMA as an example of a new way of conducting aboriginal/Crown relations, in which aboriginal groups can approach the federal government to negotiate solutions that may benefit all yet do not require all First Nations to participate against their wishes. Yet the FNLMA only partially addresses the needs of First Nations because it does not provide a model land code or any other institutional support for the development of useful property rights. In the absence of such templates, First Nations land codes will proliferate, making life more complicated for those who want to do business on Indian reserves.

CONCLUSION

It is clear from this brief historical chapter that the British and Canadian governments intended the introduction of property rights to lead to the integration and assimilation of aboriginal peoples into mainstream society. Western-style property rights, in their view, would not only safeguard the interests of aboriginal peoples with respect to their lands but would also allow them to escape poverty by integrating into the Canadian economy. As such, the Canadian Government developed and generally respected a number of different forms of on-reserve private property rights, including location tickets, certificates of possession, certificates of occupation, customary rights, leases, and the land codes emerging out of the FNLMA. Yet it was clear that most of these property rights, especially the location tickets, the certificates of occupation, and the certificates of possession, were meant to be temporary measures in the march toward the complete assimilation of aboriginal peoples into mainstream society.

The Canadian Government's view was essentially the same as that of the US Government: that Indians were people without property who had to be introduced to Western-style property rights. Canadian legislative provisions for location tickets and enfranchisement were similar in spirit to the Dawes Act, which tried to break up American Indian reserves by imposing a form of fee-simple ownership. The crucial difference, however, is that Canadian legislation has always been permissive rather than mandatory with respect to property rights on reserves. Because Canada did not go down the road of coercion in the same way that the United States did, we now have an opportunity to make fee-simple ownership, both collective and individual, available to First Nations in a non-coercive way.

Before explaining how that can be done, however, we have to demonstrate why it needs to be done. That is, we have to point out the limitations of current forms of on-reserve property (mainly customary holdings, CPs, and leases), showing how they hinder the economic development of which First Nations are capable, and which they so badly want.

5

Customary Land Rights on Canadian Indian Reserves

Leonard and Mary Anne Johnstone are members of the Mistawasis First Nation in Saskatchewan. They had been farming on the
reserve since about 1960 when the band council decided in 2002 to
repossess much of their land. At the time, the Johnstones controlled
33 quarter sections, more than one-sixth of the 192 quarter sections
on the reserve. They held 13 of these quarters under certificates
of possession issued by the minister of Indian Affairs, while the
other 20 were "ad hoc" or "customary" holdings approved by band
council resolutions at various times. For about ten years (1986–96),
the Johnstones also had a certificate of right of use and occupation issued by the Department of Indian Affairs for 17 of their 20
customary quarters. This document allowed them to use their land
as collateral to borrow money from the Farm Credit Corporation;
but this certificate was temporary in nature, not permanent like a
certificate of possession.

In the words of Justice Barclay of the Saskatchewan Court of
Queen's Bench, the Johnstones

> improved, maintained, nurtured and sustained the lands
> in their occupation and possession. The applicants have
> given their whole lives to nurturing the land. They have
> picked roots, cleared stones, fenced, drained and nurtured
> piece by piece, quarter by quarter, bush by bush, pasture by
> pasture, slough by slough to create a farming environment
> which would be an all-encompassing economic, family and
> community lifestyle.[1]

Notwithstanding this decades-long investment by the Johnstone family, the Mistawasis band council decided to take back the 20 customary quarters. The Johnstones applied to the Saskatchewan Court of Queen's Bench for an interlocutory injunction to block the reversion but lost in a decision handed down on 23 May 2003. Justice Barclay held that "it is clear that the proper approval of the Minister, or his lawful designate, was never acquired with respect to the 20 quarter sections of land in issue."[2] The Johnstones might have a claim for financial damages, he allowed, but that could be litigated later, and meanwhile the reversion of the land could proceed. Welcome to the little-known world of customary property rights on Canadian Indian reserves, where various forms of quasi-ownership are conferred by political authorities, where owners are frequently confused about what rights they possess, and where rights can be withdrawn on short notice without compensation.

What follows is a conceptual survey of traditional allotments on Canadian Indian reserves. In this chapter, we discuss the emergence of customary rights, the range of their formalization, and their treatment by Canadian courts. We also analyze the strengths and limitations of customary rights as they relate to economic development on Canadian Indian reserves. To accomplish these goals, we draw upon the scanty literature and case law on the topic and rely heavily on fieldwork conducted by Chris Alcantara at Cowichan Tribes (British Columbia); Siksika Nation, Piikani Nation, and Blood Tribe (Alberta); and Sandy Lake Nation (Ontario) in 2002.

EMERGENCE AND FORMALIZATION OF CUSTOMARY RIGHTS

Traditional or customary rights are the most common system of property rights on Canadian Indian reserves. This system of allotment has no direct statutory basis; its justification in Canadian law comes from the authority of the band under the Indian Act to make use of reserve land for the benefit of its membership.[3] In essence, band council resolutions create individual interests in parcels of reserve land. A member with such an interest can build on it, improve it, farm it, sell it to another member, and, in some cases, devise it in a will. But, as shown in *Mistawasis*, chief and council can evict a member from a customary holding at any time or for any reason because they have legal authority over all reserve land not held under CPs.

Customary rights emerged in more or less the same manner on many different reserves. Historically, band memberships were small enough that land was plentiful. The abundance of land meant that members, usually families, could claim parcels of land for themselves with little, if any, risk of conflict with others. Some of these claims even go back to the period before reserves were assigned and surveyed.[4] On these lands, families built homes, grazed animals, and farmed. Land was also freely exchanged between members. In the event of death, land usually passed on to other members of the family.

Because land was abundant, conflicts were few, resulting in very little government involvement in customary claims. When governments did intervene, they did so in a minimal way. At Piikani Nation and Blood Tribe, for example, the tribal government's only involvement was to require members to erect fences around their properties within two years. Failure to do so meant that others could lay claim to the property. However, this two-year requirement was rarely, if ever, enforced. Prior to more recent government involvement in the allotment process, none of the customary allotments were surveyed or recorded in any type of registry. At all five First Nations studied in this chapter, familial customary claims to property were recognized by the community and recorded in their oral traditions.[5]

As time progressed, almost all status Indians in the provinces (but not in the northern territories) eventually moved onto reserves. On these new reserves, families once again claimed parcels of land for their own individual use. In cases where the government created reserves on lands where Indians already resided, members continued to occupy the parcels of land that they had historically lived on. Reserve status, however, created new stresses for community life. The fixed borders of reserves and the rising band populations increased the number of conflicts over land. As the number of conflicts grew, members turned to the band council to help resolve disputes. To minimize disputes and facilitate resolution, many bands established lands departments that had the task of administering all community and individual uses of land. Individual land-use policies and departments varied from band to band, depending on each

Table 5.1 | Range of Formalization of Customary Rights at Five First Nations in Canada, 2002

First Nation	Recognized by the community?	Allotted by BCR?	Formally recorded in registry?	Surveyed?	Dispute resolution mechanism?
Sandy Lake, ON	Yes	No	No	No	No
Cowichan Tribes, BC	Yes	No	No	No	Yes
Piikani, AB	Yes	Yes	Yes	Yes	Yes
Blood Tribe, AB	Yes	Yes	Yes	Yes	Yes
Siksika, AB	Yes	Yes	Yes	Yes	Yes

reserve's population, culture, history, and territorial makeup. The result was wide variation in the formalization of customary rights, ranging from very little (Sandy Lake and Cowichan Tribes) to much greater (Piikani Nation, Blood Tribe, and Siksika Nation).

The level of formalization involves several factors: whether customary rights are recognized by the community, whether they are allotted to members by band council resolution (BCR), whether they have been surveyed and formally recorded in a land registry, and whether a dispute-resolution mechanism other than chief and council is in place to deal with conflicts. The range of formalization for the five First Nations that we studied in 2002 is summarized in table 5.1.

Community Recognition

At all five First Nations, customary rights were recognized and respected by the community. Originally, families obtained usage rights to individual properties on these reserves by fencing or clearing the land.[6] As time progressed, the community membership acknowledged that certain properties were owned by certain families or individuals. Community recognition was recorded in oral tradition, and elders were unofficially given responsibility for verifying ownership of property. Community members continued to acknowledge that certain families and individuals had ownership or usage rights to certain parcels of land regardless of band council approval. Members respected these parcels and usually did not trespass on them even though they could do so legally if they wished. Although there were many disputes over customary rights, most disputes were over boundaries rather than ownership. When disputes occurred over actual ownership, it was usually because there was a conflict between community and band council recognition of ownership.[7]

In contrast to the other four First Nations examined in this chapter, community respect for customary rights at Cowichan Tribes has waned considerably. In 1876, Cowichan customary land tenure was changed when all of the land outside of the seven villages in the reserve was allotted to members through location tickets. Since then, almost all of the reserve has been subdivided and allotted to individuals using CPs. According to its website, "Cowichan's practice of alloting parcels of land to individual families pre-dates colonisation, and it [today] has one of the largest per-capita CP allocations among First Nation bands."[8] Moreover, at present "almost all Cowichan Reserve land is allocated or claimed by individual band members. The only communal land holdings are the site of the Administration complex and a parcel by St Ann's Church leaving virtually no land for overall community development purposes unless the Band purchases it from the CP holder(s)."[9]

Band Council Resolutions, Land Registries, and Surveys

At Cowichan Tribes and Sandy Lake, customary allotments were never formally recognized by chief and council. Therefore, customary land rights in both reserves were never surveyed or recorded in a land registry.[10]

In contrast, Piikani Nation, Blood Tribe, and Siksika Nation took over the customary allotment process in response to a growing membership and shrinking land base. At these three First Nations, existing allotments were respected. For new allotments, however, members had to submit a land-usage plan for consideration by the Lands Department and chief and council. If the plan was acceptable and if the member was in good standing with the band, the Lands Department forwarded the application to the council. Chief and council then passed a BCR allotting the member the tract of land for individual use. At Piikani, a member received "Occupation Rights and Utilization Privileges"; at Blood, a "Land Use Area"; and at Siksika, a "Land Use Agreement."[11]

Rather than requiring surveys, both Piikani Nation and Blood Tribe used to demand that their members fence off their land within two years. Failure to do so meant that other individuals could claim the property. Now, however, both reserves have been completely surveyed; a new survey for an allotment is only required when a lot is being subdivided. Siksika Nation, on the other hand, used surveys from the beginning when it first took over the customary allotment process and continues to use surveys whenever land is allotted to a member. For all three bands, once an allotment is made and surveyed, it is recorded in the band's Land Registry.[12]

Dispute-Resolution Mechanisms

Dispute-resolution mechanisms at the five First Nations that we studied vary from no mechanism (Sandy Lake), through structured and somewhat effective (Piikani, Blood, Cowichan Tribes), to highly structured and effective (Siksika). At Sandy Lake, there was no dispute-resolution mechanism other than chief and council. Members pleaded their case to individual councillors or to the entire council at a formal hearing. The council either made a ruling in the form of a BCR or declined to do so. Frequently, chief and council preferred to allow members to work out their own disputes, leaving them to negotiate, exchange goods, or intimidate each other to come to an agreement.[13]

Piikani Nation, Blood Tribe, and Cowichan Tribes all had mechanisms that are effective to varying degrees. At Piikani, the Lands

Committee, made up of the department head, three administrators, and a secretary, had the task of resolving disputes. The committee allowed disputants to present their case to it before sending its recommendation to the council, which then accepted or rejected the recommendation. It was reported that, more often than not, the council rejected the committee's recommendation and used its own criteria to make determinations.[14]

In the past, Blood Tribe also used a committee made up of land department administrators to resolve disputes. However, because of the ineffectiveness of the committee, disputants are left with the option of resolving disputes themselves or obtaining a ruling from chief and council.[15] At Cowichan Tribes, the Lands Investigation Committee, made up of eight elders, three councillors, and several Lands Department staff, held hearings to resolve customary land disputes. The committee acted as a court or mediator between the disputants, requiring them to make separate presentations to the committee, which the opposing party could observe but not interrupt. After the presentations by the disputants, the committee examined written records, oral tradition, and the recollections of elders. The committee then made a decision and sought the approval of the disputants. In the event that the parties did not support the decision, the committee sent its recommendations to chief and council.[16] Today, the Lands Investigation Committee and the band council rarely adjudicate disputes because almost all Cowichan lands have been allocated through CPs.

Siksika's mechanism seemed to be the most effective. The band employed a committee made up of several lands department officials to resolve disputes between members. The committee's mandate was to resolve disputes through consultation, mediation, and compromise. In cases where the committee could not achieve agreement between the disputants, it made a decision based on the evidence and sent a recommendation to chief and council. Chief and council almost always affirmed the recommendation because the lands department had the most expertise in land management. However, most of the time, the committee was able to come up with a resolution that was agreeable to all of the disputants. The key to the committee's success was that disputants knew that chief and council usually supported the committee's decision, thereby motivating the parties to find some sort of compromise that was acceptable to both sides.[17]

CUSTOMARY RIGHTS IN CANADIAN COURTS

Although customary rights have existed on reserves for more than a century and a half, the body of Canadian case law is quite small.[18] Courts have usually refused to hear cases involving customary rights because such rights have neither statutory nor common-law basis. They have made exceptions, however, when a customary right met the requirements needed for a certificate of possession: namely, band council consent and the approval of the minister of Indian Affairs. For instance, in *Leonard v. Gottfriedson* (1982), the court ruled that a band member can get enforceable occupation rights to reserve land only by fulfilling the requirements of s. 20(1) of the Indian Act. This ruling was confirmed in *Joe v. Findlay* (1987), *MacMillan v. Augustine* (2004),[19] *Derrickson v. Kennedy* (2006),[20] *Chief Chris Tom v. Morris* (2007),[21] *Paul v. Paul* (2008),[22] *Maracle v. Grant* (2008),[23] and more importantly, in *Nicola Band et al. v. Trans-Can Displays et al.* (2000). In the latter case, the court ruled that customary rights "cannot create a legal interest in the land that would defeat or conflict with the provisions of the [Indian] Act."[24] Although customary rights have been historically used and recognized by the band in certain instances, "recognition of an individual's traditional occupation of reserve lands does not create a legal interest or entitlement to those lands unless and until the requirements of the Act [s. 20(1)] are met."[25] Indeed, in *George v. George* (1996), the court enforced a customary allotment approved by both the band council and minister of Indian Affairs. This legal reasoning was upheld in *Cooper v. Tsartlip Indian Band* (1997), which upheld the transfer of a customary right because it was recorded in the federal Land Register and approved by the minister of Indian Affairs. A similar line of reasoning was used in *Williams et al. v. Briggs* (2001), in which the court ruled that one member's property rights claim was stronger than another's because her claim fulfilled at least one element of the requirements listed under s. 20(1): the approval of the band council.[26]

Although the Canadian Government and courts do not legally recognize customary rights, individual band members have been able to use them for personal farming and housing developments, as collateral for small bank loans, and to generate revenue through unregistered leases. The most common use of customary property for economic development is farming. Members with customarily held land frequently lease it to non-Indian farmers through s. 28(2) permits. Section 28(2) of the Indian Act states: "The Minister may by permit in writing authorize any person for a period not exceeding one year, or with the consent of the council of the band for any longer period, to occupy or use a reserve or to reside or otherwise exercise rights on a reserve."

Such leases may be organized as a cartel. At Piikani, 80 percent of the band's five-year renewable agricultural and grazing s. 28(2) permits were issued to off-reserve farmers on behalf of members who had customary rights to parcels of reserve land. To acquire a permit, a member with customary rights approached the band council. The Piikani Lands Committee interviewed potential farmers, conducted a credit check, verified that the farmer had financial support from a bank, reviewed the proposed crops to be grown and the soil quality of the land, and assessed how much the farmer planned to spend per acre. Once a farmer was chosen, the committee forwarded its decision to chief and council, which then passed a BCR approving the permit. The application and BCR were sent to Ottawa, where the permit was registered in the Indian Lands Registry. Piikani permits ran for a maximum of five years, at which time they could be renewed with any necessary adjustments. Farmers were charged land rent, ranging from $18.50 to $43.00 an acre. All of the land rent went to the individual member, with the exception of a $1.00 per acre fee, which the band charged for administering the permits on behalf of the member.[27]

Blood Tribe also allowed members with customary rights to recruit off-reserve farmers to farm their land using s. 28(2) permits. The acquisition of a permit at Blood Tribe was identical to the process at Piikani except for the fees charged. Most of the farming permits were based on cash rent paid to individual members with occupancy rights. Very few of the permits were based on crop share. Land rent at Blood ranged from $20.00 to $42.50 an acre, with the band taking a 5 percent administrative fee. In 2002, chief and council determined that all new and renewing permits would have a set rate of $40.00 an acre and a renewable term of three years.[28]

At both Blood and Piikani, members have been able to use their permits as collateral – called "grain assignments" – for small bank loans up to $10,000.[29] For example, an occupant has 100 acres of land rented to an off-reserve farmer for $40.00 an acre. The off-reserve farmer pays the occupant $4,000, minus $200 (5 percent), which goes to the band as an administrative fee. Payments are made to the member in three installments of $1,266.66 on the first of April, October, and December. A bank will lend the member an amount equal to up to a year and a half of a permit ($3,800 + $1,900), so in this case the member is eligible for a loan of $5,700. Once the first payment of $1,266.66 is issued, a portion of the $5,700 loan can be paid off and that same amount ($1,266.66) borrowed again, resulting in an endless cycle of borrowing and repayment until the permit expires permanently.[30] At Blood Tribe, the band did not play a role in these small bank loans. At Piikani, however, banks required members to have a BCR stating that all future rent monies coming from the permitted land were to go directly to the bank to pay off the loan.[31]

The second major use of customary rights is for securing financing for individual members to construct their own housing. Siksika had an on-reserve housing program under which eligible members could apply for a $35,000 grant from the Housing Department to subsidize the construction of their own house or to purchase a new mobile home. This $35,000 came from a federal fund administered by the band. Eligible members had to be registered band members or eligible members under Bill C-31, had to have the ability and credit rating to pay off a bank loan, and had to be able to contribute at least 25 percent of the total cost. The member was also given $28,200 to service the site. In addition, the band guaranteed an individually obtained mortgage from a bank for up to $75,000 over a twenty-five-year amortization period. In exchange, borrowing members signed an agreement stating that in the event of a default or an action to foreclose, they agreed to relinquish to the band their claim to the property and house. Members who wished to access this program but did not yet have a customary right to land had to submit three sites where they would be willing to build their house. The Lands Department chose an unencumbered site and granted the member customary rights to the land and the house. All applications under this program had to be approved by chief and council.[32]

Members at Cowichan Tribes were also able to use customary rights to build a small number of houses through personal mortgages from the Canadian Mortgage and Housing Corporation (CMHC). To acquire a ministerial guarantee for a mortgage, the member had to demonstrate a legitimate claim to the land to the Lands Investigation Committee. Once this was established, the holder transferred rights to the land to the band in return for guaranteeing the mortgage. Possession of the land was returned to the member when the mortgage was paid off and any other conditions set by the band were met.[33] Today, the majority of homes at Cowichan Tribes are privately owned (300), with the rest being band-owned rentals (60) or CMHC-owned rentals (154).[34]

At Piikani, customary rights played a somewhat smaller but still important role for the housing needs of two members. In 1995, their houses were destroyed by flooding. Using the insurance money paid to them and their customary rights to their properties, the members were able to acquire ministerial guarantees to secure mortgages from a bank to rebuild their homes. The key to these arrangements was the presence of the down payment and the traditional land-holding.[35]

In 2005 the Lac La Ronge Indian Band (Saskatchewan) introduced a new housing program based on the innovations of two bands in Ontario and Quebec. Building on the experiences of the Bay of Quinte Indian Band and the Six Nations Band in Ontario, the Lac La Ronge Indian Band applied for and received a $1.7 million grant from DIAND (the federal Department of Indian Affairs and Northern Development) to start a revolving loan fund. The purpose of the fund is to loan monies to individual members to renovate or build their own homes on the reserve. The fund is meant to be self-sustaining. As members repay their loans, other members can make use of the returned monies to build their own houses.

A member seeking to build a house on the Lac La Ronge reserve must apply to the band for a customary allotment. The band issues a letter to the individual, stating that the land is available to the member for six weeks pending financing. The member then must apply to the Bank of Montreal for a mortgage. If approved, the member can access up to 20 percent of the down payment from the revolving loan fund. As an incentive for repayment, the band adds 0.5 percent to each monthly payment the member makes. The member must also sign a lease with the band stating the details of the mortgage and the repayment schedule for the funds borrowed from the revolving loan fund. During and after the life of the mortgage, the member owns the house and any improvements personally made to the land (shed, fence, etc.). The member can sell the home, but only to fellow band members. Non-band members, including spouses and children, cannot own the house. Title to the land remains with the band, which will only intervene if the terms of the lease, such as failing to make regular repayment, are violated.[36]

Beyond such uses, Indians on reserves have also used customary rights to engage in informal and unregistered contracts called "buckshee leases." These agreements, signed by band members with nonmembers, non-Indian businesses, or corporations, are used for a variety of purposes including farming, cutting timber, and erecting billboards. The danger with these leases is that they are not registered with Indian Affairs and therefore do not receive any of the legal protection afforded to registered leases. Some band councils, such as at Siksika, and to a lesser extent Cowichan Tribes, actively opposed buckshee leases because they went against the cultural identity of the band. They viewed such leases as benefiting the individual at the expense of the entire community[37] because no revenue flowed from such leases to the band administration. Nonetheless, across the country, many band members prefer to use buckshee leases rather than registered leases to avoid the transaction costs of dealing with the band and the Department of Indian Affairs and Northern Development.

Many native people defend customary rights as being consistent with their perception of their culture. With the exception of Cowichan Tribes, all of the bands studied in this chapter resisted adopting CPs, citing fears that they were destructive to the reserve's land base and antithetical to the nation's culture.[38] These fears seem to be less prevalent in those parts of eastern Canada where the indigenous culture included agriculture and family ownership of land (the Six Nations reserve, for example, is almost entirely subdivided into CPs); but they are particularly acute on the western prairies, where cultural traditions originally based on buffalo hunting included individual ownership of chattels but not of land.

At Piikani, Blood, and Siksika, band members reportedly felt that the community rather than the individual should benefit from the land. Customary rights give the band some tools to accomplish collective goals because the band has legal control over all land not held under a CP. At Piikani, for example, the band council wanted to build a school on land to which a member had occupation rights and utilization privileges. The property was perfect for the school because it was on a major road and was in a central location near most of the homes on the reserve. The member agreed to give up his occupation rights and utilization privileges, provided that the band compensated him with $20,000. The band refused to negotiate and evicted the member. The member responded by obtaining legal advice. He was told, however, that he had no basis for a legal challenge because the courts have refused to recognize customary rights unless they meet the requirements of a CP.[39] The member, therefore, had no legal recourse and no means of preventing eviction or extracting compensation. Nonetheless, the band did provide him with some compensation.[40] Customary rights, in short, are easily subordinated to collective purposes. This may be an advantage in the sense of being compatible with the prevailing cultural beliefs and political system on many reserves.

Customary rights fit into the communal control prevalent on reserves such as Blood Tribe and Siksika Nation. At these two First Nations, all members shared in the revenue generated from oil, gas, and farming activities. If oil or gas was found on an individual's property, the band took control of it and extracted the resource. For farming permits, the band took a portion of rent paid to individuals. Members accessed these funds through various band services such as free housing, housing repairs, and band council jobs.[41]

Individual band members also value customary rights because these rights give them a direct connection to their pre-contact cultural heritage. Indians employed customary property rights based on usage and traditional occupation long before the arrival of Europeans.[42] On all the reserves examined in this chapter, most of the individual properties were obtained prior to the band council regulating the allotment practice, resulting in many members having rights to land based on their traditional occupation or fencing of it. In almost all cases, the band council respected these traditional holdings because they were seen as being an integral part of the band's cultural and social makeup. In contrast, band officials viewed CPs as a foreign instrument based on western European notions of land tenure and ownership and designed to achieve cultural assimilation and the destruction of Indian life. Officials at Piikani, Siksika, Blood, and Sandy Lake mentioned how CPs were a foreign institution that could destroy their reserve's land base. They were emphatic about their intentions to keep their customary land-tenure systems as these systems supported their cultural beliefs and practices.[43]

Customary rights have another practical advantage over CPs and leases. Since customary rights are administered by the band, INAC is rarely, if ever, involved in land transactions. Therefore, in contrast to First Nations that extensively use CPs and leases, bands with customary rights do not experience the additional time delays involved in waiting for ministerial approval. Compared to CPs,[44] customary land tenure is more time-efficient – an advantage of what in the United States would be called tribal sovereignty.

Customary rights, however, also have important limitations, especially for those First Nations interested in participating in the Canadian economy. First, they are not enforceable in Canadian courts unless they amount to an incomplete CP. Courts will sometimes enforce customary rights if such rights have been approved by the band council through a BCR recorded in the band's land registry and/or have been approved by the minister, but otherwise there is a legal vacuum. Of the five First Nations examined in this chapter, only Siksika had a customary allotment system that mimicked the requirements of a CP. In principle, this limitation might be overcome by a system of US-style tribal courts that could enforce customary rights, but such courts do not exist in Canada at the present time.

The fact that chief and council are the source of authority for customary rights is another problem, especially in light of Canadian courts' unwillingness to adjudicate disputes over customary rights. The relative smallness of most of these communities means politicians are usually connected to many members of the band. Thus politics can and does intrude into the allotment of customary holdings as well as dispute resolution. For instance, common to all five First Nations examined in this chapter was the problem of boundaries. None of the allotments at Cowichan Tribes and Sandy Lake was ever surveyed, registered, or recorded. In places such as Blood and Piikani, where INAC unilaterally imposed a square survey onto the reserves, disputes occurred over the validity of the INAC survey as compared to the original allotments based on physical features, fencing, and oral tradition. In the end, members were forced to turn to chief and council for resolution. Frequently, however, the council chose not to make a decision, passing the buck to the band's lands department because it did not wish to antagonize the disputants at election time. When chief and council made a ruling, decisions were sometimes based on nepotism.[45] Even then, losing disputants sometimes waited for a more friendly council to get elected in two or four years before appealing a ruling because BCRs can be overturned by the council at any time.[46] Band constitutions establishing stable decision-making processes might alleviate some of these difficulties, as they do in larger democratic systems.

Another limitation of customary rights is that the lack of security of tenure discourages individual band members from pursuing on-reserve development. This insecurity of tenure comes in three forms. First, although a member can transfer customarily held land to another member through a quit claim, band council must approve it. Second, members' ability to devise their property is limited because wills devising customarily held land are not legally recognized or enforceable. Some Nations have developed more secure ways to get around this problem. Piikani, for example, used conditional quit claims in which members state they will sell their property to another member upon their death for a fee. However, these documents were restricted and had to be approved by chief and council, thus limiting their usefulness. Nonetheless, the council at Piikani more often than not respected these conditional quit claims. In contrast, Siksika's chief and council were vehemently opposed to any type of document that devised customarily held land in the event of a member's death.[47] Also, as mentioned previously, the individual is constantly threatened by the council's ability to seize land at any time and for any reason, leaving the member with no legal recourse, beyond the band council, to seek justice. Councillors can be easily swayed into action or inaction due to the smallness of Indian communities.

The insecurity of tenure and the lack of legal protection afforded by the courts are the key weaknesses of customary rights. Without security of tenure, individuals have little incentive to engage in innovative projects to raise their standard of living. The threat of the band taking over an economic development project or house saps the individual's entrepreneurial spirit. The danger of politics intruding into the cancellation of an allotment, quit claim, or will is a constant fear, especially in a small community where politicians are connected to many members of the community. This, in turn, affects the entire community, as members may move away or invest off-reserve, taking away potential sources of employment for other members.

Finally, customary rights in practice tend to produce band-owned rather than individually owned and financed housing. As noted previously, there are some exceptions. At Cowichan Tribes, one member was able to use his customarily held land as collateral for a band-guaranteed mortgage from the CMHC to build his own house.[48] At Piikani, two members used a cash down payment and a transfer of their customary interest in land to the band to acquire band guarantees for bank mortgages to rebuild their flooded houses.[49] However, the bulk of housing on-reserve is band-owned rental housing. Rather than building their own homes, members preferred to receive rental housing with rates of $307 a month at Siksika, $487.50 at Blood Tribe, and $600 at Cowichan Tribes. Because members can stop paying with little fear of retribution, nonpayment rates for band-owned housing ranged from medium to very high. At Cowichan Tribes, fifty of four hundred members living in rental homes were not paying in 2002;[50] at Siksika, the nonpayment rate was 60 percent;[51] and at Blood, approximately 75 to 80 percent.[52] At Piikani, 97 percent of members living in rental housing were not paying.[53] Members did not fear that the band council would evict them for nonpayment because the evicted members could punish councillors by voting against them in the next election. In addition, in all of the reserves studied, the community was said to frown upon the use of evictions, thereby further weakening council's will to act. In some cases, First Nations have had to turn to external institutions to recoup unpaid rent. For instance, the Champagne and Aishihik First Nation in the Yukon Territory filed a $100,000 lawsuit against some of its citizens "after all other efforts to recover unpaid rents failed." The lawsuit targeted five Champagne and Aishihik citizens who each owed between $10,000 and $30,000 in unpaid rent. Chief James Allen blamed DIAND for developing a dependency through "handouts to our First Nations people." The result was "an odd situation where some First Nation citizens seem to be making distinctions based on who's collecting the rent. Down the street, you may have a First Nations person with a white landlord and they're willing to pay that white landlord every month. But when it comes to paying your own First Nation, it's a different story."[54]

Nonpayment of rent reduces the amount of capital available to First Nations to build more housing and engage in repairs. According to one estimate, Cowichan Tribes was losing approximately $600,000 a year from nonpayment. For those First Nations that have few economic development resources available, this problem is even more acute. At Piikani, which was poor compared to the other Treaty 7 First Nations, the high nonpayment rate had crippled the housing department, leading to deteriorating housing conditions and very few new housing constructions per year.[55] For Blood Tribe, which did have some agricultural and oil and gas developments, nonpayment resulted in the closing of the housing department for one full year.[56] Siksika, on the other hand, managed to keep its housing stock in good condition and had done a relatively good job in meeting the demands of its membership for new construction and repair. However, they accomplished this feat because they had extensive oil and gas reserves that helped make up for the lost revenue in uncollected rents.[57]

CONCLUSION

Customary property rights on Indian reserves are probably the least economically efficient property rights system available to aboriginal peoples in Canada. The main problem limiting their usefulness is the lack of security of tenure. Customary land rights tend to be poorly documented, unsurveyed, and subject to the authority of the band council, itself frequently and inordinately influenced by band politics because of the small size of reserves. These weaknesses, together tend to generate a large number of disputes between band members, sometimes involving the band council, especially when the lands in question acquire some sort of value. The overall result is significant economic disincentives for individuals seeking to participate in the Canadian economy.

6

Certificates of Possession and Leases: The Indian Act Individual Property Regimes

Although the customary-rights system described in the previous chapter is the most widely used, it is not the only option available to First Nations. Since 1951, First Nations have had access to two statutory property rights systems: certificates of possession and leases. This chapter examines these systems in more detail. It begins by focusing on the certificate of possession system as it is currently used at the Six Nations Indian reserve near Brantford, Ontario, and ends by looking at the leasing system as it is used on reserves in Ontario, British Columbia, and Alberta.

CERTIFICATES OF POSSESSION

General Considerations

A certificate of possession is proof of an individual's lawful possession of reserve land. It is issued under the authority of the Indian Act by the minister of Indian Affairs after approval by the band council.[1] Only band members can hold and transfer CPs.[2] Since inception of the system in 1955, more than 140,000 of these certificates have been issued to property holders on 288 reserves.[3] Between 2002 and 2004 alone, approximately 40,000 new CPs were issued. Some reserves may have only one or two certificates, in contrast to the Six Nations reserve in Ontario, which has allotted almost all of its lands through 6,500 certificates.

The main provisions governing CPs can be found in sections 20-29 of the Indian Act. A CP gives its holder an interest in property falling somewhere between a fee-simple and life-estate interest. An "interest in reserve lands is a right to possession ... not a fee simple interest."[4] Underlying legal title still resides in the Crown, as reserves are set aside by the Crown for the use and benefit of First Nations.[5] Yet band members in possession of a CP do have security of tenure over their land. They can build a house, farm, or other buildings on the property without much fear of external interference from squatters, the band council, or other third parties.[6] To obtain a CP, however, requires the approval of the band council and the minister of Indian Affairs, and in this way is quite different from fee-simple ownership.

To transfer a CP requires the use of s. 24 of the Indian Act, which allows a CP holder to convey title to another band member or members. These transfers, however, are contingent upon the approval of the minister of Indian Affairs and can only occur between members of the same band, adding potentially significant transaction costs and limitations on the size and scope of on-reserve land markets. Similarly, CP holders can devise their land to another band member through a will, but it only becomes legal if the minister approves it under s. 45. CP holders can also lease their land to either a fellow Indian or to a non-Indian through s. 58(3). Again, the consent of the minister is necessary.

Besides the need for ministerial approval, there are several other differences between CPs and fee-simple rights that deserve mentioning. One is the lack of clear rules governing the division of matrimonial property in the event of a divorce. Off-reserve, provincial laws allow the courts to award partial or full ownership of matrimonial property to spouses not listed on the ownership papers. On-reserve, however, provincial matrimonial property laws do not apply. CPs can only be transferred through s. 24 of the Indian Act, meaning that Canadian courts cannot award possession of CP-held property in the event of a marriage breakdown.[7]

Another difference between CPs and fee-simple rights is that land held under a CP is safe from legal seizure under sections 29 and 89 and is exempt from taxation under s. 87 of the Indian Act.[8] Sections 29 and 89 are particularly important because they restrict the ability of the CP holder to mortgage property or use it as equity to expand a business.[9] As such, banks and other financial institutions are reluctant to lend CP holders money due to their inability to collect on defaults.

Yet CPs do provide individuals with significant security of tenure because Canadian courts have been willing to enforce them. In *Watts v. Doolan*, the band was ordered to pay the CP holder damages and rent for unlawfully erecting communication equipment on his property.[10] In *Westbank Indian Band v. Normand*, the Federal Court of Appeal ruled that a CP vested in its holder "all incidents of ownership."[11] The courts have also upheld a CP holder's right to transfer a CP to a fellow band member and lease property regardless of the objections of the band council.[12] In short, CPs provide members with well-defined, legally enforceable property rights that are safe from illegal seizure and squatting. This security of tenure has encouraged many members to build homes or farms on their land, or to lease it for commercial and agricultural purposes.

Certificates of Possession at Six Nations: A Case Study

Of the approximately 950,000 acres originally allocated to Six Nations under the 1784 Haldimand grant, only 47,374 acres remained under Six Nations control as of 2002.[13] Approximately 95 percent of the land was individually held under 6,500 CPs, while the balance was band land used for administrative buildings and municipal services.[14] Of the approximately 22,000 members of Six Nations, only half actually lived on the territory.[15] Demand for land was high at Six Nations, as many off-reserve members wanted to move back onto the territory. However, they found it difficult to do so for two reasons. Current landholders were reluctant to give up their land, and CPs provided their holders with the necessary security of tenure to prevent any band-led redistribution of land.[16]

The high value of reserve land made the process of allotting and transferring CPs extremely important. Since most of the Six Nations reserve had been allotted to members, the main type of CP transaction was the transfer under s. 24 of the Indian Act. The Six Nations Lands/Membership Department typically handled twenty to twenty-three transfers a month during the period when housing was being allotted, and ten to fifteen transfers during the rest of the year. Overall, they handled approximately two hundred transfers a year. Land prices depended on location. For instance, in the main commercial area called "the village," a typical lot sold for $15,000 an acre. Outside of the village, prices ranged from $500 to $3,000 an acre.[17]

There were two main types of transfers. In the first, CP holders transferred their undivided interest to another for a fee. The second type occurred when CP holders wished to divide their interest in the land among several people, usually their children. In that case, each person was issued a CP to the smaller individual tracts. A transfer began when a CP holder came to the Lands/Membership Office to apply for a transfer. If the applicant was a band member, had a legal CP to the property, and had no one disputing the transfer, the application was recommended for approval to the Six Nations Lands Membership Committee (LMC). If the transfer involved the subdivision of land into smaller tracts, then a survey of the property was conducted by the Department of Indian Affairs and Northern Development (DIAND). According to the DIAND District Office in Brantford, it took between six months and a year to complete a survey.[18] According to Six Nations, however, the survey process usually took a lot longer, citing a case that took eleven years to finish.[19]

Once the LMC received an application from the Lands/Membership Office, it reviewed the documentation and either approved or rejected it. If an application was approved, it was sent to the band council for a final review.[20] If the band council approved it, which it almost always did, it passed a General Council Memorandum (GCM) supporting the transfer. The documents, including the transfer and the GCM, were then sent to the DIAND District Office in Brantford, which forwarded them to Ottawa.[21]

In Brantford and Ottawa, the CP was reviewed for a final time by the Lands Registry Office. If all of the legal requirements were met, the lands examiner cancelled the old CP and issued a new CP or CPs, depending on the type of transfer. The CPs were recorded in the Reserve Lands Register as required by s. 21 of the Indian Act, and were sent back to the band, which then forwarded the CPs to the individuals. The average turnaround from mail out to mail back was supposed to be two weeks. Depending on the type of allotment, however, the turnaround could be much longer. For instance, if CP holders decided to subdivide their lot among their children, it took additional time to create the lots in the department database and to verify all of the documentation and data submitted.[22] According to the Lands/Membership Office at Six Nations, the turnaround for transfers was rarely two weeks.[23]

How long does it take to complete a transfer from start to finish? For a simple transfer from one individual to another, the total amount of time was three to four months.[24] For a transfer where CP holders divided their interest in the land among several people, the process could take much longer. The average time was supposed to be six months to a year; but the long wait for a survey, coupled with possible bureaucratic delays at the Lands/Membership Office, the DIAND District Office, and DIAND in Ottawa, could lengthen the approval process to anywhere from a year to eleven years.[25] The long waiting time from this added level of document review by DIAND inflicted significant time and monetary costs on anyone seeking to acquire an interest in reserve lands for economic development or for construction of a house.[26] This could have an adverse impact on meeting land and housing demands on-reserve, as well as discouraging economic development projects by both on-reserve and off-reserve entities.

However, private property rights do not have to be complete and absolute in order to be useful. Notwithstanding the restriction on sales, several First Nations in Ontario,[27] Quebec,[28] and British Columbia[29] have made an imaginative use of the CP system to promote private ownership of homes on reserves using two means: a band-administered revolving loan fund, and ministerial and band guarantees for loans from private lending institutions.

At Six Nations in Ontario, members could use their CP to obtain a housing loan from the band's revolving loan fund, or to obtain a band guarantee for a loan from the Bank of Montreal or Royal Bank of Canada.[30] The Six Nations revolving loan fund was established in 1968 with band monies and DIAND funds. The idea was that the band would use the fund to loan money to members, at a fixed interest rate, to build their own homes. The fund was to be a self-perpetuating internal financing mechanism for on-reserve housing.

To access funds, a member formally transferred the CP to the band, using section 24 of the Indian Act, in exchange for a $75,000 loan at a fixed simple interest rate of 7 percent. When the loan was paid off, the band formally transferred the CP back to the member. In the event that the member defaulted on the loan, the band evicted the member from the land and disposed of the property to make up for the lost funds. This could be accomplished because the band had possession of the CP. As members repaid their loans, more money would be available to more members to build more houses.[31]

Members of the Six Nations also used their CPs, in conjunction with band guarantees, to obtain mortgages directly from the Bank of Montreal or the Royal Bank. A member with a CP approached one of the banks for a housing loan. If the member met that bank's lending criteria (e.g., credit history, job history), then the member asked the band council for a band guarantee. In exchange for the band guaranteeing that it would immediately pay off the loan to the bank in the event of a default, the member formally transferred the CP to band council for the length of the loan. Once a band guarantee had been obtained, the bank released up to $95,000 to the individual at market interest rates. When the loan was paid off, the band returned the CP to the member. In the event of a default, the band immediately paid off the remaining balance of the loan and perhaps evicted the member from the land and disposed of it to recoup its losses.[32]

Both the revolving loan fund and the Bank of Montreal and Royal Bank mortgage programs have been very successful at Six Nations. Due to low default and nonpayment rates,[33] Six Nations has raised the total amount that individuals can obtain from both programs. In the case of the revolving loan fund, members can now borrow up to $120,000, up from $75,000 in 2002, at 7 percent simple interest. For the bank mortgage programs, band members can now borrow up to $150,000, up from $95,000 in 2002. As well, the band council has raised the total amount of funds guaranteeing these loans from $18 million in 2002 to $25 million in 2008, providing more band members with money to build their own homes.[34]

Revolving loan funds and band guarantees for bank loans are also used by other First Nations in Ontario, Quebec, Saskatchewan, and British Columbia to provide a means for members to build and own their own homes. Although these other Nations have private housing ownership programs that basically operate in the same manner as at Six Nations, there are some differences. For instance, some First Nations[35] use a revolving loan fund and/or private institutional funds,[36] while others use Canadian Mortgage and Housing Corporation (CMHC) monies.[37] There are also differences in who issues the guarantees. Some First Nations use band guarantees,[38] while others use ministerial guarantees,[39] which are essentially the same as band guarantees except that the minister of Indian Affairs guarantees the loan.[40] Finally, while most First Nations require the member to transfer the CP to the band for the duration of the loan, the Mohawks of Kahnawake require the CP to be transferred to a three-person trustee.[41] These trustees are politically independent band members and volunteers, not having been appointed by the federal, provincial, or band governments.[42] As status Indians, they have the authority to dispose of the property in the event of default.[43]

LEASES

The second property right found in the Indian Act is the leasing system. Leases can be granted on the band's collective land as well as on any type of individually controlled reserve land. However, the courts have held that Indian land can only be leased through a federal statute, such as the Indian Act.[44] The Act provides for three types of leasing arrangements for reserve land: short-term leases, long-term leases, and leases granted on behalf of a CP holder.

Governing these three leasing arrangements is *Surrey v. Peace Arch Ent. Ltd*,[45] in which the British Columbia Court of Appeal ruled that Indian land could only be leased through a government official. In other words, the band council or individual Indians wishing to lease reserve land cannot do so themselves. Rather, they must seek the approval of the federal government.

Short-Term Leases

Short-term leases or "permits" are governed by section 28(2) of the Indian Act, which gives the minister the power to grant to any person the right to reside on, use, or occupy reserve land for a period no longer than one year. For permits longer than a year, the minister must obtain the consent of the band council. In a number of rulings, the courts have confirmed that bands can engage in short-term leases only through the use of section 28(2).[46] In *Hofer v. Canada*,[47] Hofer, a non-native farmer, had signed a conditional agreement with the Blood Tribe Council extending his lease permits to tribal land for another five-year term. The validity of the agreement was conditional on "any final agreement set forth by Chief and Council and Permittees."[48] When Hofer was issued fifteen permits for three years, he took the federal government and the Blood Tribe to court for breach of contract. The Federal Court ruled that there was no evidence that the conditional agreement containing the five-year term had been approved either by the band council or by the minister, as required under section 28(2) of the Indian Act. Moreover, the conditional agreement itself provided that the chief and council had the right to change the final agreement before issuing the permits. Therefore, the change in the length of the permits from five to three years was valid.[49]

The influence of band councils over short-term leasing arrangements is limited by the need for a permit from the minister. In *Millbrook Indian Band v. Northern Counties Residential Tenancies Board*,[50] the band, which operated a mobile home park on unsurrendered reserve land, leased a space to Mrs Rushton, a non-Indian. At issue was whether the band council could lease land to a non-Indian without a permit from the minister, even if the band council believed that such a lease would be beneficial. The Nova Scotia Court of Appeal ruled that since the minister did not issue a permit, the lease she had signed with the band was void.[51] Thus, permits do not give local aboriginal governments much in the way of land-management authority.

Further limiting the influence of band councils over section 28(2) permits is the case of *Mannpar Enterprises Ltd. v. Canada*,[52] in which the plaintiff sought damages against DIAND and the band for failing to renew a permit to extract sand and gravel from the reserve. The term of the permit was five years and had a five-year renewal clause, "subject to [the] satisfactory performance and renegotiation of the royalty rate and annual surface rental."[53] At the end of the term, the company sought to renew the permit; however,

DIAND refused at the request of the band. The court ruled that section 28(2) permits do not require the "consent [of the band] at every stage of the permit process, including renewal."[54] Therefore, the band was bound to the renewal clause.[55]

All three cases illustrate another difficulty with short-term leases. The fact that both the band council and the minister are involved in giving approval can jeopardize the interests of innocent third parties. The duality of decision-making means that third parties have to invest more heavily in getting legal advice to protect their own interests, leading to inevitable delays and additional expense.

Despite these difficulties, bands and members with individual interests, especially those with customary rights to reserve land, have been able to use permits to generate revenue. The most common use of the permit is to rent farmland to off-reserve farmers. For example, at the time of our case study of the Piikani Nation in Alberta, a member with customary rights to land approached council. Council directed the Lands Committee to interview potential farmers, conduct credit checks, verify that the farmers had financial backing from a bank, review the crops to be grown and the quality of the soil, and determine how much the farmers planned to spend per acre. Once a farmer was chosen, council sent the permit to Ottawa, which approved it, registered it, and sent it back to the band. Piikani permits typically had a term of five years with the possibility of renewal. Land rent ranged from $18.50 to $43.00 an acre. Almost all of that revenue went to the individual, although the band did extract $1.00 an acre from the land rent as payment for administering the permit.[56] At other nations, such as Blood Tribe in Alberta, the process was essentially the same.[57] A less common use of permits, already described in the preceding chapter, was to obtain small bank loans, called "grain assignments."

Back at Piikani, the process was a little different. Members could sometimes obtain small loans for up to $10,000 from banks, using crops as security. Banks would only do this, however, if the member provided a BCR stating that all future rent monies derived from a permit would be paid directly to the bank. The band would only provide the BCR if the member had the ability to repay the loan.[58]

Although at first glance these uses seem to be beneficial, they may in fact prevent the band and its members from realizing the full potential value of the reserve land. For instance, at Blood Tribe, off-reserve farmers working on individually held and band-held reserve land under permits were earning approximately $45,796,500 gross a year from the land. From this, Blood Tribe netted $7,013,953, half of which went to the land's occupants and the rest to the band. The farmers, not the band, collected the remaining $38,783,453. Therefore, rather than using permits, the Lands Department was encouraging members to farm these lands themselves, or to allow the band, through band corporations, to farm the land, in order to acquire this revenue for themselves.

This same phenomenon occurred with the grain assignments. Although in theory the use of grain as collateral helped create additional capital for individuals to pursue economic development, the reality was rather different. Most people who obtained such financing, at least at Blood Tribe, relied on the permits as their main source of income and, once the first loan was obtained, remained stuck in an endless cycle of borrowing and repayment until the permit permanently expired.[59]

Long-Term Leases

For long-term leases of reserve land, section 38(2) of the *Indian Act* allows the band to "conditionally surrender" or "designate" land to the federal government for the purpose of leasing. The Supreme Court of Canada ruled in *Opetchesaht* that, "[i]n the case of ... long-term leases ... surrender is required, involving the vote of all members of the band."[60] After the band receives the approval of its members, the federal government can lease the land to an Indian or non-Indian development company, which can subdivide and sublease the land. The Cowichan people in British Columbia have successfully used the designation process to create revenue for both the band and its individual members. For instance, the Duncan Mall and the Wal-Mart superstore in downtown Duncan were built on designated land originally held as several CPs.[61] The Cowichan government and the former CP holders were able to work out an agreement in which the latter received 90 percent of the leasing revenue, while the band got the remaining 10 percent.[62] Land leased in this way remains reserve land, with the Crown retaining legal title and jurisdiction.

Besides allowing off-reserve companies to build economic development projects on-reserve, another frequent use of long-term designations is to obtain financing for band corporations to develop reserve land. Section 89(1) of the Indian Act hinders the ability of bands to raise financing for on-reserve economic development projects because Indian lands are "not subject to charge, pledge, mortgage, attachment, levy, seizure, distress or execution in favour or at the instance of any person other than an Indian or a band." By using section 38(2), the band can obtain financing from private lending institutions and maintain absolute control over the way in which the land is developed. This can occur because section 89(1.1) of the Indian Act expressly allows leasehold interests in designated land to be "subject to charge, pledge, mortgage, attachment, levy, seizure, distress and execution."

One band in western Canada, which asked not to be identified in our research, used section 38(2) to greatly enhance its financial situation. The band designated reserve land for seventy-five years to develop 1,200 housing lots for members, non-members, or non-Indians to build houses on. The Crown issued a head lease to the band, which then created a band-owned development company to service the lots and give out subleases. Residents paid the entire lease upfront, with prices ranging from $35,000 to $55,000, depending on the location and size of the lot and no possibility of renewal. Once residents signed the sublease, they had to secure financing from a bank to build homes according to construction guidelines set out by the bank. After paying for the lease and obtaining a mortgage from the bank, the only fee that residents had to pay to the band was a form of municipal tax for certain services that the band provided, such as garbage collection and street maintenance.

A serious problem with long-term leasing is that the terms incorporated in the agreement may make the lease land less valuable than its off-reserve equivalent. This need not always be true; one econometric study found that extension of the lease term from five to twenty-five, and then to sixty-five years, had made Indian reserve leasehold land in the Palm Springs, California, area almost as valuable as neighbouring freehold land.[63] But value of Indian leasehold land has certainly been an issue in Canada, as illustrated by the high-profile case of *Musqueam Indian Band v. Glass*.[64] The Musqueam Band in Vancouver surrendered forty acres of land for leasing in 1960. The Crown in turn leased the land to a development company, which subdivided the land and gave out ninety-nine-year leases to individuals who subsequently built houses. Contained in the leases was a rent review clause stating that, after the first thirty years and every twenty years thereafter, annual rent would be reassessed at 6 percent of the current land value. The dispute in the case was over the method of determining the "current land value" of reserve land designated for long-term lease. The trial division of the Federal Court of Canada held that land designated under section 38(2) remained Indian land, and that such land must be valued in terms of leasehold rather than freehold interest. The court also considered that the unique nature of Indian land would have an effect on its current value, reducing it by 50 percent as compared to similar property in the city of Vancouver.[65] However, the Federal Court of Appeal overturned the decision of the trial judge, arguing that the land designated under section 38(2) should be valued in terms of freehold rather than leasehold interest.[66]

The case was subsequently appealed to the Supreme Court of Canada. Writing for a 5-4 majority, Justice Gonthier ruled that since the leased land had not been surrendered for sale, the value of the land should be assessed as freehold title, even though there was "no such thing as freehold title on a reserve."[67] But the restrictions on sale and use that come with being reserve land, coupled with the power of the band council to levy property taxes and pass bylaws such as zoning laws, greatly reduces the current value of designated land.[68] Therefore, the majority held that the trial judge was correct in assessing a 50 percent reduction in the current land value.[69]

This case raises serious questions about the usefulness of long-term leases for Indian bands because rent calculations are based on the fair market value of the land. With this ruling, the Supreme Court of Canada set a precedent that land designated for long-term lease under section 38(2) may be worth much less than its off-reserve equivalent due to "Indian reserve feature[s]."[70] This means that bands may obtain less revenue for their land because the amount of rent collected will be lower, making long-term leases under the current regime not as useful and effective as leasing arrangements in the wider economy. The land manager of the Westbank First

Nation in British Columbia said in 2002 that the *Musqueam* dispute had a serious effect on the band's ability to designate land for leasing. Although the WFN assured potential buyers and developers that the *Musqueam* case was a unique situation and completely different from the way in which the WFN structured its leases, potential customers were still wary about purchasing or developing WFN land.[71]

The effect of the *Musqueam* decision has also been felt in the lower courts. In 1998, the Federal Court Trial Division was asked to determine the market value of devised lands for the purpose of rent calculation in *St Martin v. Canada (Minister of Indian Affairs and Northern Development)*.[72] The court ruled that the process for determining the new rent was as follows: "estimate the fee simple market value of the subject sites, reduce this value by a percentage which reflects the difference between fee simple interest and the interests inherent in the demised lands, and, apply a market oriented interest rate to arrive at [a] fair market rent."[73] Based on that process, the discount factor was 40 percent. This decision was subsequently overturned by the Federal Court of Appeal in light of the *Musqueam* decision.

In *Morin v. Canada*,[74] the Trial Division of the Federal Court increased the value of designated land by choosing an appraisal that seemed to apply the principles of the *Musqueam* decision. The court preferred the approach of the Crown's appraiser, Mr Bell, because he had taken

> great pains to understand and to apply the principles established in *Musqueam* with respect to the determination of the fair market value of Indian reserve land surrendered for leasing purposes ... In contrast, Mr Rueck testified in cross-examination that: I didn't go through the *Musqueam* decision in great detail. I used it just as a very preliminary guide as an indication that there is a difference between the two types of properties [freehold and leasehold].[75]

Therefore, the court accepted Bell's determination of the fair market value of a typical lot to have been $42,000 in 1994 and $51,500 in 1999, as compared to Rueck's appraisal of $19,200 in 1994 and

$24,000 in 1999. This decision was later appealed and upheld by the Federal Court of Appeal in 2005.[76]

It would be a mistake to think of the *Musqueam* decision itself as the root of the problem. There are underlying difficulties in this area that have to be faced. A lease, even a long-term lease, is simply not the same property right as outright ownership. A lease can be sold in the market, thus transcending some of the limitations of CPs and customary holdings; but, particularly as one approaches the renewal date, it does not carry the same security of tenure as a freehold. The market will always impose some discount on entailed land as compared to freehold. However, the discount need not be the 50 percent proclaimed by the Supreme Court in *Musqueam*. One knowledgeable observer opined that leased reserve land in the Kelowna area should be worth about 85 percent of comparable freehold land, given properly constructed lease agreements.[77]

This is a matter of considerable practical importance. There are now tens of thousands of leases on designated reserve land in Canada, creating the basis for shopping centres, industrial parks, vacation communities, and year-round residential housing projects. The commercial, recreational, or residential potential of their land is the greatest economic asset of many First Nations; and the lease of designated land will be the chief instrument for realizing the value of that potential, for marketizing the land while retaining the permanent title for the benefit of the band. These court decisions have created uncertainty for those bands and off-reserve companies who may wish to pursue on-reserve economic development. Further disputes of the *Musqueam*-type may deter potential developers and purchasers of leases, leading to devaluation of reserve land and impoverishment of the residents.

Leases Granted on Behalf of a CP Holder

At the individual level, the Indian Act also provides for Indians in lawful possession of reserve land to lease it in two different ways through the Department of Indian Affairs, but they cannot simply enter into an agreement on their own. Section 58(1)(b) says that "where the land is in lawful possession of any individual, [the minister may] grant a lease of such land for agricultural or grazing purposes or for any purpose that is for the benefit of the person in possession." Section 58(3) states that "the Minister may lease for the benefit of any Indian, on application of that Indian for that purpose, the land of which the Indian is lawfully in possession without the land being designated." Band council consent is not required in the latter case.

At the Westbank First Nation (WFN) in British Columbia, CP holders have successfully used section 58(3) to commercialize their real-estate assets. Much of the WFN land is held under CP by a small number of individuals and families. Taking advantage of the lack of band council involvement in a section 58(3) lease, these CP holders have leased their land to private development companies to build adult gated communities and residential neighbourhoods, ranging from lower-middle-class housing to $400,000 homes. These companies gave individual ninety-nine-year prepaid subleases for these homes; after ninety-nine years, the house and land revert back to the CP holder. This reversionary feature of the lease is a ticking time bomb whose effects will eventually have to be faced. Another problem with this arrangement is that all of the profit goes to the individual CP holders, while the band receives no revenue.[78]

Provisions of this type were first tested in *Boyer*.[79] John Corbière, a member of the Batchewana Indian Band, obtained lawful possession of a tract of land on his reserve in 1973. In 1980, he asked his band for a BCR approving his intention to lease the land to a corporation in which he and his wife were sole shareholders. In 1982, he applied to the minister under section 58(3) to approve the transaction. However, the band council disputed Corbière's claim to a lease. They wrote to the minister stating that the lease did not address several causes of direct harm to the band. Ignoring the band's protests, the minister issued a lease to Corbière's development company in 1983. The Federal Court of Appeal held that the 1980 BCR only consented to the principle of leasing the land and did not in fact reflect the council's approval of the particular lease granted in 1983.[80] Furthermore, the court ruled that the minister was not required to obtain the consent of the band council when issuing leases under section 58(3) since the band loses its collective right to the land when it is allotted through a CP or a certificate of occupation.[81]

The Federal Court of Appeal modified the *Boyer* decision in 1999 with its ruling in *Tsartlip Indian Band v. Canada*.[82] In that case, the respondents had CPs to reserve land upon which they wanted to build a home park for non-Indians through Clydesdale Estates Holdings Ltd, of which they were shareholders. However, the Tsartlip band council had misgivings about the lease and the use of the land, citing concerns such as a shortage of band member housing, the lack of adequate water and sewer capacity, and the longstanding opposition of band members to home parks for non-Indians.[83] Despite the concerns of the band council, the minister granted the lease and the respondents built the home park. The band then challenged the validity of the lease. The Federal Court of Appeal ruled that, although the minister does not have a fiduciary duty to the band when issuing a lease under section 58(3), the minister must still take into account the concerns of the band council, especially when a lease may harm the overall interests of the band. Parliament intended the Indian Act to be band- and reserve-oriented, and the band council should continue to have some influence on whether or not to allow non-Indians onto reserve land. "The mere fact that the Band has originally agreed to let a locatee occupy and use a lot on the reserve cannot mean, in my understanding of the whole of the Act, that the Band has implicitly abandoned the right it has under s. 28(2) to control the use of the lot by a non-member of the Band."[84] In this case the court ruled that the minister did not adequately address the concerns of the band council, and therefore the lease made under section 58(3) was null and void.

This decision once again highlights the uncertainty stemming from dual control. Under the *Tsartlip* doctrine, a band council can apparently overturn a lease made in good faith by a CP holder and approved by the minister. The net result is reduced security of expectations and increased time and expense involved in negotiating business arrangements involving CP land. However, this particular problem could be overcome partially by First Nations opting into one of the federal devolutionary programs like the FNLMA (discussed in the next chapter), which would eliminate the need for ministerial approval.

CONCLUSION

Although both Indian Act property regimes are preferable to customary land rights, they are still weighed down by some significant impediments. In the case of certificates of possession, high transaction costs and limits on transfers create significant economic disincentives for band members interested in participating in the Canadian economy. In the case of leases, transaction costs in the form of federal or band level approval as well as the potential of lost rents due to undervalued reserve lands are also significant disincentives. Certificates of possession and Indian Act leases were meant to be temporary measures to allow aboriginal people to eventually enter the mainstream economy; but First Nations are now stuck with a set of outdated property rights that severely impede their successful participation in the Canadian economy.

The First Nations Land Management Act: An Alternative to the Indian Act

For much of Canadian history, aboriginal peoples have had access only to the three property rights regimes discussed in the preceding chapters: customary rights, certificates of possession, and leases. In the early 1990s, however, a number of aboriginal groups became extremely dissatisfied with the current regimes and decided to meet with federal officials to discuss alternative strategies that would allow them to achieve more efficient, useful, and localized land management practices on their reserves. The result was the First Nations Land Management Act (FNLMA), a piece of federal legislation designed to allow First Nations to opt out of the land management provisions of the Indian Act to develop their own land codes.

THE FIRST NATIONS LAND MANAGEMENT ACT: BACKGROUND CONSIDERATIONS

In the early 1990s, a number of chiefs, led by Robert Louie (Westbank First Nation), Austin Bear (Muskoday First Nation), and Strater Crowfoot (Siksika First Nation), became extremely dissatisfied with the significant economic drag created by the Indian Act. In 1994, this group of chiefs approached Indian Affairs Minister Ron Irwin about the possibility of thirteen First Nations opting out of the land-management provisions of the Indian Act to develop their own land-management administrative regimes under a new legislative framework. In 1997, another First Nation was added to the group and in 1999 the federal government passed the First

Nations Land Management Act (FNLMA), bringing into effect the Framework Agreement on First Nations Land Management negotiated by the federal government and thirteen First Nations on 12 February 1996.

In essence, the FNLMA allows its signatory First Nations to opt out of thirty-four land-administration sections in the Indian Act to develop their own land codes for administering their lands according to their own rules and customs. A First Nation must develop and draft a land code, submit it to a jointly appointed verifier, negotiate a funding agreement with INAC, and hold a community vote on both the land code and the funding agreement. If the community approves, the verifier certifies the land code and the First Nation takes over all land-management responsibilities from the Crown. On the day the land code takes effect, it acquires legal standing and becomes enforceable in Canadian courts.[1] The average time to draft and ratify a land code is 1,068 days.[2]

Since 1999, fifty-eight bands have opted into the FNLMA, ninety have inquired about doing so, and twenty-three have put their land codes into operation.[3] A land code can address the following issues:

(a) the use and occupancy of First Nation's land, including licences, leases, and allotments under s. 20(1) of the *Indian Act*; (b) the transfer of land interests and the revenues from natural resources obtained from reserve land; (c) requirements for accountability to First Nation members for land management and moneys derived from reserve land; (d) community consultation processes for the development of rules respecting matrimonial property issues, use, occupation and possession of First Nation land and the division of interests in First Nation land; (e) publication of First Nation laws; (f) conflicts of interest in the management of First Nation land; (g) the establishment of a forum for the resolution of disputes in relation to interests in First Nation land; (h) granting or expropriating interests in First Nation land; (i) delegation by the council of its authority to manage land; (j) approvals of an exchange of First Nation land; and (k) amending the land code.[4]

In essence, the main goal of the FNLMA was to allow participating First Nations to develop locally sensitive land codes that mitigated the economic drag associated with the Indian Act. A number of signatory chiefs mentioned that many investors and band members were unhappy with the Indian Act because it imposed significant transaction costs upon on-reserve economic development and investment. The land codes, it was hoped, would eliminate ministerial interference and allow First Nations to pass more locally sensitive and efficient rules, thus making reserves more attractive to investment.

In the following section, we look at two case studies to determine what effect the FNLMA has had on economic development. These two case studies are the Mississaugas of Scugog Island in Ontario and the Muskoday First Nation in Saskatchewan. The Mississaugas of Scugog Island (Ontario) are a good case because the band's land base is small (240 hectares), as is its on-reserve population (sixty-five members). Previous research speculated that small reserves might not benefit from the FNLMA because of economies of scale.[5] The Muskoday First Nation represents a more typical reserve both in land size (9,700 hectares) and in population (five hundred members).

TWO CASE STUDIES

The Mississaugas of Scugog Island

Located 65 km northeast of Toronto, the Mississaugas of Scugog Island First Nation was one of the original signatories to the *Framework Agreement,* ratifying its land code on 11 March 1997. The code officially came into effect on 1 January 2000.

The Scugog Island land code attempts to facilitate on-reserve development in two ways. First, it creates a more formalized and efficient system of customary rights. According to s. 15 of the land code, all interests and licenses in Scugog Island lands must be documented and filed with the band before they can receive legal recognition and enforcement. Written documentation is also necessary for all land transfers, wills, subdivisions of land, and allotments of land (s. 13.2). According to s. 16.2, only band members can be allotted a residential lot. Once allocated, an allotment grants to its holder "the exclusive use and occupancy of that lot for residential purposes" (s. 16.3). Moreover, the holder is entitled to any resources or revenue arising from the sale of resources on that lot (s. 16.5). In addition to use and occupancy rights, allotment holders are free to transfer or devise their land to any band member without the need for band council approval (s. 16.6).

Customary allotments are also safe from expropriation by the band council (s. 29). This is significant because previously under the Indian Act, customary rights were unenforceable and thus could be "cancelled" at any time and for any reason. In the past, some First Nations have evicted band members from their customarily held lands because the band councils wanted to build a school or extract renewable and non-renewable resources from the members' lands.[6] Under the Scugog Island land code, however, members do not have to fear expropriation by the band.

Finally, the Scugog Island land code establishes a new dispute resolution process for protecting individual interests. Previously, customary holders had no legal recourse for disputes with fellow band members or the band council except to petition the band council for redress. Under the Scugog Island land code, however, disputants begin by petitioning either the band council or the lands advisory committee (composed of five members appointed by the band council, of which one member must be a non-resident of Scugog Island) for resolution. If either of these bodies is unable to resolve the matter, the dispute is referred to the Scugog Island dispute resolution committee. This committee has the power to confirm, alter, or reverse a previous decision, issue a new decision, or order a new hearing. The committee's decisions are final and binding. To insulate the dispute resolution committee from undue influence, s. 26.5 of the land code states that "any attempt by a person making an appeal to improperly influence the decision of the dispute resolution body will result in the automatic rejection of the appeal."

The second way that the Scugog Island land code tries to facilitate development is by eliminating the involvement of the federal government from all land transactions. The land code establishes that the Scugog Island First Nation is the sole administrator of lands on its reserve. Administrative powers include the ability to pass laws regulating development, conservation, protection, and the management and ownership of Scugog Island reserve lands, including water, waterbeds, riparian rights, and renewable and non-renewable resources (ss. 7–8). The band council is free to grant interests and licenses in community lands, except in the case of leases that exceed twenty-five years, at which point community approval is required.[7] It can also grant permits to extract resources from community lands, again subject to community approval if the terms of the permits are longer than one year. Individual leasehold interests can be used as security to obtain mortgages. In the event of a default, seizure can occur only if: a) the mortgage received the proper approval from either the band council or the community; b) the mortgage was properly registered with the band; and c) the lessor is given a reasonable opportunity to redeem the mortgage (s. 18.4).

The Scugog Island land code is a clear attempt at strengthening customary rights and reducing transaction costs. Preliminary evidence suggests that there has been significant progress toward these goals. Previously, according to former Scugog Island Chief Rennie Goose,

> Getting a business going under the Indian Act is a long path. By the time information flows from the First Nation, through the federal government regional offices to headquarters, then back down the line, the process can easily take anywhere from 6 to 18 months. By that time, any business that may have been interested in partnering with the First Nation has likely moved on.[8]

Now, under its land code, the band has the authority to move quickly on business proposals. For instance, the Scugog Island land code was crucial in the construction and management of a casino on the reserve. According to former Chief Goose,

> It [our land code] definitely helped in our negotiations with our partner in operating the casino. Our lease arrangement required that we borrow a significant sum of money and it's likely that we would not have been able to do so under INAC land management. Under FNLMA, we were able to secure the loan and hold ourselves out as a stable potential partner.[9]

The revenues from this casino have enabled the band "to expand its Administration office during 2006 with another addition which houses 14 offices, a small conference room, and a staff lounge." As well, the band has been able to develop a sixteen-unit residential subdivision and is in the process of examining the possibility of a water/sewage treatment plant for the region.[10]

The Scugog Island land code has also reduced the transaction costs involved in allotting and administering leases and CPs. With regard to leases, former chief Goose has observed that "even a relatively simple agricultural lease would take a long time to process under the *Indian Act*."[11] With regard to CPs, Jill Thompson, former land manager and now economic development officer for Scugog Island, has observed that it could take up to two years to process CP applications under the Indian Act.[12] Now under the band's land code, the administration of leases and CPs is much more efficient as the band no longer has to wait for applications to go through multiple approval stages at the federal level. Instead, most land transactions can be completed by the First Nation in a matter of hours or, at a maximum, a couple of days.

Muskoday First Nation

Muskoday First Nation is located 20 km southeast of Prince Albert in the province of Saskatchewan. It has an on-reserve population of five-hundred members and a reserve area of 9,700 hectares, of which a significant portion is excellent farmland. The Muskoday First Nation was one of the original signatories of the Framework Agreement, drafting and ratifying its land code by 31 October 1997. Its land code came into effect on 1 January 2001.

Compared to Scugog Island, the Muskody First Nation land code is less successful in formalizing and strengthening customary rights. Although the land code does require that all interests and licenses in Muskody lands be documented in writing and registered with the band council before they are recognized and enforced (s. 14.1.11; s. 17), it does not specify what ownership rights individuals acquire when they are allotted an interest. This is in contrast to Scugog Island, where the land code clearly specifies that holders gain exclusive use and occupancy rights to their allotment. The Muskody land code also states that "there shall be no transfer or assignment of an interest in Muskody land without the written consent of the council" (s. 18). At Scugog Island, the band council's consent is not required for these transactions. Furthermore, a customary right under the Muskoday land code does "not entitle the member to benefit from the resources arising from the interest" (s. 20). Again, this is in contrast to Scugog Island, where holders are entitled to the resources on their property and any revenues derived from their sale. Finally, whereas the Scugog Island land code forbids the band council from expropriating customarily held lands, section 21 of the Muskoday land code allows the band council to expropriate all reserve lands as long as the expropriation is for community purposes. Community purposes can include, but are not limited to "a fire hall, sewer or water treatment facility, community centre, public works, roads, schools, day-care facility, hospitals, health-care facility, and retirement home." Before expropriation can occur, the band must make "a good faith effort to acquire, by mutual agreement, rights or interests in Muskoday land" (s. 21). If the good faith effort fails, the band can go ahead and expropriate the land as long as it offers the band member reasonable monetary compensation.

As in the Scugog Island land code, the Muskoday land code offers a dispute resolution process. Disputants begin by petitioning either the band council or the lands advisory committee. The lands advisory committee, which is made up of seven band council-appointed members, one of whom must not be a resident, is supposed to advise the band council on all issues related to Muskoday lands, including disputes involving reserve lands (s. 15). If the band council and the lands advisory committee are unable to resolve the dispute, the matter is referred to the dispute resolution committee, which has exactly the same powers as the Scugog Island committee (s. 30).

As at Scugog Island, the Muskoday land code attempts to reduce transaction costs by eliminating federal involvement. The land code states that the Muskoday band has sole ownership of all rights and resources in the band's reserve lands; this includes water, waterbeds, riparian rights, and renewable and non-renewable resources (s. 7). The band also has a wide range of law-making powers over its lands, including the "development, conservation, protection, management, and the use and possession of Muskoday lands" (s. 8). For greater certainty, the code states that the band council has the sole power to grant interests, licenses, and permits for using Muskoday community lands or to extract natural resources. Mortgages on leasehold lands are permitted, but before such lands can be seized in the event of a default it must be proven that the band council consented to the mortgage and that the mortgage was registered with the band or the First Nations Land Registry in Ottawa. Finally, the band council must be given "a reasonable opportunity" to redeem the mortgage before it can be seized (s. 19).

In general, the Muskoday land code does reduce transaction costs but it falls short in strengthening individual property rights on its reserve. The only significant differences between Muskoday customary rights before and after the adoption of the land code are the legal requirements for written documentation and the creation of a formal dispute resolution process. Otherwise, the nature and usage of customary rights under the code remains the same as before. As described above, transfers and other dispositions of lands under the land code remain subject to the approval of the band council; the exact nature of individual ownership remains unclear; the resources found on individual allotments continue to belong to the band council; and finally the language in s. 21 of the land code is sufficiently broad to allow the band council to expropriate individual interests in reserve lands for almost any purpose.

Despite these weaknesses, preliminary evidence suggests that the Muskoday land code has had a positive effect on economic development. Prior to the FNLMA, third parties were reluctant to invest in Muskoday lands. According to Band Manager Leroy Bear, a manufacturer of farm equipment wanted to set up shop on the reserve. The band told the manufacturer that they were interested but that the manufacturer would have to send a proposal to INAC. "After getting caught up in 'red tape,' they were unable to come to an agreement," and the manufacturer ended up establishing his operation in a nearby town.[13] Now, with its land code in effect, Muskoday First Nation is much more attractive to off-reserve investment. In 2004 it was approached by the Canadian Forestry Service to plant trees on the reserve. The project employed fifteen part-time workers and transferred $35,000 over five years to the First Nation, while at the same time beautifying the area beside a new school on the reserve. A number of private entrepreneurs have opened, or have expressed an interest in opening, businesses on the reserve. In October 2004, the First Nation agreed with an off-reserve resident to lease a band-owned restaurant. "The time frame involved from tendering to signing the lease was less than three months – a fraction of the time that is required to complete commercial leases under the *Indian Act*." Others have inquired about opening up "a mini strip-mall, a car wash/oil change business, and a gift shop dealing mainly in native artwork," all of which the First Nation is actively pursuing under its land code.[14]

The investment climate has clearly improved since the adoption of the land code. In August 2006 the band entered into two-year and five-year lease agreements with investors and farmers to open a new restaurant in the same building as the community Store and Gas Bar and to farm some of the reserve's most valuable agricultural lands.[15] Moreover, the band "continues to lease billboard space on its lands to three different companies in the City of Prince Albert. Businesses from other surrounding communities have approached the Lands department on leasing billboard space along Highway #3, one of the busiest routes in the province."[16]

The land code has also had a positive effect on the band's administration of permits. Since the code came into effect in 2001, the band has issued and is administering 170 cash permits. As opposed to the months that it took to issue a permit under the Indian Act, the average time to issue a permit under the Muskoday land code is less than a month.[17] Moreover, the Muskoday First Nation directly controls its permits and leases. This means it receives rents directly from the sublessees and can enforce the terms of its leases without having to rely on INAC to do so. In essence, the land code allows the Muskoday First Nation to avoid the problems that the Musqueam Indian band encountered when it had to rely on a reluctant INAC bureaucracy to enforce the terms of its leases.[18]

The effects of the land code on individual property rights at Muskoday First Nation, however, are less clear. According to Land Manager Ed Bear,

In pre-FNLMA times, we had Traditional Land Holdings to acknowledge our members on the parcels of land that they occupy. The problem was that the Indian Act did not allow for the land to be registered in the Indian Lands Registry.[19] Under our newly adopted code, our Traditional Land Holdings are recognized and a certificate is given to the person holding the land. It is also registered in our lands registry. Lots of our community members were excited to have that piece of paper. Previously, they had been concerned that if a new Chief and Council were elected, their land holdings may be called into question. Now, with the registered certificate, that is no longer a concern.[20]

However, his enthusiasm may be overly optimistic because the band still retains significant control over traditional landholdings. Members must still seek band council approval before any land transactions can occur, and their traditional landholdings remain subject to expropriation by the band council for community purposes. As such, it is not certain that the Muskoday land code will in fact prevent a "new Chief and Council" from interfering with or expropriating members' traditional landholdings. The spectre of nepotism and personal politics still hangs over the land-management regime at Muskoday First Nation.

CONCLUSION

In general, the FNLMA has had a positive impact in improving economic development conditions on Canadian Indian reserves. Its strength lies in allowing First Nations to opt out of the archaic land-management provisions of the Indian Act. Once free from these provisions, First Nations can develop land codes that encourage economic development while respecting locally sensitive needs and issues. The Scugog and Muskoday cases clearly illustrate the significant positive improvements that can occur under the FNLMA. Other First Nations report similar improvement. At Beecher Bay (or Scianew) First Nation in British Columbia, "there have been positive developments that are a direct result of the community having the authority to decide what land management priorities are important and to be able to work towards these goals in a quicker manner than under the *Indian Act*."[21] Similarly, observers suggest the FNLMA has had a positive effect at Shxwha:y First Nation in British Columbia: "The approval of the Shxwha:y Village's Land Code has proven to be of great benefit to the community ... Shxwha:y Village's first concrete example of this was in their ability to obtain a Timber Mark from the BC Ministry of Forestry. The process took them less than 10 days. With INAC, it took them 6 months." Moreover, "they have been approached by several large developers who do not currently deal with First Nations because of INAC bureaucracy. The developers have reviewed their Land Code and are excited to work with Shxwha:y Village as they see Shxwha:y Village has the final decision making authority."[22] At Whitecap Dakota First Nation, in Saskatchewan, the band has been able to approve sixteen new commercial leases, including leases that led to the development of an award-winning golf course and a world-class casino. Officials attribute these successes to the "ease of negotiating land leases under the land code."[23] Finally, at Nipissing First Nation, in Ontario, the band has used its land code to attract off-reserve investors to build a motel, a travel agency, a storage facility, a recreational vehicle sales and servicing facility, a coffee shop, convenience stores, gas stations, a tobacco product manufacturer, and an office complex on its reserve.[24]

These success stories are not isolated incidents. The Department of Indian and Northern Affairs, the First Nations Land Advisory Board, and individual First Nations are constantly publicizing the positive effect that the FNLMA is having on all of its participating First Nations. This is not to say that the FNLMA is problem-free; indeed, some of these problems are potentially significant. At Tsawwassen First Nation, for instance, "the transition from the *Indian Act* management regime was not without its challenges, particularly because the costs of training staff and developing laws and procedures are significant."[25] As well, due to the diversity of the land codes themselves, investors may face significant learning costs if they are interested in doing business with multiple FNLMA First Nations. The task of learning the rules for investment for multiple First Nations may discourage some investors from on-reserve development.

Although the FNLMA is clearly an important step forward for First Nations in Canada, it is subject to a double limitation that, we believe, prevents it from becoming a comprehensive pathway to economic success. One side of that limitation is that the FNLMA leaves each First Nation on its own to develop its own system of property rights. Taken to the extreme, this could lead to 630 different First Nation land codes in Canada, each with uniquely defined property rights – a nightmare scenario for developers interested in doing business on Indian reserves. The other side of the coin is that the FNLMA did not set up any central machinery to provide First Nations with technical assistance in the form of model land codes and zoning regulations. The absence of such templates throws First Nations back on their own resources, leading to a proliferation of legal regimes as well as the inability of some First Nations to make progress on their own. Part 3 of this book suggests a further step forward, the First Nations Property Ownership Act, to provide indefeasible title while providing the necessary advisory institutions and legal templates for successful participation in the market economy.

PART THREE

Beyond the Indian Act

Whereas part 2 showed the limitations of existing property rights on Indian reserves, in part 3 we try to sketch out the "other path" of a First Nations Property Ownership Act, which, for First Nations who want to take this path, would recognize their collective to their current landholdings while also facilitating the introduction of fee-simple ownership. Chapter 8 explains with case studies how transaction costs under existing regimes of property rights are so high that they delay and even deter many potentially profitable developments on reserve land. Chapter 9 describes the many attempts of First Nations to get "beyond the Indian Act" through incremental legislative change as well as comprehensive negotiations over land claims and self-government. Chapter 10 concludes by describing the contents of a hypothetical First Nations Property Ownership Act, based on the work that the Nisga'a Nation has already done in developing their own land-title system, which will soon include the possibility of fee-simple ownership of land by individuals.

8

Why Markets Fail on First Nations Lands

Markets exist when voluntary exchanges take place between buyers and sellers, facilitated by informal and/or formal rules and infrastructure. Markets are social institutions, in which both parties recognize and receive a benefit from trade. They are able to realize this benefit because at least one of the parties has a competitive advantage in location, technology, labour, product, or service. Trade, however, cannot take place unless there is infrastructure to enable the exchange and rules to provide certainty about property ownership.

The inhabitants of the Americas had markets long before any contact with European explorers and settlers. Recognizing the benefits of exchange, they established far-flung networks for trading corn, pipestone, oolichan grease, and many other products.[1] They exploited competitive advantages by specializing, e.g., the Secwepemc in salmon fishing, the Woodland Cree in pemmican, the Nootka in whaling, and the Kwakiutl in woodworking and iron and metal extraction.[2] Some nations, such as the Maya and Norte Chico, built trade-enabling infrastructure such as roads and marketplaces.[3] In addition, commerce-friendly social institutions also emerged, such as the Chinook trading language, used among pre-contact First Nations from Alaska to California, and the Aztec system of commercial law.[4] And, as has been discussed earlier in the book, there were many systems of property rights.

Markets, however, are largely absent on First Nations lands now. It is not that there are no competitive advantages; indeed, many

First Nations have competitive advantages related to location, natural resources, and labour. But the rules, powers, and administration necessary to establish secure property ownership and infrastructure to facilitate trade are not in place. The result is that trade is too expensive and markets fail on First Nations lands. This chapter explains why.

A MARKET HERO

Economists seldom acknowledge that it sometimes takes heroism to make markets work. If there were a hall of fame for people who have reduced transaction costs and made markets work where they had failed before, it would include Clarence Jules, Sr, who worked to establish a pioneering industrial park on the Kamloops Indian Reserve. Under his leadership as chief, the Kamloops band council in 1962 passed a bylaw to establish the Mount Paul Industrial Park. Chief Jules made sure the necessary infrastructure was built, and he personally convinced a number of businesses to invest and lease land on the reserve. His powers of persuasion must have been impressive, because securing a property right on Indian land in the 1960s was difficult. Potential investors faced uncertainty about tenure, lease registration, tax liability, and local service provision; moreover, they had plenty of options on non-Indian lands. It is a testament to his vision that the Mount Paul Park has grown from 11 original businesses in 1964 to more than 150 today, with annual sales of more than $250 million.

To put Clarence Jules's accomplishment in perspective, consider what he said during the White Paper consultations of 1968, when he was asked about how the Indian Act should be changed:

> We feel that we are in a better position to judge the needs
> of our people than officials of the Department located in
> Ottawa. We point out that much of the dissatisfaction with
> the present Act arises from the lack of power and authority
> to Band Councils. To give just one illustration: We operate an
> Industrial Subdivision on part of our reserve and lease lots in
> the Sub-division to various individuals and companies. Before
> a lease can be granted not only must the Band Council pass its

resolution but the lease is then routed through the Kamloops Indian Agency, then to the Vancouver office and finally to Ottawa. The same process is followed on the return trip.

We can document instances where months have gone by before a lease is finally issued. In many cases by the time the lease has been returned the lessee has gone elsewhere because people today require almost instantaneous decisions. These delays cost us money and we don't like it. There must be a change to grant more power and authority to Indian Band Councils. After all, our Indian people elect us to represent them; they do not elect officials of the Indian Department.[5]

To our knowledge he was the original First Nations leader to recognize the high transaction costs associated with establishing tradable property rights on reserves. Out of practical experience, he arrived at the same conclusion that the discipline of economics has reached.[6] As one economist has written, "In the absence of institutional adaptations, high transaction costs lead to market failure, impede economic growth, and hamper competitiveness."[7] Chief Jules was also the first person to publicly identify that the Indian Act system of governance was to blame.

UNDERLYING PROPERTY RIGHTS AND MARKETS

As Hernando de Soto has observed, we take for granted the legal, governmental, and fiscal framework in Canada that supports individual property rights.[8] When this supportive system is absent, as among First Nations, the result is high transaction costs, because the buyer and seller must create these rules for themselves. It is no coincidence, therefore, that the costs of completing a real-estate deal on some of the best-located First Nations lands in Canada are so high.

Most homeowners in Canada are familiar with indefeasible or fee-simple property rights. In seven of the ten provinces, Canadian landowners enjoy some version of the Torrens system of land titles,[9] which includes insurance to secure property ownership. Canadians' use of their property is governed by local rules such as zoning and building codes, but the chronological term of fee-simple property ownership is unlimited. Fee-simple ownership must coexist with the underlying title that remains with the government, symbolized by the Crown in the British tradition. It is in virtue of its underlying title that the government can regulate land use, impose property taxes, and reclaim ownership of land if such taxes are not paid.

Certainty with respect to both individual and underlying property rights is required for markets to work effectively. In Canada, it is mainly provincial and local governments that provide the rules to clarify property rights in support of markets. Provincial governments provide the legal and administrative framework to protect and enforce property ownership. Local governments provide local service quality, security, and reliable information; make rules for land development and zoning; and build the public infrastructure, such as roads and utilities, necessary to facilitate trade.

When these jurisdictions are not recognized or there are insufficient resources to exercise them, the result is high transaction costs and market failure, as has happened to First Nations. They do not have the provincial type of powers necessary to protect and enforce marketable property rights on their lands. Moreover, from 1876 until 1918, First Nations were prevented from raising tax revenues to fund local governments that could have developed local rules and supplied commercial-grade infrastructure.[10]

In 1875, the Mohawk community of Tyendinaga tried to create a tax system, collecting property taxes from their lessees to pay for local services. The band, the township, and the local Indian Agent agreed to this innovation, but the Department of Indian Affairs ordered it stopped.[11] Other attempts to develop sources of revenue for First Nations and to participate in the Canadian fiscal relationship were also frustrated. In 1908, Six Nations was denied a share in the Dominion subsidies received by every other local government at the time, as well as the right to collect a rail tax.[12]

Traditional methods of redistributing wealth among First Nations were also banned: thirst dances due to the permit and pass system of 1881, which prevented Indians from leaving their reserves or trading outside their communities;[13] potlatches in 1884;[14] sun dances, giveaways, and similar ceremonies in 1890.[15] Agricultural production was diminished by the 1889 policy of peasant farming, whereby each family on western Indian reserves was supposed to become self-sufficient with one acre of wheat and one acre for vegetables and a cow or two.[16] A 1918 amendment to the Indian Act enshrined some of these previous restrictions:

> Every Indian or other person who engages in, or assists in celebrating or encourages either directly or indirectly another to celebrate any Indian festival, dance or other ceremony of which the giving away or paying or giving back of money, goods or articles of any sort forms a part, or is a feature, whether such gift of money, goods or articles takes place, before, at or after the celebration of the same, or who engages or assists in any celebration or dance of which the wounding or mutilation of the dead or living body of any human being or animal forms a part or is a feature, is guilty of an indictable offence.[17]

In effect and in intent, the legislation turned Indians into economic wards of the state. When these amendments were passed, Calgary MP Thomas Mitchell Tweedie said, "Well, the Indian may be satisfied and he may not. My personal view with regard to the Indian is that he is the ward of the Government, and being a ward he is bound to accept the treatment given him."[18] In 1951 the Indian Act was amended to remove this and other provisions. It was not until 1988, however, with the so-called "Kamloops Amendment," that First Nations obtained the authority to levy property taxes. Finally, First Nations would have access to independent revenue sources to build a supportive market framework.[19]

FIRST NATIONS LANDS ARE WORTH LESS

There is a great deal of potentially valuable First Nations land; but, if there is little effective demand for it, the land's worth will remain low. As has been established in the preceding chapters, there is a variety of individual property rights on First Nations lands. Generally however, the markets for these individual titles fail because the rules governing these individual rules of ownership and the nature of underlying collective property rights are poorly specified in the Indian Act and poorly administered by Indian and Northern Affairs

Canada. As the institutional economics literature demonstrates, capitalism requires an appropriate legal, administrative, and institutional framework.[20]

A method called "transaction cost analysis" can be used to study the development process on Indian reserves. This approach, which dates back to earlier forms of efficiency studies, such as process mapping, Taylorism, and Fordism, is now called transaction cost analysis among software engineers. It is where engineering meets economics.[21] Based on a series of First Nations case studies, the Fiscal Realities consulting firm has mapped out the seven steps required to bring a development into being.

1. *Project Initiation/Concept.* In this initial phase of the project, the developer and/or community leaders identify suitable land and pitch the idea to the community. It also includes initial due diligence and economic and financial feasibility studies. In the First Nations context, finding appropriate land is difficult because the real-estate industry is usually not present on the reserve. Moreover, few First Nations have land development offices to help facilitate economic projects. Neither of these constraints exists off First Nations lands.

2. *Land Tenure Certainty.* At this stage, the community creates land tenure certainty for the development. First Nations using the Indian Act and wishing to provide longer-term certainty normally resort to the land designation process as laid out in the Act (designation is not required on certificate of possession lands for leases less than fifty years).[22] For municipalities, it is land-use planning and zoning.

3. *Land Leasing.* For First Nations, this is the negotiation of the actual land lease agreement between the developer and the community, or between the developer and the certificate of possession holder. It includes all the standard elements of an Indian Affairs lease agreement and features unique to a First Nations context, such as employment policies or guarantees of tax rates. In a municipality this may involve a lease or a fee-simple title transaction, often facilitated through a provincial land titles office.

4. *Financing.* This refers to financing the costs of the development. Financial institutions have less familiarity with First

Nations and generally demand greater security from them than from other borrowers. For example, it is very common for on-reserve developers to pledge the title to off-reserve property as part of their financing. This is true for both First Nations and non-First Nations developers.

5. *Infrastructure Development and Services.* Most significant projects require upgrading the existing physical infrastructure, building new infrastructure, or obtaining access to services and infrastructure in other jurisdictions. There are fewer infrastructure financing options for First Nations than for municipalities. Off First Nations lands, infrastructure is financed using a combination of local revenues, local revenue savings, development cost charges, public-private partnerships, debentures, and contributions from the federal and provincial governments. On First Nations lands under the Indian Act, only local revenues, savings, and contributions from the federal government are available.

6. *Local Legal Framework for Markets.* Investors need certainty with respect to development costs and taxes, local service quality, local land-use and other laws and rules, and recourse in the event of a dispute. In other words they need certainty about local collective property rights. In comparison with provincial legislation and municipal bylaws, most of this has to be created by First Nations from scratch as little or none of it exists in the Indian Act. To cite one example, the Westbank First Nation has more than thirty local laws covering matters from fire hydrants to pest management to the development approval system.

7. *Construction.* This is probably the most heavily regulated of all components. It includes all the regulations associated with building standards, development approval processes, and risk, heritage, and environmental assessments. Once again much of this is well known in the provincial/municipal context but has to be invented for each First Nation wishing to undertake a development. Off First Nations lands, the engineering and construction industries are far more familiar with provincial environmental and building standards and procedures than they are with the federal procedures and standards that apply for Indian Act developments.

Table 8.1 summarizes the differences between establishing marketable property rights off and on First Nations land. Our hypothesis is that the costs of establishing a tradable property right on First Nations land are significantly higher than off First Nations land.

LET'S MAKE A DEAL

In 1998, Fiscal Realities did a study for the Indian Taxation Advisory Board and the Department of Indian Affairs investigating real-estate transaction costs under the Indian Act.[23] We dissected four case studies of successful commercial and residential real-estate deals on First Nations lands. The intent was to compare how long it took to establish a secure property right using the Indian Act to similar deals in the appropriate provincial/municipal setting.

One inspiration for the study was a casual observation made from the top of a hill overlooking Kamloops. Separated by nothing more than a river was the underdevelopment of the best land in the valley on the Kamloops reserve compared to substantial development up all the hills in the city of Kamloops. Another inspiration was the Master's thesis of Jason Calla,[24] a managing economist at the time with Fiscal Realities and a Squamish Nation member.

We considered time to be an adequate proxy for the professional and opportunity costs associated with a real-estate transaction. This approach for measuring transaction costs is common,[25] because there are no other industry standards for the costs associated with the components of land development. In general, assuming community interests and regulatory safeguards are met, the shorter the time frame for finishing each component of a land deal, the lower the costs and the greater the net benefit produced. Also, in general the shorter the time from concept to construction, the lower the opportunity costs and the greater the net benefit.[26] Thus, the time from start to finish was used as a proxy for the cost of each component. The analysis looked only at the costs of establishing property rights and not at the other costs of business. For example, it did not compare transportation costs or labour costs on and off First Nations lands. It only assessed costs that are a function of establishing tradable individual property rights.

Table 8.1

Stage	Off First Nations Land	On First Nations Land (using the Indian Act)
Project Initiation/ Concept	Search available real estate and approach local government development services office	Little or no real estate information and generally no development services office
Land Tenure Certainty	Defined and managed through provincial legislation and bureaucracy	Requires land designation for long term certainty and Indian Affairs bureaucracy
Land Leasing	Transaction almost always facilitated by real estate industry	Modify Indian Affairs lease as required
Financing	Financial industry has substantial experience with many financing models	Little or no experience of financial industry
Infrastructure Development and Services	Local governments have many infrastructure financing options and deliver local services	Fewer financing options for First Nations and service agreement with local government usually required
Legal Framework for markets	Investors generally know their expected costs/taxes, the local laws, investor recourse, and land use	Much of this legal framework has not been established by the Indian Act or First Nations; therefore significant investor uncertainty
Construction	Building and engineering standards and bonded construction common	Building and engineering standard uncertainty and possible bonding issues

In separate case studies, we looked at four First Nations that successfully developed their lands using the Indian Act. All information is based on interviews with the developer and First Nations principals involved in each of the case studies. We will briefly discuss two of these studies[27] in this chapter:

- Real Canadian Superstore at Seymour Creek I.R. No. 2, a Squamish Nation reserve in North Vancouver, British Columbia;
- Sun Rivers golf course and residential development at Kamloops I.R. No. 1, British Columbia.

These are not typical First Nations communities; they have favourably located reserves and a strong historical association with trade and markets. The Squamish reserve is located on an old overland trade route; and the Kamloops reserve, at the confluence of the North and South Thompson Rivers, also has a long history of trade.[28] In both cases the developer had a proven off-reserve track record and significant financial capacity. The economic viability of both developments was self-evident; the Real Canadian Superstore was to be located just off the Ironworkers Memorial Bridge in North Vancouver, and the Sun Rivers golf course was to be sited in the sunniest part of Kamloops, where winter is regularly two to four weeks shorter than in the rest of the Kamloops region. These location advantages should have provided a favourable setting for economic development on First Nations land.

Real Canadian Superstore

A Real Canadian Superstore is located on Seymour Creek Indian Reserve (I.R.) No. 2, one of twenty-three reserves held by the Crown for the sole benefit and use of the Squamish Nation membership. The Superstore is operated by Westfair Foods Ltd ("Westfair"), a subsidiary of Loblaw Companies, Ltd. The building comprises approximately 115,000 square feet on eight acres of I.R. No. 2.

The Squamish Nation is comprised of approximately three thousand members, two thirds of whom live on the reserves. These reserves are located on the North Shore of Vancouver, the Howe Sound, and the Squamish Valley. Seymour Creek I.R. No. 2 is located on the North Shore in close proximity to downtown Vancouver and adjacent to the District of North Vancouver. The strategic location of Squamish Nation reserves near Vancouver has meant increasing demand for development that has challenged the

Squamish Nation Council and administration to adapt rapidly and develop additional capacity to respond to development proposals.

The Squamish Nation expected the Superstore project to take no more than two years to complete. In reality, it took fifty-three months from expression of interest until the doors of the store opened. A similar development in Vancouver would have taken fourteen months, as determined by process mapping of a hypothetical commercial real-estate development in the city.[29]

There were two main causes of delay in this project. The first holdup was caused by a lack of local government administrative infrastructure. A similar project in Vancouver would proceed through the planning department as per the city's land-use plan and development approval and zoning process. No such department or rules existed in Squamish. Instead, Squamish had an economic development committee, consisting of band councillors and members of the administration. The team had varying levels of previous experience in terms of lease negotiations, service negotiations, rent reviews, construction, and environmental issues. It took approximately twenty-four months from the initial meetings until an agreement in principle was drafted to be presented to Squamish Nation Council. The community and developer expected this process to take approximately six months.

Securing a clear commercial property right caused the second major delay. This is a relatively straightforward process off First Nations lands, with numerous templates to work from. Based on interviews with developers who have completed commercial deals within Vancouver, it can take as little as a few days and no longer than six months to secure their commercial property right. The eight-acre site for the Superstore had complex leasing arrangements, including two head leases and a sublease. The Squamish Nation formed a holding company called Stitsma Holdings Ltd, which entered into head lease agreements with Her Majesty the Queen in Right of Canada for reserve lands and roads as well as a head lease agreement with the British Columbia Hydro and Power Authority for the hydro lands. The lease negotiations were lengthy. The head leases and the sublease were negotiated simultaneously. As there were few precedents for this type of lease structure, legal advisors for the Squamish Nation, the Department of Justice (on behalf of the federal government), and Westfair Foods Ltd took great care in ensuring their respective clients' interests were protected. In particular, the Department of Justice was particularly concerned about protecting the obligations of the Crown. In total, securing the property right took eighteen months in Squamish.

Sun Rivers

The Sun Rivers development is located on approximately 460 acres on the Kamloops I.R. No. 1. The project is comprised of an eighteen-hole championship golf course, approximately two thousand residential units, a school, and office/commercial space.

The main reserve for the Kamloops Shuswap (Secwepemc) people is located near the junction of the North and South Thompson Rivers near the city of Kamloops. Current reserve lands of the Kamloops Shuswap cover 33,000 acres,[30] and total membership is just over 1,100. The Kamloops reserve consists of prime development lands, generally on the south-facing, sunny side of the valley bottom. The City of Kamloops, with a population just under 100,000, has nearly reached its infrastructural limits. As demographic pressures increase on the city, pressure to have a residential development on the Kamloops reserve has also increased.

The Sun Rivers proposal was similar to the Superstore at Seymour Creek I.R. No. 2 in that both projects were proposed for sites that were defined as "band lands" by the Indian Act. This meant that the land had to be designated for lease through the process set forth by the Department of Indian Affairs. The designation and associated environmental approval processes were a major source of delay in this project.

Similar to the Squamish project, the Crown as represented by various federal departments was determined to protect its interests. In 1995, an official from the Department of Fisheries and Oceans visited the Kamloops Indian Band. The Department was concerned that the proposed Sun Rivers development would disturb salmon habitat along Mount Peter and Mount Paul. It appeared in the aerial photograph they viewed in their Vancouver office that there were streams running along these two mountains and that this proposed development would prevent salmon from spawning. But in reality Kamloops has a semi-arid climate and there have been no such streams in this area for at least five hundred years. The developers' attempt to secure a property right was put on hold for a further four months until the official DFO visit confirmed the lack of streams.

Also, similar to Squamish, the acquisition of a secure property right involved major delay. The Kamloops Indian Band entered into a head lease with Her Majesty the Queen in Right of Canada. The head lease has an initial term of ninety-nine years expiring in 2095. This expiry date can be amended to 30 June 2115, as the final development of Sun Rivers nears completion. This ensured that all residential units will have a lease of at least ninety-nine years. In addition to the complexity of the lease agreements, there was an additional need to draft development standards bylaws, development approval bylaws, zoning bylaws, and permanent building regulations. These were all contained in the Master Development and Servicing Agreement, and they filled in the local government component of property rights that are common off First Nations land. The result for the Sun Rivers development was extra time and high legal and professional fees.

As with the Superstore, it was expected that it would take about two years before construction could begin on the Sun Rivers development. In the event, delays in completing a residential market framework, writing a sublease document acceptable to financial institutions, and building infrastructure meant that it took more than fifty-four months. Based on an interview with the Kamloops city planning department, a similar project in the city of Kamloops would have taken about sixteen months in 1998.

CONCLUSIONS

The Kamloops and Squamish case studies likely *underestimate* the true cost of establishing marketable property rights on-reserve because both represent successful projects on First Nations lands where the costs of establishing property rights were relatively low in the first place.[31] These case studies suggest, therefore, that the cost of establishing a marketable property right on First Nations land is at least four times more expensive than establishing the same property right off First Nations lands. Transaction costs this high are likely to lead to market failure.

The implications of this conclusion for First Nations policy are significant. Any effort to improve the well-being of First Nations through economic development will fall short of its goal unless these transaction costs are reduced. It is imperative for Canada to address this problem. The current costs of First Nations poverty are estimated at about $4 billion a year,[32] and these costs will continue to grow because of the above-average First Nations population growth rate.

Making markets work on First Nations lands can be accomplished by recognizing and implementing jurisdictions that provide individual property ownership and protect underlying First Nations property rights. The next two chapters explain how to accomplish this.

9

Escaping the Indian Act

In 1975, a meeting was held at Chilliwack, British Columbia, by the Union of BC Indian Chiefs, which at the time represented all First Nations communities in BC. The purpose of the meeting was almost unheard of: to reject government funds. The First Nations who attended wanted to escape the Indian Act and the Department of Indian Affairs above all. Almost as importantly, they also wanted to escape poverty. A number of prominent Indian leaders at the time, including Phillip Joe, Forrest Walkem, and Don Moses, spoke. One particular speaker, Willis Morgan, representing the Kitamaat Indian Band, cautioned that First Nations were not ready for this because they lacked the economic base and tax systems to pay for local services, education, health, and welfare.[1]

Morgan's caution was ignored, and First Nations throughout BC rejected government funding in the late spring 1975. But, by autumn, reality set in, and Willis Morgan was proved right. First Nations had neither the capacity to deliver local or other services, nor the jurisdiction or systems to collect revenues, nor the infrastructure to attract investment. Within six months, most communities began accepting government funding again.

This battle was lost, but the struggle continued as a group of First Nations embarked on a different strategy to escape the Indian Act and poverty. They sought to incrementally implement the jurisdictions and systems they needed to support an economy. While the constitutional debates of the 1980s and early 1990s raged, they fought behind the scenes for federal legislation giving them power

Table 9.1

Incremental Approaches	Selected Comprehensive Approaches
• First Nations Property Tax – 1988 • First Nations Sales Tax and GST – 1997 and 2003 • First Nations Land Management Act – 1999 • First Nations Fiscal and Statistical Management Act – 2005 • First Nations Commercial and Industrial Development Act – 2005	• Council of Yukon First Nations Umbrella Agreement – 1993 • Nisga'a Treaty – 2000 • Westbank Self-Government Agreement – 2003

over taxes, lands, and local services. These incrementalists began to exercise their powers during the 1990s, gradually escaping while others were using self-government agreements and legislation to completely escape. Table 9.1 lists what we consider incremental and comprehensive strategies.

Regardless of the particular strategies, the intent was always the same: to reduce the influence of the Indian Act and the Department of Indian and Northern Affairs on their lives, enlarge their fiscal independence, and increase their community members' standard of living. This chapter tells some of these stories. It evaluates how successfully these First Nations have utilized their Indian Act escapes to reduce their poverty and become more fiscally independent. It also suggests how First Nations can begin to exercise their emerging jurisdictions to provide certainty to individual property rights and clarity to First Nations underlying title. In so doing, it sets the stage for the proposed First Nations Property Ownership Act in the final chapter.

ESCAPING FIRST NATIONS POVERTY

First Nations don't just want to escape the Indian Act and the Department of Indian Affairs. They also want to escape poverty by reducing the influence of INAC. This means they need more independent revenues. Escaping both poverty and INAC means they need sustainable economic growth.

This section focuses on two questions. What is the root cause of First Nations poverty? And how can escaping the Indian Act unlock the economic potential of First Nations?

Beginning with the root cause, it is important to recognize that the engine of economic growth is private investment, whether this is investment in capital, research, and new technology, or improvements in human capital. In Canada, private-sector investment outweighs public-sector investment by nearly five to one. Four times as many jobs are created in the private sector as in the public sector. Therefore, attracting private investment is the key for First Nations to escape poverty.

The role of investment in community-building is straightforward. Investment creates jobs and business opportunities. This supports further entrepreneurial initiatives by people, which create further profits and hiring. Ultimately, this supports more training and the development of a management cadre, which builds the fiscal capacity of government to pay for increasingly broad-based social improvements. It also builds toward a natural constituency for accountable, fiscally responsible government because the investment climate is enhanced.

The aim of investment is to produce more goods and services with the same or fewer inputs. This is the definition of higher productivity, which is necessary for improving the standard of living and maintaining the ongoing capability to compete with other producers. First Nations communities are plagued by low rates of private investment and, as a result, suffer from high unemployment and a host of social ills. On the surface, then, the solution to these ills seems simple: generate more private investment. However, many factors must be in place to attract private investment.

In order to attract investment through a competitive rate of return, a community must generally be able to publicly provide all of the following:

- responsive local public institutions,
- competitive public infrastructure,

- secure property rights, and
- an appropriate mix of taxes and services.

Moreover, it must also possess at least one of the following private competitive advantages:

- a natural resource endowment or access to natural resources,
- a competitive location for markets or technology,
- a human-resource advantage either in skills, demographics, or location, or
- competitive access to or ability to use a new productivity-improving technology or innovation.

Investors need cost, service, and infrastructure and property ownership certainty. This is what the public sector provides. The combination of the certainty provided by the public sector to potential investors and the local competitive advantages make up a community's investment climate. The question for First Nations communities wishing to escape poverty is: what is wrong with their investment climate that prevents more private investment?

Is it a lack of access to natural resources? No. Possessing access to resources or having a good location is important, but it is not enough to create economic growth. For example, both Russia and Peru are well endowed with natural resources; indeed, Russia is also well endowed with technology and human resources. However, neither country provides a high standard of living because they have been unable to offer the supportive public sector input that is also required.

By contrast, countries such as Singapore and Japan have achieved very high standards of living with relatively poor natural resources. Japan, until the rise of China, was the second largest economy in the world, despite being natural-resource poor, by virtue of public institutions that created and supported human and technological advantages.

First Nations economies are not without potential. Most have at least one of the following competitive advantages: location, human resources, technological or innovative strengths, and access to natural resources. In those few cases where no competitive advantage exists on First Nations land, the possibility of settling outstanding land claims or adding land to existing reserves or integrating into markets in other jurisdictions provides hope. In other words, lack of competitive advantage is not the barrier to First Nations prosperity. Moreover, to the extent that First Nations can translate their existing competitive advantages to markets outside First Nations communities, the potential for First Nations economic development is much higher.

The barrier to prosperity on First Nations lands is an inability to provide sufficient certainty to investors. The previous chapter illustrated this by demonstrating that the transaction costs for creating this certainty in an investment deal on First Nations lands are much higher than they are in the rest of Canada. Investment transaction costs are principally a function of an economy's public sector mix of revenues and services, its economic and governance institutions, its property right system, and its economic infrastructure. These factors are uncompetitive or substandard for almost all First Nations. As a result, a plan for First Nations to escape poverty must focus on building a public sector that reduces investor transaction costs on their lands. This means moving decision-making closer to First Nations themselves and diminishing the power of the Indian Act and INAC. First Nations must use their new powers to lower investor transaction costs.

Federal legislation will be required to replace parts of the Indian Act. This legislation should open up independent revenue sources for First Nations so they can implement their new powers. They will also need their own national First Nations institutions to provide them with template laws and training and support for their administrations. The focus of these national institutions must be the reduction of transaction costs.

Legislation requires federal political will combined with an accurate understanding of the problem. We cannot supply the will, but we hope our book contributes to clarifying the economic aspects of aboriginal poverty and dependency. Unfortunately, politicians and policymakers generally view First Nations problems as social and not economic, and they generally favour programs over reform. For First Nations to escape, the Indian Act needs to be replaced by legislation that allows them to use the power of markets, but to date no political party has truly embraced this approach. Nonetheless, finding a place for First Nations within the Canadian federation and allowing them to participate in the global economy remains one of Canada's greatest political challenges.

A group of First Nations must support any legislative change as well. Sometimes it seems as if First Nations don't want to escape. First Nations governments fear the loss of current entitlements, especially relating to lands. Many are deeply mistrustful of policies advanced by other governments. Even economic development is a controversial goal because many First Nations fear it masks an agenda for the federal government to abandon its fiduciary obligations. These apprehensions are exacerbated because the business constituency within First Nations is small and many First Nations opinion leaders were educated in law or history rather than business or economics. This is why all escapes generally require strong First Nations leadership and a voluntary approach so that interested First Nations can make the break when they are ready.

In summary, the escape plan has two elements. The first part is for First Nations to utilize federal legislation, independent revenues, and supportive national institutions to reduce transaction costs and facilitate investment. If they are successful with the first part, the second element of the plan is straightforward. First Nations sell their particular competitive advantage in location, resources, labour, or technology to investors and consumers.

THE FIRST TUNNEL — FIRST NATIONS PROPERTY TAX

First Nations property tax represented the first escape tunnel from under the Indian Act. It gave First Nations a stable independent revenue option – the power to collect property tax from their leaseholders. Property tax revenues meant that First Nations could begin to effectively and sustainably implement local property rights. It also illustrated how federal legislation could recognize First Nations jurisdictions. It dramatically changed incentives for First Nations governments by creating a tangible link between economic growth and government revenues. Most importantly, it provided a template for future escapes.

To begin, a province cannot tax federal lands, but the province can tax a "user of federal land in respect of the user's occupancy." However, the provincial Crown cannot affect that occupancy by enforcement of the tax to displace the federal interest in lands. Therefore, non-federal-Crown users of federal Crown land could be taxed by a province on the basis of their occupancy of the land, but for a province to enforce the tax it could not displace the occupant.[2]

This is significant because under the Constitution, as interpreted by the Judicial Committee of the Privy Council in *St Catherine's Milling*, provinces have the reversionary title to Indian reserves, even though the federal Parliament has legislative jurisdiction. Thus provinces could collect property tax from non-Indian leaseholders on First Nations lands, although they would have difficulty enforcing their power. Perhaps because there were few such leaseholders or perhaps because provinces did not wish to create a potential conflict, few chose to implement their property tax authority on First Nations lands. The exceptions were British Columbia and Quebec. This is why the history of First Nations property tax is so closely associated with British Columbia.

In the words of Manny Jules, here is how First Nations property tax jurisdiction was eventually established:

> In the seventies, my community was engaged in a property tax battle with the province of BC and the city of Kamloops. We tried the courts to resolve our issue. We lost at all levels. The advice we received was always the same. You must change the Indian Act to collect property taxes. In December 1984, I became Chief of my community.
>
> My first issue was property tax jurisdiction. The provincial government collected property taxes from our leaseholders and provided no services in return. This meant we had to charge service fees to pay for services that property taxes would usually pay for. This is double taxation. Double taxation makes it difficult, to say the least, to attract investors. To add to this insult, when I asked the provincial government what we were getting from the tax money they were collecting from our lands they responded good government.

Although the solution is simple – transfer property tax jurisdiction to us – implementing this solution was difficult. In January, 1985 we wrote letters to every First Nation community in Canada asking their support to change the Indian Act. We received letters and band council resolutions of support from 120 communities across Canada.[3]

For three years Kamloops and other supportive First Nations worked to change s. 83 of the Indian Act to transfer property tax jurisdiction to the local level. The passage of Bill C-115 in 1988 was the first Indian-led amendment to the Indian Act in Canadian history.[4] It was initially suggested that perhaps 20 First Nations would adopt property tax jurisdiction, but 120 have now done so.[5] A big reason for this growth is the Indian Taxation Advisory Board (ITAB), which was established in 1989 to implement First Nations tax jurisdiction and replaced in 2007 by the First Nations Tax Commission.

First Nations quickly recognized that property tax revenues expanded as a result of economic development. To cite just two examples, the assessed values of Westbank and Squamish have each increased fourfold since they established their tax jurisdiction.[6] At the most, one-fifth of this increase was caused by real estate inflation; a much greater four-fifths of the increase resulted from new development.

Property tax revenues meant First Nations could more effectively deliver local services. They could begin to clarify how their jurisdiction would impact individual property by providing services such as water, sewerage, and garbage collection as well as police and fire protection. First Nations could provide reliable information and develop rules for land development and zoning. They could begin to improve public infrastructure related to transportation, communication, and environmental health. In short, property tax allowed First Nations to more competitively implement those local powers necessary to attract and facilitate private investment. This creates a virtuous circle in which tax revenues lead to improved services, which lead to more investment and increased tax revenues. This is how every other Canadian community grows.

The ITAB developed the concept of model laws for First Nations, providing model laws for taxation, assessments, expenditures, and tax rates in 1994. Model laws create national standards for the First Nations property-tax system, and standards mean lower transaction costs for investors. Model laws reduce the costs of implementing tax systems. In this regard, some of the early adopters of property tax created their own property-tax laws. Estimated costs were over $100,000,[7] whereas the estimated cost of adopting a model property-tax law is considerably less than $10,000 for a First Nation.[8]

The ITAB began to publish the First Nations Gazette so that First Nations laws could be promulgated to the public like other laws in Canada. The ITAB also established the Tulo Centre of Indigenous Economics to provide accredited training in First Nations tax administration and applied economics.[9]

The ITAB also demonstrated that First Nations inherent jurisdictions can be established through federal legislation. This is important because these are the jurisdictions that First Nations must exercise to clarify individual property rights. In 1992, the Matsqui and Siska First Nations sent tax notices to Canadian Pacific Railway (CPR). CPR appealed to the Matsqui assessment appeal board that it was not liable to taxation since its tracks were not on reserve lands, but the board ruled that CPR line was indeed located on reserve lands. CPR then challenged the authority of the assessment appeal board to determine issues of tax jurisdiction. This challenge eventually made it to the Supreme Court of Canada, where CPR's challenge was upheld on the grounds that assessment appeal boards do not have the expertise or the mandate to determine whether a railway is on the reserve or not. Although this matter would later be settled by negotiation and clarified in a federal regulation, some dicta by Justice Lamer are still important:

it is important that we not lose sight of Parliament's objective in creating the new Indian taxation powers. The regime which came into force in 1988 is intended to facilitate the development of Aboriginal Self-government by allowing bands to exercise the inherently governmental power of taxation on their reserves.[10]

The Supreme Court used the phrase "inherently governmental powers." Investigating this choice is beyond the scope of this book, but is it possible that the Court was ruling that First Nations could have their jurisdiction recognized as a result of federal legislation?

Since 1988, five more pieces of legislation that create specific First Nations authorities have been passed. In chronological order, they are:

- First Nations Sales Tax on Selected Products Act – 1997 and 1998
- First Nations Land Management Act – 1999
- First Nations Goods and Services Tax Act – 2003
- First Nations Fiscal and Statistical Management Act – 2005
- First Nations Commercial and Industrial Development Act – 2005.

The story for each of these is interesting, but for our purposes only three questions need be answered. First, what new authorities did each provide to First Nations to clarify their collective property rights? Second, how easily were these new authorities adopted and implemented? And, most importantly, how have these new powers improved the investment climate to reduce the poverty of First Nations and increase their government revenues?

The First Nations Sales Tax on Selected Products Act was initiated by the Westbank First Nation (1997) and the Kamloops Indian Band (1998). This legislation allowed First Nations to collect the GST on the sale of all fuel, alcohol, and tobacco on their lands, including sales to First Nations people. Between 1998 and 2007, eleven First Nations implemented this authority (nine in BC, one in Manitoba, and one in Saskatchewan).[11] It is no coincidence that ten out of eleven of these sales-tax-collecting First Nations also collect property tax.[12]

The Department of Finance eased the transition to the exercise of this power by providing model First Nations legislation and tax collection agreement templates. The ITAB provided information and made presentations to any interested First Nations. Exercising this authority was straightforward, and First Nations apparently feel they have benefited, because all who have utilized this power are still doing so.

In 2003 Canada passed the First Nations Goods and Services Tax Act to expand this power to all GST-eligible products and services.[13] To encourage First Nations to exercise this expanded authority, Canada placed a moratorium on selective tax agreements for fuel, alcohol, and tobacco. Since that time, eleven First Nations in the Yukon, one in the Northwest Territories, and six in British Columbia have implemented the expanded sales tax power. Currently, there are thirty-seven First Nations throughout Canada that are on the FNGST schedule. Of these, eleven have implemented a comprehensive FNGST system. The ITAB assisted six of these.[14]

The tax collection agreements for all GST-eligible products are much more complex than for just three products. The Department of Finance supports First Nations with model laws and agreement templates, but take-up has not been as strong as hoped. In particular, only one of the First Nations that implemented the three-product tax is now exercising the expanded power. The growth of First Nations GST agreements is much slower than that of the First Nations property tax system.

There are two reasons for this. First, the revenue gain from the First Nations GST did not appear to be sufficient to balance the political cost of raising taxes on their members. Second, the complexity of these arrangements meant that institutional support was required to provide confidence and capacity to interested First Nations. As pointed out by Graham and Bruhn, more First Nations would adopt this power if the First Nations Tax Commission were directly involved.[15]

Despite its relatively slow take-up, First Nations GST represents a significant independent revenue source for interested communities. These revenues can be used to build competitive infrastructure, implement local laws and administrative systems that clarify individual property rights, and generally improve the First Nations investment climate. To the extent that these community investments generate more FNGST for First Nations, they reinforce the potential cycle of wealth creation for First Nations.

Canada has also begun to enable First Nations to make use of sales-tax powers. So far the provinces of BC and Manitoba have developed models for provincial tobacco taxes, Saskatchewan has developed them for fuel and alcohol, and Quebec and New Brunswick have created them for provincial sales taxes.

The First Nations Land Management Act has already been discussed at length in chapter 7, so this chapter will only add three points. First, it follows the same escape plan as property tax by allowing First Nations to assume powers over sections 18–20, 22–8, 30–5, 37–41, 49, 50(4), 53–60, 66, 69, 71, 93 and regulations made under sections 42, 57, and 73 of the Indian Act.[16] Fourteen First Nations led the development of the Act. Participation is voluntary, and it creates an indigenous institution, the Lands Advisory Board, to help implement the jurisdiction. Since 1999, fifty-eight First Nations have expressed an interest in joining the First Nations Land Management Act.[17]

Second, because it is federal legislation, it allows First Nations to provide certainty to investors with respect to a number of land-management responsibilities, including land-use planning, zoning, development processes, and rules associated with land usage. In particular, First Nations have the power to make laws in respect of the development, conservation, protection, management, use, and possession of their First Nations land. These powers are common to all local governments in Canada.

Third, it has the potential to significantly reduce the costs of doing business on First Nations lands. Well-crafted laws will provide transparency and certainty to investors. The FNLMA allows First Nations to establish secure and tradable land tenure. Local administrations can provide these services and reduce investor transaction costs. To date, however, there is no clear evidence that the FNLMA is facilitating more investment. In this regard, the Lands Advisory Board has not developed a model land code and accompanying land laws that are focused on reducing transaction costs for interested First Nations.

The First Nations Fiscal and Statistical Management Act (FSMA) was passed in March 2005. This legislation was designed to raise First Nations local revenue-raising powers to the same level as other local governments in Canada, improve First Nations access to capital markets for infrastructure financing, and enhance the First Nations investment climate. In 2007, four national institu-

tions were created under this legislation to support First Nations –
the First Nations Tax Commission as the successor to the Indian
Taxation Advisory Board, the First Nations Finance Authority, the
First Nations Financial Management Board, and the First Nations
Statistical Institute.[18]

For our purposes, there are four essential features of FSMA.
First, in combination with the FNLMA it enables many of the local
government powers required to provide certainty to individual
property owners in Canada. First Nations can create laws that
specify that in the event of property tax non-payment or a viola-
tion of land-use rules, individual property rights can revert or be
appropriated back to the First Nation. Because these reversionary
rights to First Nations have yet to be recognized, however, neither
piece of legislation can confer indefeasible title to First Nations
lands. Second, by providing greater investor certainty and financing access to improved economic infrastructure, the FSMA should
reduce some investment transaction costs on First Nations lands. It
will not, however, completely reduce the high costs of doing business. To cite but one missing element, the FSMA does not provide
First Nations – the governments with the highest fiscal imbalance
in Canada – with sufficient revenue options to provide a certain
and stable investment climate. Third, it is popular. It was thought
that only ten First Nations would join in the first year, but fifty-four
First Nations have already added their names to the FSMA schedule.[19] Fourth, it received all-party support, because it was led by
First Nations and participation is voluntary.

The First Nations Commercial and Industrial Act (FNCIDA) was
passed in November 2005, in the dying days of Paul Martin's Liberal
Government. Like the FSMA, it is also an optional, First Nations–
led legislation that received all-party support. The FNCIDA is an
innovative piece of legislation designed to fill the regulatory gaps
on First Nations lands. In particular, it enables the federal government to develop regulations that allow provincial legislation and
regulations to apply on First Nations lands, with the concurrence
of the relevant province.[20] These regulations would also allow First
Nations to contract with provincial regulatory bodies as required.

For example, FNCIDA could be used as proposed for Fort
McKay, Alberta, to fill in environmental regulations gaps so that a

resource project could proceed.[21] It could also be used as proposed in Squamish, British Columbia, to improve tenure certainty and enable property transfer taxes for a condo project.[22] By so doing, FNCIDA would create a new, independent revenue-raising power for First Nations.

FNCIDA, however, is costly and time-consuming to implement. It took Fort McKay two years to develop their regulation. Squamish expects their regulation won't be finished until the end of 2009, and there are still potential conflicts with both levels of government. In both cases the cost to the First Nations is thought to be over $1 million.[23] Moreover, although the clear policy objective of FNCIDA is to reduce transaction costs, it is difficult to evaluate its success in this regard until it is successfully implemented.

Despite this, it is quite possible that the combination of FSMA, FNGST, FNLMA, and FNCIDA could significantly reduce transaction costs on First Nations lands. To accomplish this, it is first necessary to design laws and regulations that reduce transaction costs. As was mentioned previously, it is not clear that this is the objective of very many FNLMA land codes. If this shortcoming with the FNLMA is overcome, which arises in part because the Land Advisory Board does not provide model land codes and land-use laws that reduce transaction costs, then a First Nation could utilize these pieces of incremental legislation to significantly clarify individual property rights on its lands and facilitate more private investment.

Table 9.2 summarizes the First Nations powers that these pieces of legislation enable, discusses how these clarify underlying property rights, and specifies the parts of the Indian Act from which First Nations can escape.

Of the 103 different First Nations on the FNLMA, FSMA, and FNGST schedules, 20 percent have opted into both the FNLMA and the FSMA, 9 percent are on both the FNLMA and FNGST schedules, and 13 percent are on both the FSMA and FNGST schedules. Moreover, there are 5 First Nations that have opted into all three pieces of incremental legislation (St Mary's, Skeetchestn, Tsawout, Tzeachten, and Muskeg Lake First Nations).

In sum, a First Nation that opted to use these laws would have (a) significantly expanded revenue options related to the GST and

Table 9.2

Legislation	Powers	Property Right Clarification	Sections of Indian Act and number of Escapees
First Nations GST Act	GST revenue raising over consumption on First Nations lands	Payment and administration of GST on First Nations lands same as rest of Canada	37 First Nations
FNLMA	Land management and processes; Land use; Possession of land; Conservation and protection of lands; Land registry	Clear land-use laws and procedures similar to local governments. Creates a deeds type land registry system similar to some provinces. Facilitates long-term tenure but does not create indefeasible title.	s. 18–19, 20, 22–28, 30–31, 32–33, 34, 35, 37–41, 49, 50(4), 53–60, 66, 69, 71, 93, and regulations made under 42, 57, 73. 58 First Nations
FSMA	Property tax; Local Improvement taxes; Tax for provision of services; Development Cost Charges; Taxes on business activities; Long term borrowing; Financial management; Local services; Taxpayer representation	Similar revenue laws and standards to other local government governments in Canada. Local services comparative to relevant regional standard. Tools and rules for financing infrastructure similar to local governments in BC, Alberta, and Saskatchewan.	s. 83. 54 First Nations
FNCIDA	Possibly property transfer tax; Possibly strata title act	Identical to BC power and rules	3 First Nations

local revenues; (b) substantially more powers outside of the Indian Act; (c) less market failure on its lands; and (d) institutional support to implement these new powers. Moreover, through the exercise of their jurisdictions, the rules with respect to individual property ownership would not differ substantively from any other jurisdiction in Canada. The only differences would be that, unlike other jurisdictions in Canada, a First Nation could still not provide the most secure form of individual property ownership, indefeasible title, and as a result the costs of doing business on its lands would remain higher.

THE BIG DIGS

A few First Nations have eschewed the incremental escape approach of using specific federal legislation in favour of a complete escape using comprehensive self-government agreements and legislation. We will briefly discuss three of these recent big digs: Council of Yukon First Nations (1993), Nisga'a (2000), and Westbank (2005).

We chose these cases for three distinct reasons. The Yukon First Nations were chosen because they significantly expanded potential independent revenue-raising powers for First Nations. The Nisga'a are of particular interest to us because, through their agreement, they obtained and, as is discussed in the last chapter, implemented land-title powers. Westbank demonstrates how to utilize self-government powers that are not significantly different from those contained in the incremental legislation to create an attractive investment climate. It is noted that the James Bay and Northern Quebec Agreement (JBNQA) is absent from this discussion. The JBNQA was significant because it was the first Comprehensive Land Claim Agreement signed by First Nations in Canada.[24] The three comprehensive arrangements discussed here build on the foundation of JBNQA.

Each of these escapes is characterized by five similar features:

- The authority of the Indian Act no longer applies to their lands.
- Their continued reliance on federal transfers to fund some or all of their programs and services requires a continued relationship with the Department of Indian Affairs.

- Each comprehensive agreement and legislation took a great deal of time and money:
  - Council of Yukon First Nations – eighteen years and $63 million[25]
  - Nisga'a Nation – twenty-four years and $150 million[26]
  - Westbank First Nation – thirteen years and an unknown amount of local revenues.[27]
- None of these groups received much or any support from First Nations institutions to implement their new powers.
- Each of these agreements was met with public concern and some opposition.

To illustrate the time and cost required for a self-government agreement, let us look more closely at the Yukon case. In 1973, the federal government accepted a claim by the Yukon Native Brotherhood (representing status Indians) and the Yukon Association of Non-Status Indians called "Together Today for Our Children Tomorrow."[28] In 1984, the federal and territorial governments reached an agreement-in-principle that was rejected by the Council of Yukon Indians (CYI) General Assembly.[29] In December 1986, a new federal policy on comprehensive claims was announced.[30] Consistent with the new federal comprehensive claims policy, in 1987 CYI claim negotiations resumed. In 1988, a new agreement-in-principle was reached. In 1990, eighteen years after negotiations began, the Umbrella Final Agreement (UFA) was completed.[31] On 29 May 1993, four Yukon First Nations signed the UFA and final agreements with the federal government, the Yukon Territorial Government, and the CYI. The four First Nations, the Vuntut Gwitchin First Nation, the First Nation of the Nacho Nyak Dun, the Champagne and Aishihik First Nations, and the Teslin Tlingit Council, also signed self-government agreements on 29 May 1993.[32]

Each final agreement outlines that specific First Nation's share of financial compensation from the Government of Canada, i.e., its portion of the $242,673,000 total (in 1989 dollars). It also specifies the repayment terms of each First Nation's share of funds borrowed for negotiation costs, which is roughly 25 percent of their total compensation. The payments are made over a fifteen-year period after the Final Agreement comes into effect.[33] According to the Report of the Royal Commission on Aboriginal Peoples, "In the case of the

CYFN, the federal government requires First Nations communities to repay $63 million in loans spent on the negotiations."[34] This was in reference to the Umbrella Final Agreement and individual First Nations final agreements.[35]

The Yukon Agreements expanded the powers of First Nations governments well beyond those of the incrementalists. Yukon First Nations now have the powers to make laws concerning:

- social and welfare services
- health care
- training programs
- adoption, guardianship, custody, care and placement of children, education programs
- inheritance, wills, intestacy, and administration of estates
- solemnization of marriages
- pollution and protection of the environment
- administration of justice
- direct taxation.[36]

These powers would be considered mainly provincial or territorial in scope in the Canadian context. Other than estates, environment, and possibly administration of justice, their impact on clarifying individual property rights is minimal. However, the Yukon First Nations did receive more tax powers than any other First Nations in Canada. Canada was confident that other First Nations would accept this expansion of tax power and issued a white paper offering to develop legislation to facilitate these expanded independent revenue options for any interested First Nations,[37] but there has not yet been much take-up of the offer.

The Yukon First Nations' new powers would have to be harmonized with territorial and/or federal concurrent powers, but few of them have been implemented because of a lack of institutional support.[38] As a result the Yukon Agreements have met with considerable criticism.[39] In the fifteen years since the umbrella agreement was finalized, implementation has not been successful and the investment climates of the participating First Nations have not been enhanced. According to the 2003 Report of the Auditor General, "INAC seems focused on fulfilling the letter of the land claims' implementation plans but not the spirit. Officials may believe that they have met their obligations, but in fact they have not worked to support the full intent of the land claims agreements." In addition, the report comments that the dispute-resolution measures outlined within the agreements are ineffective. Without UFA implementation and landownership certainty, opportunities such as the Alaska Highway Pipeline Project have been difficult to realize.[40]

The Nisga's agreement took even longer. Almost 120 years ago, the Nisga'a formed their original Land Committee (1890). However, between 1927 and 1951, federal legislation made it illegal for First Nations to raise funds to advance land claims, so the Nisga'a were unable to negotiate any treaties during these years. In 1951, this provision of the Indian act was repealed, and in 1955 the Nisga'a Land Committee re-established itself as the Nisga'a Tribal Council.[41] In the late 1960s, the Tribal Council initiated the Calder legal action in the BC Supreme Court, and by 1973 it had reached the Supreme Court of Canada. The result of that decision led Prime Minister Trudeau to state that "perhaps you [First Nations] had more legal rights than we thought when we did the White Paper."[42]

In 1976 the federal government commenced negotiations with the Nisga'a, which the provincial government joined in 1990. The Nisga'a Final Agreement Act was ultimately passed on 13 April 2000, twenty-four years after negotiations began.[43] The cost of negotiating the Nisga'a treaty is estimated at $150 million.

The Nisga'a Agreement went beyond the Yukon Agreement by allowing First Nations authorities to make laws relating to traffic and transportation and, most importantly for this book, land title.[44] The scope and implications of the agreement were met with considerable criticism.[45] Political concerns eventually led to a referendum on treaties in BC.[46]

We have not found any formal evaluation of the implementation of the Nisga'a agreement. Despite criticisms, in our opinion the benefits of this agreement could far exceed its costs if, as we discuss in the next chapter, the Nisga'a can create a model for indefeasible individual title on First Nations lands that could be transferred to interested First Nations throughout Canada.

Negotiations concerning Westbank Self-Government began under the Community-Based Self-Government Policy in 1990 and continued after 1995 under the Inherent Right of Self-Government Policy. In July 1998, a Self-Government Agreement-in-Principle was signed. The Westbank First Nation and the Government of Canada signed the Westbank First Nation Self-Government Agreement on 3 October 2003, to end thirteen years of negotiations. This agreement was brought into effect by the Westbank First Nation Self-Government Act, which received Royal Assent on 6 May 2004 and came into force 1 April 2005.[47] According to Graham and Bruhn, "the tax revenues collected by the Westbank First Nation allowed it to fund its self-government negotiations in a period where the federal government had frozen all funding for that purpose."[48]

The Westbank Agreement implementation story has been one of economic success. Westbank is located adjacent to Kelowna, and two of its five reserves are densely populated. It is estimated that ten thousand non-members live on Westbank lands. The Westbank First Nation has the distinction of having the largest residential tax base of any First Nation in Canada. Because of its independent revenues, Westbank has been able to establish an efficient administrative system for implementing this legal framework. The result has been that the cost and time for facilitating investment in Westbank is as low as or lower than elsewhere in Canada.[49]

As a result of the self-government agreement, Westbank lands are governed under the most comprehensive system of community laws for any First Nation in Canada. These laws are passed under the authority of the Westbank Self-Government Act, the Westbank Self-Government Agreement, and Westbank First Nation Constitution. Land use in Westbank is subject to the rules specified in part 11 of the Constitution. However, the self-government powers of Westbank First Nation are no greater than those of the Nisga'a and Yukon First Nations. In fact, many of the provincial/territorial powers in the former agreements do not appear in the Westbank agreement. Perhaps Westbank was not interested in absorbing the potential financial liabilities of health care and social assistance.

The ability of the Westbank First Nation to implement its powers and establish investor certainty in a short time frame has been impressive. Below is a short list of some of the laws that now apply on Westbank lands:

- 2005-01 – WFN Long-Term Debt Liability and Guarantees Law
- No. 2005-06 – WFN Garbage Collection Law
- No. 2005-07 – WFN Unsightly Premises Law
- No. 2005-08 – WFN Noise and Disturbance Control Law
- No. 2005-11 – WFN Fire Protection Law
- No. 2005-13 – WFN Traffic and Parking Control Law
- No. 2005-14 – WFN Building Law
- No. 2005-15 – WFN Subdivision, Development and Servicing Law
- No. 2005-16 – WFN Waterworks Law
- No. 2005-17 – WFN Business Licence Law
- No. 2005-18 – WFN Sanitary Sewer Systems Law
- No. 2008–03 – WFN Residential Premises Law
- No. 2008-04 – WFN Advisory Council
- No. 2006-02 – WFN Family Property Law
- No. 2006-03 – WFN Allotment Law
- No. 2007-01 – WFN Land Use Law
  - Land Use Plan – Schedule "A"
  - Zoning Regulations – Schedule "B"
  - Servicing Maps – Schedule "C"

Many of these laws are similar in nature to those of any local government in Canada. All of these could be passed using the authorities contained in the FSMA and FNLMA. In short, the Westbank First Nation has created the administrative and legal framework to support the most secure individual property-rights system now possible on First Nations lands. It allows certificate of possession holders to establish leases of a term and structure necessary to provide certainty to investors. It has also established a deeds land registry system that has attracted the interest of title insurance companies. Despite this, the Westbank agreement does have critics. Some are concerned about the powers of the Westbank First Nation and others about tax and representation.[50] The passage of the WFN taxpayer advisory law was intended to address the latter concern.

For Westbank, the economic results of establishing a comprehensive set of rules that apply to individual property rights are evident.

In the few years since the comprehensive legal framework has been established, a number of Westbank certificate of possession holders have attracted investors to their lands. According to interviews with developers, the value of an acre of land in Westbank has risen from about $15,000 in 1991 to about $1 million in 2007.[51] Most importantly, by implementing its powers in a manner that supports marketable individual property rights, the Westbank First Nation has almost escaped the Indian Act.

There is no magic in the Westbank story. Other First Nations can escape along a similar path. They can also create the fiscal, legal, and administrative framework to support markets using the FNLMA, FNGST, FSMA, and FNCIDA. They can build competitive infrastructure. They can combine certainty and infrastructure to investors with the best possible leasehold tenure system. By doing so they will have a competitive investment climate from which they can realize their potential advantages in location, access to resources, or labour. To cite just three examples: the Osoyoos First Nation has created an attractive investment climate for its agricultural competitive advantage (growing grapes); the Whitecap Dakota Sioux have accomplished the same for its advantages related to resources (water) and location; and, in the United States, the Agua Caliente Tribal Nation near Palm Springs has used its location advantage near Palm Springs to create a competitive residential real-estate market on its lands.[52]

CONCLUSIONS

First Nations can escape and are escaping the Indian Act and poverty using federal enabling legislation. Some are taking an incremental approach and are leaving selected sections of the Indian Act behind. The escape route is similar in all these cases. First, identify the specific sections of the Indian Act required to deliver a service or collect revenue. Second, draft legislation that allows First Nations to assert this jurisdiction when they choose. Third, create national institutions to help First Nations implement these new powers in a manner that support markets.

These escapes have been mainly successful. More than one hundred First Nations have chosen the property-taxation and land-management route. There has been general public support; indeed, since 2005, all federal legislation relating to First Nations using this approach has received all-party support.

Other First Nations have negotiated comprehensive agreements allowing them to completely escape the Indian Act. Of the three we looked at, only one has so far achieved economic success, and this is because it had significant property-tax revenues to support the development of a competitive investment climate. The other two have yet to realize their economic potential because they lack independent revenues and First Nations institutional support to assert their new powers in a way that supports markets. Perhaps most importantly, big escapes take many years to negotiate, are expensive, and seem more susceptible to public concerns.

Together, however, the combination of the incremental and grand escapes has defined a set of First Nations jurisdictions relating to revenues and services. The potential for First Nations to use these jurisdictions to clarify individual property ownership now exists. Moreover, they can define and implement these jurisdictions in a way that it is familiar to Canadians and facilitates investment. Indeed, the Westbank First Nation has almost completely escaped the regressive Indian Act property-rights systems.

To allow more escapes in a timely and cost-effective fashion, optional legislation is required that (a) recognizes reversionary rights to First Nations title, (b) reduces transaction costs and supports markets on First Nations lands, and (c) provides institutional support so that interested First Nations can develop with confidence the legal and administrative framework for individual property ownership. This will allow them to establish the marketable system of property rights that the rest of Canada takes for granted. How to do this is the subject of the final chapter.

Back to the Future: Restoring
First Nations Property-Rights Systems

The Nisga'a Nation is located in northwestern BC, in the Nass Valley. To get to the Nisga'a Nation government from southern BC, you fly from Vancouver to Terrace; then you drive an hour along the new Nisga'a Highway 113 to the village of New Aiyansh, which, along with three other villages, is home to a total population within Nisga'a territory of roughly 2,500. Along the way you pass Nisga'a Memorial Lava Bed Park, the site of Canada's last volcanic eruption, which occurred approximately 250 years ago.

I (André Le Dressay), along with Manny Jules and Wayne Haimila, visited the Nisga'a Nation in November 2006. We met with the president, Nelson Leeson; CEO Ed Allen; Secretary Treasurer Edmond Wright; and the Nisga'a registrar, Diane Cragg. They had invited Manny to speak about taxation and some of the issues related to implementing the taxation provisions in their treaty. Manny wanted to discuss an idea he had been advocating since the early 90s, related to First Nations property ownership and the Torrens registry system. They were happy to speak to someone about matters outside the parameters of the Indian Act. It was difficult for them to communicate with other First Nations because, since the implementation of their treaty, they have virtually nothing in common with Indian Act First Nations.

During the conversation, Allen and Cragg mentioned that they understood land-title systems very well and that they already had one. They all had read a copy of Hernando de Soto's *Mystery of Capital* and were looking forward to realizing the benefits of property ownership and the Torrens registry system. I could hardly contain my amazement. Here we were about 650 miles north of Vancouver, and the Nisga'a Nation already had a land-title system. It was like the moment during the movie *Monty Python's Holy Grail* when the French tell King Arthur to go away because they already had a Holy Grail and it was very nice. However, unlike the movie, the Nisga'a did let us see the legal and administrative framework to support a Nisga'a land-title system, and it spawned an idea that is the subject of this chapter. We are proposing that the federal government pass a First Nations Property Ownership Act so that First Nations across Canada can have clear underlying and individual property ownership, should they so choose.

The benefits of a First Nations property ownership would be substantial. In combination with existing federal legislation, it would fill in most of the gaps in the First Nations investment climate and dramatically reduce transaction costs. With a stroke of a pen, First Nations land values could rise to those prevailing in the rest of Canada. It would recognize underlying First Nations title, and thus formally bring First Nations governments into the federation. It could increase home equity for homeowners on First Nations lands so they can be more entrepreneurial, plan for their retirement, and bequeath their wealth just like other Canadians. It would help resolve issues relating to matrimonial real property and estates. It would provide market incentives for improved financial management and for completing self-government and land-claim negotiations.

This chapter goes into more details about these benefits, but first we discuss the historic accomplishment of the Nisga'a Nation and provide an outline of the objectives of a proposed First Nations Property Ownership Act based on the Nisga'a model.

THE FIRST INDIGENOUS LAND-TITLE SYSTEM IN THE WORLD

After the failure of the Charlottetown Accord in 1993, First Nations wishing to fully escape the Indian Act through a self-government agreement or treaty faced a dilemma. Once outside of the Indian Act, should the ultimate title of their land be transferred to the provincial system or maintained in the federal one? The dilemma arose because, constitutionally, there appear to be only two types of underlying title in Canada – the Crown in the right of the province and the Crown in the right of the federal government.[1]

This is important because there are a number of situations when land is "transferred" from an individual to the state. These include dying intestate without heirs, not paying taxes, violating land or environmental rules, or having land that the state happens to want for its own purposes, subject to compensation to individual property owners. These are the state's reversionary and expropriation rights. From an economist's perspective, the government that obtains title through reversionary or expropriation rights holds the characteristics of allodial title.[2] Therefore, the question for First Nations is who holds the allodial title to their land when reversionary or expropriation rights are to be exercised.

For reference purposes, it is assumed that, in some limited cases related to expropriation and the unlikely disappearance of the Nisga'a Nation, Nisga'a lands revert to the Crown in the right of the province. The other reversionary rights remain with the Nisga'a. By comparison, in the Westbank self-government agreement and all the incremental legislation presented in the previous chapter, it is assumed that these lands could revert to the Crown in the right of the federal government.[3]

Phrased differently, the legislative intent of the Nisga'a treaty and its accompanying self-government agreement was to recognize First Nations underlying title. This means that Nisga'a lands will remain Nisga'a in the exercise of almost all jurisdictions. This is made clear in sections 4, 5, 6, and 9 of the Nisga'a Nation Entitlement Act and to a lesser extent in chapter 3 of the Nisga'a Nation constitution.[4] The specific name of this underlying title might be the Crown in the right of the Nisga'a, or Nisga'a aboriginal title, Nisga'a treaty title, or simply Nisga'a.

To protect and assert their reversionary title, one of the first pieces of legislation passed by the Nisga'a Nation was the Nisga'a Land Title Act, enacted on 11 May 2000. After a series of technical and policy amendments, a consolidated version of this legislation appeared on their website in August 2008.

The following brief description of the Nisga'a land-title system is drawn from a research paper developed by Diane Cragg for the First

Nations Tax Commission, entitled *Best Practices in First Nation Land Title Systems.*[5] Diane Cragg is the land-title registrar for the Nisga'a Nation, charged with developing the legal and administrative system to support their land-title system.

The Nisga'a chose to implement a Torrens land-title system. Invented by Sir Robert Torrens of Australia in 1858,[6] the Torrens system does away with the need for a chain of titles to a property as is common in a deeds registry system. In the Torrens system the state guarantees title to a property. It is not necessary to go beyond this guaranteed certificate of title, as it contains all the information about the title. The Torrens system provides a straightforward method for determining title to land and interests in land based on several elements that generate secure title including:

1. registration;
2. certainty of title in the registry;
3. a system of priorities for ranking competing interests; and
4. assurance that the registered owner is the true owner of the title.[7]

In a Torrens system the registrar is responsible for assessing the legal validity of the instrument being registered, and cannot accept an instrument that does not conform to the requirements of the enabling legislation. The information is recorded in the land-title system in relation to a legally surveyed parcel of land with a distinct identifier. The record of the information is itself the evidence of title. A state of title certificate is provided setting out the registered interests associated with a parcel that can be relied upon. The registrar in this case is responsible for both the administrative process of document registration and the validity of the registered documents.[8]

The Torrens system is often contrasted with a deeds system. In a deeds registry system, instruments relating to land are deposited and recorded in a registry. The registrar maintains the records but does not have any involvement in the actual effect of the documents and does not determine if the documents are valid or lawful. In this sense a registry system is really just a filing system. The risk associated with the transaction rests with the parties, rather than with the registrar. The only risk carried by the registrar is related to the administrative process of registering the documents.[9] For reference purposes, the Indian Lands Registry is a poorly managed and almost completely ineffective deeds system.

This guarantee of title of the current owner in a Torrens system significantly reduces the transaction costs compared to a deeds system. In a land or property transaction, the amount of time for a lawyer or other professional to review the current guaranteed title is minimal. In a deeds system that contains all of the particular property's transaction, this cost could be rather significant. To address some of this risk, deeds systems are often supported by title insurance. There is very little requirement for title insurance in Torrens systems, and most property owners in Torrens systems do not purchase it.[10]

In a recent speech recognizing the 150th anniversary of the Torrens system, Diane Cragg explains why the Nisga'a Nation felt that a Torrens system was the most culturally appropriate system for them:

> In a Torrens system, as opposed to a deeds registry, the recorded information is itself evidence of the right to the land, and a state of title certificate that sets out the registered interests associated with a parcel can be relied upon. The records are publicly searchable.
>
> This is, in an interesting way, a way of expressing the traditional Nisga'a way [method] of recording property interests, using a new technology [a modern Torrens system].
>
> It is no longer necessary to bring hundreds of people to one place to witness a transaction, because the public record of the transaction is available to everyone.
>
> It is the public recording of the interest (formerly the passing of the name) that establishes title, and the adaawak, or history, can be obtained through a long form of the certificate of title, which shows every transaction related to the specific parcel of land since the treaty.[11]

Technically, the Nisga'a have chosen to implement a modified Torrens title system. In particular, they will be able to provide guaranteed fee-simple title that is protected by an assurance or insurance fund. It will have all the elements of a Torrens system. It is modified only to the extent that the Nisga'a system would allow for the registry of some cultural land interests that are not common in other Torrens systems.

Torrens-type title systems are currently used by seven provinces and all three territories.[12] In addition to being culturally appropriate, table 10.1, developed by Diane Cragg, summarizes why the Torrens system is considered superior to deeds type registry systems and the current Indian Lands Registry.

Other features of the Nisga'a title system include:

Underlying Title. The Nisga'a Nation owns its land in fee simple; and through the exercise of jurisdictions related to estates, land management, and possibly the environment and taxation, the underlying title will either revert to them or can be appropriated by them. This provides the Nisga'a Nation with the necessary authority to take responsibility for its land-title system and determine what kind of interests it will grant.

Individual Title. The Nisga'a Nation is contemplating an amendment to its Land Title Act in autumn 2009 to facilitate individual fee-simple title on its lands. As a result it would be the first indigenous government in the world to provide a guarantee of fee-simple individual property rights on lands over which it maintains jurisdiction. In the event that the Nisga'a system also is able to provide an assurance fund as protection against fraud, it will provide an individual property right that is as secure as anywhere else in Canada.

Provincial Land-title System Compatibility. No interests in the Nisga'a system are registered in the BC land-title system. However, the legislation stipulates that all documents and plans in the Nisga'a system should be at an equivalent standard to the BC system, so both systems could be utilized if desired. In particular, Nisga'a land-title administrative standards related to accuracy, reliability, independence, priority registration, and document and data security are in keeping with the standards of the BC Land Title office.

Reduced Transaction Costs. The Nisga'a land-title system significantly reduces the costs of doing business on Nisga'a lands in at least three ways. First, collective and individual property rights on Nisga'a land are similar to these property rights in the rest of BC.

Table 10.1 | Comparison of the Torrens, Deeds, and Indian
Lands Registry Systems

	Land-title Registry (Torrens)	*Deeds Registry*	*Indian Lands Registry (Deeds)*
Accuracy and Reliability	BEST PRACTICE Standards of document registration established by statute; Guarantee & assurance fund	Standards of document registration established by statute; No guarantee	Standards of document registration established by policy rather than statute; No guarantee
Document and Data Security	BEST PRACTICE Responsibility for document security set out in legislation; Single registry – all relevant records are in one place	Responsibility for document security may be set out in legislation; May be multiple registries	Responsibility for document security established by policy; Multiple registries
Protection Against Fraud	BEST PRACTICE Participants in fraud do not acquire interest in land; Mechanisms to protect against registration of fraudulent interests; Fraud victims are compensated by assurance fund	Registry has no role in establishing the verity of a transaction; Fraudulent transactions may be determined by law to have no effect; Not all documents are registered	Fraudulent transactions are determined by policy to have no effect; Eligibility requirements may reduce opportunities for fraud
Guarantee and Assurance Funds	BEST PRACTICE Guarantee of title and assurance fund established by statute	No guarantee of title; Assurance fund may not be provided	No guarantee of title; No assurance fund
Priority Registration	BEST PRACTICE Priority of Registration establishes priority of interests	Priority of registration may establish priority of interests; Unregistered documents may affect priority	Registration in priority sequence based on policy, rather than legislation; Unregistered documents may affect priority

	Land-title Registry (Torrens)	Deeds Registry	Indian Lands Registry (Deeds)
Resolution of Competing Interest	BEST PRACTICE Allows the registration of interests in priority sequence; Initial title recognition is only role; Does not allow the establishment of competing interests	Has no role in resolving competing interest when initial title determined; Registered documents may create competing interests	Has a role in granting interests (via ministerial approval); Registered documents may create competing interests
Matrimonial Real Property	BEST PRACTICE Clear and consistent practice regulated by statute	Clear and consistent practice regulated by statute; Property may not be registered	Court orders with respect to matrimonial real property have no effect
Estates	BEST PRACTICE Clear and consistent practice regulated by statute	Clear and consistent practice regulated by statute; Property may not be registered	Complex process using both federal and provincial legislation; Property may not be registered
Legal Surveys	BEST PRACTICE Standards for surveys set out in legislation; All parcels surveyed and allocated a unique legal description	Standards for surveys set out in legislation; Multiple surveys may exist	Standards for surveys set out by policy; Multiple surveys may exist

Second, the Nisga'a land-title office and database makes it relatively inexpensive to register or search for a particular individual property right. Third, the system provides for a clear process with timelines related to surveys and subdivision approvals, thus saving potential developers time and money.

Dispute Resolution. When the Nisga'a system eventually provides guaranteed individual title, it will have effective mechanisms for resolving disputes related to estates and matrimonial property. Land title means property can be sold to resolve these disputes, whether required by provincial family and estate laws or by equivalent First Nations laws.

In sum, it should be clear that the world's first indigenous Torrens system that provides indefeasible title is located in the far northwest corner of British Columbia, Canada. If the Nisga'a can do this in spite of their isolation, why aren't there more of these systems? The reason is time. In the modern context, it has taken the Nisga'a Nation thirty-five years to have enough security in their underlying title to have the jurisdiction to confidently provide individual fee-simple title.

TOWARD THE FIRST NATIONS PROPERTY OWNERSHIP ACT

What if it were possible to develop federal legislation that recognized First Nations underlying title and established a First Nations Torrens registry system so that individual property ownership or fee-simple title was possible on First Nations lands? Answering this question has been part of the life's work of Manny Jules. In the early 1990s he worked with then Chief Stephen Pointe, now the lieutenant governor of BC, to develop a First Nations property ownership system. This attempt was unsuccessful because they were unable to generate the political will for the necessary federal legislation.

Since then, two important developments have improved the chances of success. First, over the last fifteen years, the combination of federal legislation that enables First Nations powers and institutional support to implement these powers has been demonstrated as an effective method to escape the Indian Act while enhancing the economic and social union of Canada. In particular, those First Nations who want to exercise their jurisdiction must at least escape the Indian Act to collect property taxes and local revenues through the FSMA and sales taxes through the FNGST, and implement comprehensive land management rules through the FNLMA or other means.

Second, as expressed in their 2008 election platforms, both the federal Conservative and Liberal parties support the development of legislation to create an optional First Nations land-title system. On 22 September 2008, Joe Friesen wrote in the *Globe and Mail* that the Liberals are in favour of private land title in those communities that want it and have the capacity to implement it. He also wrote that the Conservatives support the development of a private-property regime and the creation of a First Nations Land Ownership Act to transfer land title from the Crown to individual bands.[13]

In other words, there is sufficient support in the House of Commons to enact federal legislation to create effective individual property rights on First Nations lands. Unfortunately, political will is a necessary but not a sufficient condition for successful First Nations legislation. As was discussed in the previous chapter, successful escapes from the Indian Act must also (a) be First Nations–led, (b) enable First Nations powers that replace parts of the Indian Act, (c) support markets on First Nations lands so they can become more independent, (d) be optional, and (e) create First Nations institutions to facilitate a takeover of responsibilities from INAC.

To begin, there is little doubt that this proposal is a continuation of the First Nations–led initiatives of the 1990s. In this regard, Manny Jules recently suggested the name *First Nations Property Ownership Act* because he was thinking of what his father said in 1968: "We don't even own our own land."[14] This legislation would finally implement what his father's generation of leaders wanted – ownership of underlying title by First Nations governments and individual property ownership affirmed by guaranteed title.

Second, to facilitate an effective First Nations land-title system that is beyond the Indian Act, the legislation must accomplish six objectives. It must provide fee-simple title to current First Nations lands. It must ensure that underlying title remains with the First Nations in case of reversion or appropriation. This means that when either a First Nation or another government exercises a jurisdiction that results in a removal of the individual title, that title must revert to the First Nation. As was discussed in the last chapter, most of those jurisdictions relevant to reversion and appropriation are associated with taxation and land management. Third, the legislation must convey the fee-simple and underlying title to the First Nations while avoiding concerns from provinces about their possible rights of resumption. Fourth, the legislation should create the titling, registry, and surveying structure to support a Torrens title system. It can accomplish this by placing these requirements in the legislation, or it can enable First Nations to make laws on their lands that meet these requirements. Fifth, Torrens systems are integrated with dozens of other statutes. This integration facilitates lower transaction costs for land-development and public-service efficiencies and in so doing provides property-rights certainty. The legislation must facilitate these linkages, perhaps through future regulations, so the First Nations can quickly catch up to the modern Canadian property-rights legal framework. Finally, it must accomplish all this through federal legislation.

If the above objectives can be accomplished, this legislation will allow property markets to work on First Nations lands as they do everywhere else in Canada. First Nations could choose to provide indefeasible title to current individual landowners, such as those who possess certificates of possession or traditional or customary holdings, or even lessees. Alternatively, a First Nations could choose to maintain its fee-simple title and provide leasehold and/or strata title. Regardless of the First Nations choice, individual property rights would be registered in a Torrens system, and those with indefeasible ownership would have a certificate of guaranteed title subject to the exercise of jurisdictions on First Nations lands. As a result, individual property-rights uncertainty would no longer be an excuse for lower property values on First Nations lands. Once the market becomes comfortable with First Nations governance, property markets should work as well on reserve as they do off.

The legislation would be completely optional for First Nations. The First Nation could choose to participate through an acceptable demonstration of community support similar to passing a land designation under the Indian Act, a land code under the FNLMA, or a self-government or treaty agreement. Moreover, the First Nation would determine application of the new title system to its lands. Some First Nations will limit their land-title system to a specific area and may even limit tenure to leasehold title. Others may choose to apply their land-title system to all their lands and enable comprehensive fee-simple ownership. The legislation would facilitate either of these choices as well as an infinite number of choices in between.

The legislation would contain the complete legal framework for a First Nations Torrens land-title system. In this regard, the guarantee of title is at the heart of the Torrens system. This means that holders of title do not need to search beyond the record in the land-title office, and those transactions have a legal certainty that cannot be matched in a deeds registry system.

To support the implementation of the First Nations Property Ownership Act, education and training would have to be provided to participating First Nations. The Tulo Centre of Indigenous Economics, with its commitment to creating the legal and administrative framework to support markets on indigenous lands, might be an ideal location.

Efficiencies for registering title will be sought. Initially, perhaps the BC Land Title and Surveying Authority could serve as the registrar.[15] As in the provinces, registrations would be completed on a fee-for-service cost-recovery basis. Once sufficient economies of scale are achieved in the First Nations system,[16] registration could be transferred to a First Nations land-title registrar.

Although guaranteed title means that the requirement for title insurance is minimized, the system must still be backed by an assurance fund. An assurance fund is required because there is always a possibility of fraud, even in the most carefully monitored systems. As much as possible, effective anti-fraud measures will be included in the enabling legislation.

THE BENEFITS OF A FIRST NATIONS LAND-TITLE SYSTEM

Market economies are built on the exchange of property rights. The market cannot function without property rights that are secure, easily defined, enforced, and traded. This is especially true with respect to land. Land is the most fundamental type of property, and therefore property rights in land are the bedrock of the market economy. The success of an economy can be traced to its ability to provide secure and tradable property rights over land. A Torrens land-title system typically provides the private sector with both the requisite property rights and a mechanism for their exchange. In this regard, the ultimate objective of the First Nations Property Ownership Act is to support the aspirations of First Nations people: to assist them to unlock the tremendous economic potential of First

Nations land, to become productive contributors to the Canadian economy, and to provide a mechanism that will allow them to create the level of prosperity that other Canadians take for granted.

A First Nations land-title system will provide numerous benefits to First Nations and Canada. In spring 2007, Greg Richard, the senior economist of Fiscal Realities, and I wrote two papers for the First Nations Tax Commission describing and quantifying the benefits of a First Nations land-title system. We identified seven broad benefits that would result from a First Nations land-title system:

1. *Reduced transaction costs.* A First Nations land-title system would reduce transaction costs in two fundamental ways. First, it would create a standard for First Nations land title, surveying, and registration and eventually greater integration with land development processes and public service provisions. Standards reduce transaction costs. Second, the land-title system would accelerate the development of land-transaction skills pertaining to First Nations in land administration and also to outside professionals. It would make it easier to transfer skills from other jurisdictions and between First Nations. To the extent that these reduced transaction costs are coupled with improvements in infrastructure and greater investor certainty, a land-title system will mean higher First Nations property values, greater private investment, and increased employment. The relationship between falling transaction costs and land-title systems is supported in the literature:

   > More recently, the policy emphasis in many countries (especially under the auspices of the World Bank) has been to land registration and titling, although property rights are a complicated institution that goes beyond simple titling, to include constitutional, legal/institutional, and social norms ... Gains in trade as a result of formal property rights over land imply on the other hand, that there will be more land trading as a consequence of a reduction in transaction costs after the rights are improved or created.[17]

2. *First Nations homeownership.* A land-title system would allow First Nations to create property with all the characteristics required to participate in open-market residential developments. In this regard, First Nations citizens, especially those currently holding certificates of possession, customary rights, or leases would probably want to convert their current quasi-property right to a more valuable and tradable tenure. Further, most First Nations have long housing waiting lists, and guaranteed property ownership could facilitate financing to meet this pent-up demand. As a result, land title would allow First Nations homeowners to build equity, which they could use to support business start-ups[18] or to transfer wealth between generations. This wealth-creation cycle is largely absent among First Nations and helps explain their continued poverty. Further, as a result of tradable properties among a number of First Nations, status households will finally have the option to move to areas of greater economic opportunity, while possibly staying on First Nations land. In Peru, where more than 1.2 million households had their defective or nonexistent property rights converted to land title between 1995 and 2001, productivity rose by more than 15 percent for the recently titled households.[19]

3. *Lower costs of government.* Higher rates of employment and increased wealth generated by First Nations property ownership will reduce dependency on social, education, health, and housing programs designed to address poverty.[20] These fiscal costs of First Nations poverty will be reduced for all govern-. ments. Moreover, to the extent that First Nations people have equity in their homes like other Canadians, it will be less necessary to guarantee loans and provide maintenance costs for housing on First Nations lands.

4. *Higher First Nations revenues.* Economic growth generated by a competitive investment climate and effective property rights will increase First Nations government revenues. This is particularly true for First Nations that have exercised their authorities with respect to property tax, sales tax, and other local revenues. As a result First Nations will begin to achieve greater fiscal self-sufficiency. In this vein and to pay

for the land management costs for implementing the First Nations Property Ownership Act, the legislation should also empower First Nations to collect property transfer taxes similar to those that exist elsewhere in Canada.

5. *Reduce number of disputes.* Property ownership will help resolve disputes related to estates and marital property. There are two issues relating to wills and estates on First Nations lands that would be addressed by First Nations having title to their property. First, some informal wills designate heirs who become multiple holders of the same property. Second, the rules surrounding the resolution of intestate wills also often result in multiple holders. If a will exists, a title system will make for a more orderly transition. If a will does not exist, it may be easier to clear multiple titles through sale than in the current system. Finally, if there are no heirs, the legislation will ensure that the title reverts to the relevant First Nation. On the second issue, title systems do not directly protect matrimonial property. Title systems that effectively support matrimonial laws do, however, provide a means for transferring title in the event of marital breakdown, because they make properties transferable on open markets. This ensures that disputed properties can be sold and the proceeds from those sales can be divided in the event of marital breakdown.

6. *Improved incentives.* A First Nations land-title system would help create a political constituency to articulate and advocate for an improved investment climate. This constituency will consist of people who benefit from policies that enhance their property values. These policies include transparent financial management, appropriate land management, stable regulations, quality services, reasonable tax rates, prudent investments in infrastructure, and an accountability regime that responds to all stakeholders.[21] Further, as a result of the value and certainty provided by a First Nations property ownership system, there is a strong incentive for First Nations to resolve outstanding land claims. Finally, a First Nations land-title system would encourage the resolution of

self-government agreements so that First Nations could provide certainty about individual title and protect their underlying title.

7. *International reputation.* The development of a First Nations property ownership system would mark an international first in the recognition by federations of the rights of minorities and indigenous peoples. It would affirm a rejection of assimilation and recognize First Nations' underlying title in Canada. This would signal to the world a new stage in the evolution of federalism. It would demonstrate the commitment of Canada to the rights of indigenous people and the ability of a federation to accommodate the unique aspirations of indigenous people without compromising the economic and social union of the federation. Recently, Canada was criticized for not recognizing the United Nations declaration of indigenous rights.[22] This legislation would not only demonstrate Canada's response but would instantly make Canada the world leader on this matter.

In short, a First Nations land-title system will improve economies in participating First Nations' communities. It will create a better functioning property market, provide business equity, lead to the creation of improved governance regimes, foster the development of land transaction and investment professionals, and improve Canada's international reputation.

Table 10.2 represents an attempt to quantify the benefits of First Nations property ownership supported by a land-title system on a sample of First Nations.[23] Benefits were based on increases in real-estate values, employment, residential development, tax revenues, infrastructure, and reduced First Nations poverty that would occur in the next fifteen years in sixty-eight tax-collecting First Nations in BC. We assumed that each of these adopted land-title systems and improved their investment climates. These First Nations were chosen because land valuation data through property tax assessments were available for them.

Conservative estimation methods relating to the amount of land developed, pace of development, and value of development result-

Table 10.2: First Nations Benefit Estimates

Benefits	Benefit Estimates (over 15 years) for 68 First Nations
Increase in real estate value	$3.8 billion
New employment	62,700 FTEs and $410 million in increased productivity
Increase in housing stock	2,750 residential units
Increase in property tax revenues	$150 million
Increase in economic infrastructure	$156 million
Increase in sales tax revenues	$92 million
Reduced cost of poverty	$1.1 billion
TOTAL	$5.7 billion in benefits over next 15 years

ing from a First Nations land-title system were used. First, it was assumed that these First Nations would only develop 40 percent of their lands in the next fifteen years. Second, it was assumed that none of these First Nations would reach the point of 40 percent development until year 15. Third these developments would not be different from the current pattern of development within their region. If it was a rural First Nations (and over 70 percent of the First Nations in the sample were rural), then they would achieve levels of rural development similar to what currently exists within their region. Fourth, the developable lands of four First Nations (Squamish, Musqueam, Campbell River, and Westbank) were restricted to 25 percent because their strategic locations significantly raised benefit estimates. Fifth, these are net benefit estimates, as it was assumed that in the absence of the FNPOA, these First Nations would still develop an additional 10 percent of their lands. Sixth we did not quantify all the benefits from the FNPOA, such as the reduced costs of dispute resolution, improvements in public service delivery from a Torrens registry system, or new business loans resulting from home equity. Finally, it is important to note that these estimates were not projected nationally. They only represent a sample of sixty-eight First Nations in Canada.

Table 10.2 summarizes our attempt to quantify the benefits from the FNPOA. Results are reported as net present values.

Questions and Answers

Although the benefits are considerable, there will certainly be concerns and questions about a proposed First Nations Property Ownership Act. We will attempt to address the ones that we are aware of so far.

Why would a First Nation want to alienate its land? The legislation would ensure that it is impossible for a First Nation to alienate its land. It will always retain its underlying, aboriginal, or treaty title to its lands. As a result of this legislation, a First Nation could no more alienate its land than could the province of Saskatchewan. However, if the First Nation introduces a system of individual title, members of the band could sell their holdings, just as a resident of Saskatchewan can sell land to a citizen of Ontario. But the land remains in Saskatchewan and continues to be subject to the regulatory authority of the Government of Saskatchewan. In the same way, any individually owned land sold by the owner would remain subject to the legislative authority of the First Nation.

Isn't this the White Paper all over again? Or, isn't this like the Dawes Act? The Trudeau-era White Paper was about removing jurisdiction over First Nations lands from the Crown in the right of the federal government and transferring jurisdiction to the Crown in the right of the province. Similarly, the Dawes Act was about moving jurisdiction over reservation land from the tribe to the state. The proposed First Nations Property Ownership Act would remove First Nations land from the Crown in the right of the federal government and transfer it to First Nations title. As was explained in chapter 3, this proposal is directly opposite to the White Paper and the Dawes Act because it recognizes and protects the inalienable reversionary right to First Nations title.

How many First Nations would be interested in this? The Nisga'a Nation is interested. The Shuswap Nation Tribal Council in south central BC has passed a resolution of support for a First Nations land-title system. Others may also be interested in this, including

First Nations that want to raise the value of their lands to Canadian norms, First Nations that want to reduce transaction costs and grow their economies by building a private sector, and First Nations that want to implement their underlying title through their self-government powers. Many First Nations don't want the lands they gain through the settlement of claims, treaty land entitlements, or additions to reserve to be reduced in value as a result of a transfer to their jurisdiction. There are First Nations that want to expedite their claims, treaty land entitlements, and additions to reserve processes. These processes will be sped up because the transfer of title from one government to another will be simplified. Holders of certificates of possession, customary holdings, and homeowners on First Nations lands who want to increase their wealth and utilize their home equity for entrepreneurial, retirement, or bequest reasons would be interested in this legislation. In other words, many if not most First Nations would potentially be interested in this legislation.

But won't it be hard to implement a First Nations land-title system? Why not just use the existing provincial systems? First, First Nations title and possible fee-simple ownership can only be established through federal legislation. Second, it will focus on creating a standardized First Nations land-title Torrens system to reduce the costs of implementation. In this regard, cost efficiencies such as provincial registry system should be sought. This might mean that for early adaptors, provincial systems may be used, but once economies of scale are achieved a First Nations registrar can be established.

How much will this cost? It should be relatively inexpensive to establish a First Nations land-title system. The principal costs are those associated with establishing an assurance fund, surveying, education, and perhaps registration. The assurance fund is essential to the guarantee of title in a Torrens title system and has a one-time start up cost of about $2 million. Education, training, and surveying should be less than $2 million annually. This is because land-surveying costs could be relatively inexpensive owing to new technologies and the potential for cost recovery from benefiting landholders. Registration costs should be based on a fee-for-service cost-recovery basis. As such, it is possible that no new resources would be required because savings found at INAC could cover this. Compared to the potential benefits, this legislation represents excellent taxpayer value for money.

As non-First Nations members become residents on First Nations lands, won't this lead to taxation without representation? One of the purposes of the First Nations Tax Commission is to address this issue. It develops standards so that the average tax bills on First Nations lands are similar to those in their adjacent jurisdictions. It encourages First Nations to develop taxpayer relations laws so that taxpayers can have meaningful input into the expenditure of local revenues. It provides a model taxpayer-relations law based on the Westbank experience. It has a formal complaints process so that taxpayers have further recourse in the event that they cannot resolve their concerns locally.

Can't First Nations achieve these benefits through self-government agreements as Westbank did? It is certainly true that a great deal of property-rights certainty can be generated using a deeds registry system and good lease documents. That said, it is also true that there is more property-rights certainty in clear underlying title, guaranteed title, and a Torrens registry system. First Nations lands should have the potential to be as valuable as those of their neighbours. While Westbank and other First Nations have been very enterprising in solving problems related to high transaction costs and poor infrastructure and land tenure systems, these solutions will never provide the investor certainty of guaranteed title. Why solve a problem indirectly when you can solve it directly?

Would this initiative solve all First Nations problems? No, First Nations still need a new fiscal relationship that provides them with sufficient revenue options to exercise their service responsibilities. This new fiscal relationship should also sort out service responsibilities between First Nations and local, provincial, and federal governments in Canada so that citizens on First Nations lands receive quality public services at a cost-effective price. There is need for a more transparent formula-driven transfer system to raise service delivery quality on First Nations land to national standards. First Nations need to build investment grade infrastructure. They need to implement their new powers such as those pertaining to land management in a way that supports private investment. So the First

Nations Property Ownership Act is not the ultimate panacea, but it is an important step in the right direction.

CONCLUSIONS

Before contact First Nations exercised property rights and utilized markets to raise individual and community well-being. The impressive Aztec, Inca, and Mayan empires are just a few testaments to their past successes. The passage of the First Nations Property Ownership Act is a step to restoring this proud history. It will recognize and implement underlying First Nations title with respect to rights of reversion and expropriation. It will allow First Nations to choose whether they want to use the legislation and how they wish to apply it to their lands. It will help them implement and assert their title.

Those First Nations who combine these new powers to create secure land tenure with better infrastructure and governance systems that support a private sector will be better able to escape poverty, the Indian Act, and INAC. And this is something that all First Nations and Canadians want. In 2003, Manny Jules said the following to the standing committee reviewing the proposed First Nations Governance Act:

> First Nations want what Canadians take for granted –
> employment opportunities, good health care, a stable income,
> and decent housing, reliable public services, good roads,
> healthy water and sewer systems and a better future for
> our kids.
>
> As a founding people of Canada, why are we not sharing
> equally in its bounty? I have grappled with this my whole life.
> Our people are not the problem. We are as innovative, entre-
> preneurial and public minded as other Canadians.
>
> Our problem is that the Indian Act has stymied the devel-
> opment of our own institutions of government. First Nations
> lack a public sector supported by modern legislation and
> standards. The First Nation public sector includes First
> Nation governments and First Nation institutions. This public

sector is critical to economic development, self-sufficiency and healthy communities.

Today, when people think of the First Nation's public sector, they are more likely to think of the Department of Indian Affairs than of our own governments and institutions. In fact, when people want to do business with us, they have to spend as much time or more responding to the regulatory requirements of the Department of Indian Affairs than to those of our own administrations. These layers of bureaucracy are a burden. This has been affirmed by the Auditor General.

The system created by the Indian Act and administered by the Department of Indian Affairs has shut us out of the economy. At best, it has ruined our investment climate. At worst, it has stolen the hope of our children. Everyone recognizes there is a need for change.

We must share a vision to build a real partnership between Canada and First Nations that is achievable in 10 years.

I see a future in 10 years where there is no Indian Act. It has been replaced by First Nation legislation.

I see a future in 10 years where there is no longer a purpose for the Department of Indian Affairs. It has been replaced by our own First Nation public institutions that protect national standards and provide a third order of government.

I see a future in 10 years where we are full participants in the economic union. I see a future in 10 years as bright as yours. In my vision, First Nations have been restored as true partners in the federation. We participate in the global economy. And we have become much more self-sufficient governments. I believe we all share this vision.[24]

The implementation of the *Nisga'a Final Agreement* on 11 May 2000 gave the Nisga'a Nation full control and jurisdiction over 2,000 square kilometers of land in northwestern British Columbia. As a first step in providing land for residential purposes to its citizens, Nisga'a Lisims Government established a modified Torrens title system to record fee simple interests in land granted by the Nisga'a Nation. Initially lands were granted in fee simple to Nisga'a Villages and a possessory right, known as an entitlement, was granted to individual Nisga'a citizens and registered as a charge against the Village's fee simple interest. That interest could not be transferred to a non-Nisga'a person.

Now, nearly ten years later, the Nisga'a Nation has experience with both the positive and negative aspects of this scheme of land ownership and is ready to take the next step. By granting full, unrestricted fee simple ownership of residential Nisga'a Lands, the Nisga'a Nation is providing its citizens with the tools to access the capital locked in their residential properties, with the intent of increasing prosperity for Nisga'a people in the Nass Valley. The act that will make this possible was announced in the news release reproduced below.

D.E. Cragg
Registrar of Land Titles
Nisga'a Lisims Government

NEW AIYANSH, BC, Oct. 30 /CNW/ – At its October 2009 sitting, Wilp Si'ayuukhl Nisga'a (WSN), the legislative body of Nisga'a Lisims Government, passed the Nisga'a Landholding Transition Act.

The Nisga'a Landholding Transition Act gives Nisga'a citizens the opportunity to own their residential properties in fee simple. A Nisga'a citizen who obtains fee simple title to their residential property under the Act will subsequently be able to mortgage their property as security for a loan, or to transfer, bequeath, lease or sell their property, to any person.

At a roundtable discussion in 2006, WSN considered ways in which Nisga'a citizens hold their residential properties. It identified the current restrictive system of Nisga'a Village Entitlements and Nisga'a Nation Entitlements as a barrier to economic development. Over the ensuing three years, Nisga'a communities in the Nass Valley and in Vancouver, Prince Rupert and Terrace were consulted, and numerous legislative options were considered, culminating in the introduction of the new Act.

"This is a significant step towards true self government. It is a process for increasing economic prosperity for our people," stated Nelson Leeson, President of the Nisga'a Nation. "It is important for us to be able to find ways of building capacity for our people so that they can stand on their own."

Under the Act, Nisga'a citizens will have the opportunity to obtain the fee simple title to residentially zoned properties of a specified size within Nisga'a Villages. Initially, the eligible properties are expected to make up approximately 1 square kilometer of the approximately 2,000 square kilometers of Nisga'a Lands. Although a Nisga'a citizen who obtains the fee simple title to their property under the Act will subsequently be able to transfer their property to any person, the property will always remain Nisga'a Lands and be subject to Nisga'a laws under the Nisga'a Final Agreement.

The Nisga'a Nation includes approximately 6,400 Nisga'a citizens.

For further information: Eric Grandison, Communications Coordinator, Nisga'a Lisims Government, (250) 633-3000

NOTES

FOREWORD

1 Chief Joseph of the Nez Perce, Lincoln Hall, 14 January 1879.
2 Charles Mann, *1491: New Revelations of the Americas before Columbus* (New York: Knopf, 2005).
3 Ibid.
4 Jared Diamond, *Guns, Germs, and Steel: The Fates of Human Societies* (New York: W.W. Norton, 1999).
5 Memorial to Sir Wilfred Laurier, Premier of the Dominion of Canada from the Chiefs of the Shuswap, Okanagan and Couteau Tribes of British Columbia presented at Kamloops, BC, 25 August 1910.

INTRODUCTION

1 Tom Flanagan, *First Nations? Second Thoughts,* rev. ed. (Montreal: McGill-Queen's University Press, 2008), chapter 11.
2 Susan Campbell, "On 'Modest Proposals' to Further Reduce the Aboriginal Landbase by Privatizing Reserve Land," *Canadian Journal of Native Studies* 17 (2007), 220.
3 David Newhouse, "Modern Aboriginal Economies: Capitalism with a Red Face," *Journal of Aboriginal Economic Development* 1 (2000).
4 Ashley Sisco and Rodney Nelson, *From Vision to Venture: An Account of Five Successful Aboriginal Businesses* (Conference Board of Canada: May 2008), 43.
5 www.duhaime.org/LegalResources/RealEstateTenancy/LawArticle-63/Fee-Simple-and-Life-Estates.aspx.
6 Statistics Canada, *Aboriginal Peoples in Canada in 2006,* tables 21 and 22, www.statcan.ca.
7 Don Sandberg, "Reserves Show Signs of Slow Progress," www.fcpp.org/main/publication_detail.php?PubID=2359.

8 Hernando de Soto, *The Other Path: The Invisible Revolution in the Third World* (New York: Harper & Row, 1989); *The Mystery of Capital: Why Capitalism Triumphs in the West and Fails Everywhere Else* (New York: Basic Books, 2000).

CHAPTER ONE

1 G.F.G. Stanley et al., eds, *The Collected Writings of Louis Riel* (Edmonton: University of Alberta Press, 1985), vol. 3, 547.
2 Rick Williams to Tom Flanagan, email 8 July 2009. Lt-Col Williams was once a DND land administrator for the Harvey Barracks.
3 Phone interview with Rick Williams, 13 July 2009.
4 Mark Lowey, "Keys to Army Base Houses Turned over to Tsuu T'ina," *Calgary Herald*, 22 August 1998.
5 Sean Myers, "Bulk of Housing Funds Unpaid," *Calgary Herald*, 17 October 2006.
6 Sasha Nagy, "Black Bear Crossing, City Join Hands," *Calgary Herald*, 17 January 1999.
7 Brock Ketcham, "Funds Found for Native Police to Patrol Former Military Base," *Calgary Herald*, 11 June 1999.
8 Sean Myers, "Bulk of Housing Funds Unpaid," *Calgary Herald*, 17 October 2006.
9 Sarah McGinnis, "Alarms Sounded over Squatter Removal," *Calgary Herald*, 15 October 2006.
10 Kerry Williamson, "Prentice Wants Squatters to Return," *Calgary Herald*, 21 October 2006.
11 Jamie Komarnicki, "Deal Houses Black Bear Evacuees," *Calgary Herald*, 16 December 2006.
12 Kelly Cryderman, "Natives Picking Up Tab for Black Bear Crossing Evacuees," *Calgary Herald*, 3 June 2008.
13 Townsite of Redwood Meadows website, www.redwoodmeadows.ab.ca (accessed 15 August 2008).
14 Paul Willetts, "The 'Right to Buy': From Public Housing to Home Ownership," 1 May 2008, Frontier Centre website, www.fcpp.org/main/publication_detail.php?PubID=2178.
15 Richard A. Epstein, *Supreme Neglect: How to Revive Constitutional Protection for Private Property* (New York: Oxford University Press, 2008), 19.
16 John Alford, Carolyn Funk, and John Hibbing, "Are Political Orientations Genetically Transmitted?" *American Political Science Review* 99

(200), 153–67; James Fowler and Christopher Dawes, "Two Genes Predict Voter Turnout," *Journal of Politics* 70 (2008), 579–94.

17 Richard Dawkins, *The Selfish Gene*, rev. ed. (Oxford: Oxford University Press, 1989), 47.

18 Ibid., 234.

19 Jane Goodall, *Through a Window: My Thirty Years with the Chimpanzees of Gombe* (Boston: Houghton Mifflin, 190), 98–111.

20 Robert David Sack, *Human Territoriality: Its Theory and History* (Cambridge: Cambridge University Press, 1986), 23.

21 en.wikipedia.org/wiki/Property_is_theft!

22 Epstein, *Supreme Neglect*, 20.

23 Thráinn Eggertsson," Open Access versus Common Property," in Terry L. Anderson and Fred S. McChesney, eds, *Property Rights: Cooperation, Conflict, and Law* (Princeton: Princeton University Press, 2003), 74.

24 Ibid.

25 Hayek's earliest and still famous statement of this principle was his article "The Use of Knowledge in Society," *American Economic Review,* 35 (1945), 519–30; for an update, see Friedrich Hayek, *Law, Legislation and Liberty* (Chicago: University of Chicago Press, 1973), vol. 1, 49.

26 Eggertsson, "Open Access versus Common Property," 85.

27 Terry L. Anderson and Peter J. Hill, "The Evolution of Property Rights," in Anderson and McChesney, *Property Rights*, 129.

28 Garrett Hardin, "The Tragedy of the Commons," *Science* 162 (1968), 1243–8.

29 Eggertsson, "Open Access versus Common Property," 75.

30 John Locke, *The Second Treatise of Government* (Indianapolis: Bobbs-Merrill, [1690] 1952), chapter 5, s. 33.

31 Harold Demsetz, "Toward a Theory of Property Rights," *American Economic* Review 57 (1968), 347–8.

32 Ibid., 350.

33 Richard Pipes, *Property and Freedom* (New York: Alfred A. Knopf, 1999), 81.

34 Fred S. McChesney, "Government as Definer of Property Rights: Tragedy Exiting the Commons?" in Anderson and McChesney, *Property Rights*, 230.

35 Jared Diamond, *Guns, Germs, and Steel: The Fates of Human Societies* (New York: W.W. Norton, 1997), 265–92.

36 Declaration of the Rights of Man and of the Citizen (1789), s. 17, printed in J. Salwyn Schapiro, *Liberalism: Its Meaning and History* (New York: Van Nostrand Reinhold, 1958), 130.

37 Fifth Amendment to the Constitution of the United States of America (1789), quoted in Epstein, *Supreme Neglect*, xi.

38 Niall Ferguson, *The Ascent of Money: A Financial History of the World* (New York: Penguin Press, 2008).

39 William Louis Coutlée, *A Manual of the Law of Registration of Titles to Real Estate in Manitoba and the North-West Territories* (Toronto: Carswell, 1890), iv.

40 *Delgamuukw v. British Columbia*, [1997] 3 S.C.R. 1010.

41 Constitution Act, 1867, s. 91(24).

42 Constitution Act, 1867, s. 109.

43 *St Catherine's Milling and Lumber Company v. the Queen* [1888], 14 A.C. 54.

44 Indian Act, s. 20.

CHAPTER TWO

1 Quoted in Richard Pipes, *Property and Freedom: The Story of How through the Centuries Private Ownership Has Promoted Liberty and the Rule of Law* (New York: Alfred A. Knopf, 1999), 19–20.

2 Quoted in Leland Donald, "Liberty, Equality, Fraternity: Was the Indian Really Egalitarian?" in James A. Clifton, ed., *The Invented Indian: Cultural Fictions and Government Policies* (New Brunswick, NJ: Transaction Publishers, 1990), 145.

3 Matt Ridley, *The Origins of Virtue: Human Instincts and the Evolution of Cooperation* (Harmondsworth: Penguin, 1996), 213.

4 Paul S. Wilson, "What Chief Seattle Said," *Environmental Law* 22 (1992), 1452.

5 Ibid., 1458.

6 Quoted in Bruce L. Benson, "Property Rights and the Buffalo Economy," in Terry L. Anderson, Bruce L. Benson, and Thomas E. Flanagan, eds, *Self-Determination: The Other Path for Native Americans* (Stanford: Stanford University Press, 2006), 31.

7 Quoted in ibid., 32.

8 Jerome A. Offner, *Law and Politics in Aztec Texcoco* (Cambridge: Cambridge University Press, 1983), 135. See also Francisco Ávalos, "An Overview of the Legal System of the Aztec Empire," *Law Library Journal* 86 (1994), 259–76.

9 Craig S. Galbraith, Carlos L. Rodriguez, and Curt H. Stiles, "False Myths and Indigenous Entrepreneurial Strategies," in Anderson, Benson, and Flanagan, *Self-Determination*, 8.

10 Ralph M. Linton, "Land Tenure in Aboriginal America," in Oliver LaFarge, ed., *The Changing Indian* (Norman: University of Oklahoma Press, 1942), 42–54.

11 Leonard Carlson, "Learning to Farm: Indian Land Tenure and Farming before the Dawes Act," in Anderson, *Property Rights and Indian Economies*, 69.

12 Bruce G. Trigger, *The Huron Farmers of the North*, 2nd ed. (Fort Worth: Holt, Rinehart, and Winston, 1990), 30–2.

13 Duane Champagne, "Economic Culture, Institutional Order, and Sustained Market Enterprise: Comparisons of Historical and Contemporary American Indian Cases," in Anderson, *Property Rights and Indian Economies*, 198–9.

14 Carlson, "Learning to Farm," 71.

15 Terry L. Anderson, *Sovereign Nations or Reservations? An Economic History of American Indians* (San Francisco: Pacific Research Institute for Public Policy, 1995), 35.

16 Leland Donald, *Aboriginal Slavery on the Northwest Coast of North America* (Berkeley: University of California Press, 1997), 26.

17 Dianne Newell, *Tangled Webs of History: Indians and the Law in Canada's Pacific Coast Fisheries* (Toronto: University of Toronto Press, 1993), 41–2.

18 Diane Cragg, "The Nisga'a Land Title System – Why a Torrens Title System Works for a Canadian First Nation," presented to the 150th Anniversary of the Torrens Title System Land Administration Conference, Adelaide, South Australia, 30 October 2008.

19 Bruce Johnsen, "A Culturally Correct Proposal to Privatize the British Columbia Salmon Fishery," in Anderson, Benson, and Flanagan, *Self-Determination*, 101.

20 Ibid., 117.

21 Carl Zimmer, "Conservation Biology: Rapid Evolution Can Foil Even the Best-Laid Plans," *Science*, vol. 300, no. 5621 (9 May 2003), 895 (www.sciencemag.org/cgi/content/full/300/5621/895).

22 Bruce L. Benson, "Customary Indian Law: Two Case Studies," in Anderson, *Property Rights and Indian Economies*, 29.

23 Donald, *Aboriginal Slavery*.

24 Catherine Bell and Michael Asch, "Challenging Assumptions: The Impact of Precedent in Aboriginal Rights Litigation," in Michael Asch, ed., *Aboriginal and Treaty Rights in Canada: Essays on Law, Equality, and Respect for Difference* (Vancouver: UBC Press, 1997), 69.

25 Benson, "Customary Indian Law," 34.

26 Benson, "Property Rights and the Buffalo Economy," 44–5.
27 Leonard Carlson, "Learning to Farm," 75.
28 Sarah Carter, *Lost Harvests: Prairie Indian Reserve Farmers and Government Policy* (Montreal and Kingston: McGill-Queen's University Press, 1990), 104.
29 Leonard Carlson, "Learning to Farm," 73; Thomas Flanagan and Christopher Alcantara, "Customary Land Rights on Canadian Indian Reserves," in Anderson, Benson, and Flanagan, *Self-Determination,* 138–9.
30 Robert J. Smith, "Resolving the Tragedy of the Commons by Creating Private Property Rights in Wildlife," *The Cato Journal* 1 (1981), 452.
31 Quoted in Ann M. Carlos and Frank D. Lewis, "Native American Property Rights in the Hudson Bay Region: A Case Study of the Eighteenth-Century Cree," in Anderson, Benson, and Flanagan, *Self-Determination,* 81.
32 Ibid.
33 Peter J. Usher, "Property as the Basis of Inuit Hunting Rights," in Anderson, *Property Rights and Indian Economies,* 46.
34 Ibid., 48.

CHAPTER THREE

1 D.S. Otis, *The Dawes Act and the Allotment of Indian Lands* (Norman: University of Oklahoma Press, 1973 [1934]), 3.
2 Leonard Carlson, "Learning to Farm: Indian Land Tenure and Farming before the Dawes Act," in Terry L. Anderson, ed., *Property Rights and Indian Economies* (Lanham, MD: Rowman & Littlefield, 1991), 67–83.
3 David M. Halford, "The Subversion of the Indian Land Allotment System, 1887–1934," *The Indian Historian* 8 (Spring 1975), 13.
4 Tom Flanagan, "Across the Medicine Line," in Rudyard Griffiths, ed., *American Myths: What Canadians Think They Know about the United States* (Toronto: Key Porter, 2008), 105–18.
5 J.P. Kinney, *A Continent Lost – A Civilization Won: Indian Land Tenure in America* (New York: Octagon Books, 1975, first published 1937), appendix.
6 Otis, *Dawes Act,* 41.
7 Carlson, *Indians, Bureaucrats, and Land,* 79.
8 Otis, *Dawes Act,* 5.
9 Ibid., 38.
10 Ibid., 18.
11 Leonard Carlson to Tom Flanagan, email, 3 June 2008.

12 Leonard A. Carlson, *Indians, Bureaucrats, and Land: The Dawes Act and the Decline of Indian Farming* (Westport, CT: Greenwood Press, 1981), 10. The Act is reprinted in Otis, *Dawes Act*, 177–84.

13 Terry L. Anderson, *Sovereign Nations or Reservations? An Economic History of American Indians* (San Francisco: Pacific Research Institute for Public Policy, 1995), 165.

14 Jennifer Roback, "Exchange, Sovereignty, and Indian-Anglo Relations," in Anderson, *Property Rights and Indian Economies,* 23.

15 Carlson, *Indians, Bureaucrats, and Land,* 48.

16 Emily Greenwald, *Reconfiguring the Reservation: The Nez Perces, Jicarilla Apaches, and the Dawes Act* (Albuquerque: University of New Mexico Press, 2002), 34; Kinney, *A Continent Lost – A Civilization Won,* appendix.

17 Greenwald, *Reconfiguring the Reservation,* 32.

18 Terry L. Anderson and Dean Lueck, "Agricultural Development and Land Tenure in Indian Country," in Anderson, ed., *Property Rights and Indian Economies,* 148.

19 Carlson, *Indians, Bureaucrats, and Land,* 12; Act of 1891, s. 3, in Otis, *Dawes Act,* 179.

20 Otis, *Dawes Act,* 139.

21 Halford, "Subversion of the Indian Land Allotment System," 14.

22 US Department of the Interior, 1981, quoted in Anderson, *Sovereign Nations or Reservations,* 122–3.

23 Halford, "Subversion of the Indian Land Allotment System," 14.

24 Kinney, *A Continent Lost – A Civilization Won,* appendix.

25 Ibid., 158.

26 Anderson and Lueck, "Agricultural Development and Land Tenure in Indian Country," 149.

27 Terry L. Anderson, *Sovereign Nations or Reservations?* 112.

28 Anderson and Lueck, "Agricultural Development and Land Tenure in Indian Country."

29 Kenneth R. Philp, *John Collier's Crusade for Indian Reform, 1920–1954* (Tucson: University of Arizona Press, 1977), 7–8.

30 E.A. Schwartz, "Red Atlantis Revisited: Community and Culture in the Writings of John Collier," *The American Indian Quarterly* 18 (1994), 507.

31 John Collier, *The Indians of the Americas* (New York: W.W. Norton, 1947), 15–16.

32 Philp, *Collier's Crusade,* 142.

33 Ibid., 153.

34 Ibid., 159.
35 Carlson, *Indians, Bureaucrats, and Land,* 18.
36 Ibid., 115–62.
37 Fred S. McChesney, "Government as Definer of Property Rights: Indian Lands, Ethnic Externalities, and Bureaucratic Budgets," in Anderson, *Property Rights and Indian Economies,* 134.
38 Diane Cragg, "The Nisga'a Land Title System."

CHAPTER FOUR

1 Brian E. Titley, *Narrow Vision: Duncan Campbell Scott and the Administration of Indian Affairs in Canada* (Vancouver: UBC Press, 1986), 1.
2 John L. Tobias, "Protection, Civilization, Assimilation: An Outline History of Canada's Indian Policy," in Ian A.L. Getty and Antoine S. Lussier, eds, *As Long as the Sun Shines and Water Flows.* (Vancouver: UBC Press, 1983), 40.
3 William B. Henderson, *Canada's Indian Reserves: Pre-Confederation* (Ottawa: DIAND, 1980), 2.
4 J.R. Miller, *Skyscrapers Hide the Heavens* (Toronto: University of Toronto Press, 2000), 85–6.
5 Henderson, *Canada's Indian Reserves: Pre-Confederation,* 2–3.
6 Olive Patricia Dickason, *Canada's First Nations: A History of Founding Peoples from Earliest Times* (Toronto: Oxford University Press, 1999), 160–1.
7 Christopher Alcantara, "Individual Property Rights on Canadian Indian Reserves: The Historical Emergence and Jurisprudence of Certificates of Possession," *The Canadian Journal of Native Studies* 23 (2003), 395; Hamar Foster, "Canada: 'Indian Administration' from the Royal Proclamation of 1763 to Constitutionally Entrenched Aboriginal Rights," in Paul Havemann, ed., *Indigenous Peoples' Rights in Australia, Canada, and New Zealand.* (New York: Oxford University Press, 1999); Miller, *Skyscrapers Hide the Heavens,* 86–8; The Royal Commission on Aboriginal Peoples, *Report of the Royal Commission on Aboriginal Peoples* (Ottawa: Canada Communications Group Publishing, 1996), 116.
8 *St Catherine's Milling and Lumber Company v. the Queen* [1888], 14 A.C., 54.
9 Peter A. Cumming and Neil H. Mickenberg, *Native Rights in Canada,* 2nd ed. (Toronto: General Publishing, 1971), 30.
10 Carl Benn, *The Iroquois in the War of 1812* (Toronto: University of Toronto Press, 1998).

11 Tobias, "Protection, Civilization, Assimilation," 40; Titley, *Narrow Vision*, 2–3.
12 John Locke, *Second Treatise of Government* (Indianapolis: Hackett Publishing Company, 1989), paragraph 27.
13 Locke, *Second Treatise*, paragraph 50.
14 Alice Kehoe, Public Lecture, Rozsa Centre, University of Calgary, 17 October 2002.
15 Locke, *Second Treatise*, paragraph 28.
16 Ibid., paragraph 34.
17 Flanagan, *First Nations? Second Thoughts*, 41.
18 Sarah Carter, *Lost Harvests: Prairie Indian Reserve Farmers and Government Policy*. (Montreal: McGill-Queen's University Press, 1990), 17.
19 Carter, *Lost Harvests*, 17.
20 Dickason, *Canada's First Nations*, 199; John L. Tobias, "Protection, Civilization, Assimilation," 40; Carter, *Lost Harvests*,17.
21 Tobias, "Protection, Civilization, Assimilation," 41.
22 Dickason, *Canada's First Nations*, 222.
23 Miller, *Skyscrapers Hide the Heavens*, 132–4.
24 *Report of the Royal Commission on Aboriginal Peoples*, 268.
25 Ibid.; William B. Henderson, *Canada's Indian Reserves: Pre-Confederation*. (Ottawa: DIAND, 1980), 12.
26 Dickason, *Canada's First Nations*, 222.
27 Tobias, "Protection, Civilization, Assimilation," 41–2.
28 *Report of the Royal Commission on Aboriginal Peoples*, 269.
29 John S. Milloy, "The Early Indian Acts: Developmental Strategy and Constitutional Change," in Getty and Lussier, eds, *As Long as the Sun Shines and Water Flows*, 58.
30 Carmen Place, *An Historical Review of the Reserve Allotment System* (Ottawa: Department of Justice, 1981), 3.
31 John E. Hall, Maureen Cowin, and John F. Rowan, *The Report of the Commission of Inquiry Concerning Certain Matters Associated with the Westbank Indian Band* (Ottawa: DIAND, 1988), 451; John L. Tobias, "Protection, Civilization, Assimilation," 42.
32 Hall, Cowin, and Rowan, *Westbank Report*, 452.
33 Ibid., 46–8.
34 Shin Imai, *The 1998 Annotated Indian Act* (Toronto: Carswell Thomson Professional Publishing, 1997), 189.
35 Hall, Cowin, and Rowan, *Westbank Report*, 481; Miller, *Skyscrapers Hide the Heavens*.
36 Canadian Parliament, *House of Commons Debates*, First Parliament, Second Session (Ottawa, 1869), 83.

37 Ibid.
38 Canadian Parliament, *House of Commons Debates*, Third Parliament, Third Session, vol. 2 (Ottawa, 1876), 751.
39 Ibid., 1038.
40 Ibid.
41 Canadian Parliament, *House of Commons Debates* (Ottawa: 1873), A1879.
42 Deanna Christensen, *Ahtahkakoop: The Epic Account of a Plains Cree Head Chief, His People, and Their Struggle for Survival, 1816–1896*. (Shell Lake, SK: Ahtahkakoop Publishing, 2000), 349.
43 DIAND, *Indian Acts and Amendments, 1868–1950* (Ottawa: Treaties and Historical Research Centre, 1981), 16.
44 Ibid., 27.
45 Ibid.; Place, *Historical Review of the Reserve Allotment System*, 6.
46 Hall, Cowin, and Rowan, *Westbank Report*, 483.
47 *Report of the Royal Commission on Aboriginal Peoples*, 283.
48 Canadian Parliament, *House of Commons Debates,* 21st Parliament, Fourth Session, vol. 2, vol. 4. (Ottawa: 1951), 1353, 1355.
49 Ibid., 1355.
50 Ibid., 1356.
51 Christopher Alcantara, "Reduce Transaction Costs? Yes. Strengthen Property Rights? Maybe: The First Nations Land Management Act and Economic Development on Canadian Indian Reserves," *Public Choice* 132 (2007), 424.
52 Tom Flanagan and Christopher Alcantara, "Customary Land Rights on Canadian Indian Reserves," in Terry Anderson, Bruce Benson, and Tom Flanagan, eds, *Self-Determination: The Other Path for Native Americans* (Stanford University Press, 2006).
53 Christopher Alcantara, "Indian Women and the Division of Matrimonial Real Property on Canadian Indian Reserves," *Canadian Journal of Women and the Law* 18 (2006).
54 Thomas Isaac, "*First Nations Land Management Act* and Third Party Interests," *Alberta Law Review* 42 (2005), 1049–50.

CHAPTER FIVE

1 *Johnstone v. Mistawasis* (2003), paragraph 24.
2 Ibid., paragraph 45.
3 Claudia Notzke, *Indian Reserves in Canada: Development Programs of the Stoney and Peigan Reserves in Alberta.* (Marburg/Lahn: Im Selbstverlag des Geographischen Instituts der Universität Marburg, 1985), 48–9.

4 Akihiko Nemoto, "Dynamics of Aboriginal Land Use Institutions: The Rise and Fall of Community Control over Reserve Systems in the Lil'Wat Nation, Canada," *Canadian Journal of Native Studies* 22 (2002), 214.

5 Telephone interview with Alan Ray, treaty and lands manager at Sandy Lake First Nation, 10 June 2002; interview with Emil Owlchild, land manager at Siksika First Nation, Alberta, 1 October 2002; interview with Lands Committee, Piikani Land Management Department, Alberta, 26 September 2002; interview with Elliot Fox, director of land management with Blood Tribe, Alberta, 16 October 2002; interview with Rhonda Sullivan, land administrator at Cowichan Tribes, BC, 16 April 2002.

6 See also Nemoto, "Dynamics of Aboriginal Land Use Institutions," 216.

7 Interview with Emil Owlchild, land manager at Siksika First Nation, Alberta, 1 October 2002; interview with Lands Committee, Piikani Land Management Department, Alberta, 26 September 2002; interview with Elliot Fox, director of land management with Blood Tribe, Alberta, 16 October 2002; interview with Rhonda Sullivan, land administrator at Cowichan Tribes, BC, 16 April 2002.

8 Cowichan Tribes, "Certificates of Possession," www.cowichantribes.com, accessed 12 August 2008.

9 Ibid.

10 Interview with Rhonda Sullivan, land administrator at Cowichan Tribes, BC, 16 April 2002; telephone interview with Alan Ray, treaty and lands manager at Sandy Lake First Nation, 10 June 2002.

11 Interview with Emil Owlchild, land manager at Siksika First Nation, Alberta, 1 October 2002; interview with Lands Committee, Piikani Land Management Department, Alberta, 26 September 2002; interview with Elliot Fox, director of land management with Blood Tribe, Alberta, 16 October 2002.

12 Interview with Emil Owlchild, land manager at Siksika First Nation, Alberta, 1 October 2002; interview with Lands Committee, Piikani Land Management Department, Alberta, 26 September 2002; interview with Elliot Fox, director of land management with Blood Tribe, Alberta, 16 October 2002.

13 Telephone interview with Alan Ray, treaty and lands manager at Sandy Lake First Nation, 10 June 2002.

14 Interview with Lands Committee, Piikani Land Management Department, Alberta, 26 September 2002.

15 Interview with Elliot Fox, director of land management with Blood Tribe, Alberta, 16 October 2002; see also the Blood Tribe website at www.bloodtribe.org, accessed 12 August 2008.

16 Interview with Abraham Joe and Angus Joe, elders and members of the Cowichan Tribes Lands Investigation Committee, BC, 17 April 2002.

17 Interview with Emil Owlchild, land manager at Siksika First Nation, Alberta, 1 October 2002.

18 Tom Flanagan and Christopher Alcantara, "Individual Property Rights on Canadian Indian Reserves: A Review of the Jurisprudence," *Alberta Law Review* 42 (2005), 1019–46.

19 2004 NBQB 160, paragraph 47 states: "From my review of the Indian Act and several decisions, some of which are referred to above, it is my conclusion that the respondents are not in lawful possession of the property in question ... They at no time ever received a valid allotment from the Band Council, they do not have any consent of the Minister and they do not have a transfer of possession from a person lawfully in possession. The respondents do not comply with the requirements of the Indian Act to substantiate a finding that they have lawful possession of the property in question." As such, according to paragraph 48, "The Band through its Council has the right to possession of the property occupied by the respondents. Technically the respondents are trespassers even though they have occupied the property in question with the apparent acquiescence of the Band or its Council since 1998."

20 *Derrickson v. Kennedy* 2006 BCCA 356 at paragraph 10.

21 *Chief Chris Tom v. Morris* 2007 BCSC 1012 at paragraphs 15–16, 21.

22 *Paul v. Paul* 2008 NSSC 124, paragraph 10 states "Neither party was able to establish an ownership interest in the lands on which the matrimonial home and variety store are located. In fact, these lands have been identified as common Band lands. Neither party had a certificate of possession, which entitled them to occupy the lands for any specific period of time ... The question of possession of common Band lands is governed by the provisions of the Indian Act. The Eskasoni Band Council is the authority which determines possession/use of these lands. This Court finds that it has no jurisdiction ... to order exclusive use of the subject lands as requested by the husband."

23 *Maracle v. Grant* 2008 (Ontario Superior Court) at paragraphs 8–9.

24 *Nicola Band et al. v. Trans-Can Displays et al.* (2000), paragraph 151.

25 Ibid., paragraph 162.

26 *Williams et al. v. Briggs* (2001), paragraph 12.

27 Interview with Lands Committee, Piikani Land Management Department, Alberta, 26 September 2002.

28 Interview with Elliot Fox, director of land management with Blood Tribe, Alberta, 16 October 2002; interview with Calvin Cross Child, technical advisor to Blood Tribe, Alberta, 16 October 2002.

29 See, for example, *Gladstone v. Blood Band of Indians* 2004 FC 856 (Manitoba).

30 Interview with Elliot Fox, director of land management with Blood Tribe, Alberta, 16 October 2002.

31 Darrel Crow Shoe, housing manager at Piikani First Nation, Alberta, 16 October 2002.

32 Interview with Darcie Royal, housing administrator at Siksika First Nation, Alberta, 1 October 2002; Siksika Chief and Council, *Siksika Housing Policy Manual,* Gleichen Alberta, 2002; interview with Emil Owlchild, Land Manager at Siksika First Nation, Alberta, 1 October 2002.

33 Interview with Rhonda Sullivan, land administrator at Cowichan Tribes, BC, 16 April 2002; Larry George, land and governance manager at Cowichan Tribes, BC, 17 April 2002.

34 Cowichan Tribes, "On-Reserve Housing," www.cowichantribes.com, accessed 12 August 2008.

35 Darrel Crow Shoe, Housing Manager at Piikani First Nation, Alberta, 16 October 2002.

36 Interview with Lac La Ronge Indian Band Government Official Kevin MacLeod, Saskatchewan, 15 July 2005.

37 Interview with Emil Owlchild, land manager at Siksika First Nation, Alberta, 1 October 2002; interview with Fran Wilgress, land manager and chair of the Land Management Committee at Cowichan Tribes, BC, 16 April 2002.

38 Telephone interview with Alan Ray, treaty and lands manager at Sandy Lake First Nation, 10 June 2002; interview with Emil Owlchild, land manager at Siksika First Nation, Alberta, 1 October 2002; interview with Lands Committee, Piikani Land Management Department, Alberta, 26 September 2002; interview with Elliot Fox, director of land management with Blood Tribe, Alberta, 16 October 2002.

39 *Nicola Band et al. v. Trans-Can Displays et al.,* 2000.

40 Interview with Lands Committee, Piikani Land Management Department, Alberta, 26 September 2002.

41 Interview with Elliot Fox, director of land management with Blood Tribe, Alberta, 16 October 2002; interview with Emil Owlchild, land manager at Siksika First Nation, Alberta, 1 October 2002.

42 See Bruce Benson, "Customary Indian Law: Two Case Studies," in Terry Anderson, ed., *Property Rights and Indian Economies* (Lanham, MD: Rowman and Littlefield, 1992); Harold Hickerson, *Land Tenure of the Rainy Lake Chippewa at the Beginning of the 19th Century* (Washington, DC: Smithsonian Press, 1967); Bruce Trigger, *The Huron Farmers of the North* (Forth Worth, TX: Holt, Rinehart, and Winston, 1990); Leland

Donald, *Aboriginal Slavery on the Northwest Coast of North America* (Berkeley: University of California Press, 1997); Cole Harris, *Making Native Space: Colonialism, Resistance, and Reserves in British Columbia* (Vancouver: UBC Press, 2002).

43 Telephone interview with Alan Ray, treaty and lands manager at Sandy Lake First Nation, 10 June 2002; interview with Emil Owlchild, land manager at Siksika First Nation, Alberta, 1 October 2002; interview with Lands Committee, Piikani Land Management Department, Alberta, 26 September 2002; interview with Elliot Fox, director of land management with Blood Tribe, Alberta, 16 October 2002.

44 Christopher Alcantara, "Certificates of Possession and First Nations Housing: A Case Study of the Six Nations Housing Program," *Canadian Journal of Law and Society* 20 (2005), 183–205.

45 Telephone interview with Alan Ray, treaty and lands manager at Sandy Lake First Nation, 10 June 2002; interview with Lands Committee, Piikani Land Management Department, Alberta, 26 September 2002; interview with Elliot Fox, director of land management with Blood Tribe, Alberta, 16 October 2002.

46 Interview with Elliot Fox, director of land management with Blood Tribe, Alberta, 16 October 2002.

47 Interview with Emil Owlchild, land manager at Siksika First Nation, Alberta, 1 October 2002; interview with Lands Committee, Piikani Land Management Department, Alberta, 26 September 2002.

48 Interview with Rhonda Sullivan, land administrator at Cowichan Tribes, BC, 16 April 2002.

49 Interview with Darrel Crow Shoe, housing manager at Piikani First Nation, Alberta, 16 October 2002.

50 Larry George, land and governance manager at Cowichan Tribes, BC, 17 April 2002.

51 Interview with Winston Day Chief, director of housing at Blood Tribe, Alberta, 16 October 2002.

52 Interview with Marilyn Little Chief, financial adjuster at Siksika First Nation, Alberta, 1 October 2002.

53 Interview with Darrel Crow Shoe, housing manager at Piikani First Nation, Alberta, 16 October 2002.

54 Canadian Broadcasting Corporation, "Rent Arrears Prompt First Nation to Take Own Members to Court," *CBC News Online*, 13 July 2005, www.north.cbc.ca.

55 Interview with Darrel Crow Shoe, housing manager at Piikani First Nation, Alberta, 16 October 2002.

56 Interview with Winston Day Chief, director of housing at Blood Tribe, Alberta, 16 October 2002; interview with Elliot Fox, director of land management with Blood Tribe, Alberta, 16 October 2002; interview with Calvin Cross Child, technical advisor to Blood Tribe, Alberta, 16 October 2002.

57 Interview with Emil Owlchild, land manager at Siksika First Nation, Alberta, 1 October 2002; interview with Matthew Ayoungman, rental coordinator at Siksika First Nation, Alberta, 1 October 2002; interview with Ferris Smith, service manager at Siksika First Nation, Alberta, 1 October 2002.

CHAPTER SIX

1 Canada, Department of Indian Affairs, "Creating Individual Interest," Directive 03-02 in *Land Management Manual*, vol. 1 (Ottawa: 1997), 7–8.

2 See *Songhees Indian Band v. Canada* (Minister of Indian Affairs and Northern Development) 2006 F.C. 1009.

3 Interview with Registrar Josée Guest and Acting Registrar Denis Gros-Louis (1 May 2001), Hull, Indian and Northern Affairs Canada. It would be interesting to know the total acreage of reserve land granted under CPs, but the Indian land registry in Ottawa cannot produce that information.

4 James I. Reynolds, *Acting for the "Purchaser" in a Conveyance of Reserve Lands* (Vancouver: The Continuing Legal Education Society of British Columbia, 2002), www.cle.bc.ca.

5 Section 2 of the *Indian Act* R.S.C. 1985, c. I-5 defines a reserve as "a tract of land, the legal title to which is vested in Her Majesty, that has been set apart by Her Majesty for the use and benefit of a band." See also Department of Indian Affairs and Northern Development, Directive 02-01 in *Land Management Manual,* vol. 1 (Ottawa: Department of Indian Affairs and Northern Development, 1995), 1; and *Eel Ground Band v. Augustine*, [2004] N.B.J. No. 161 (New Brunswick Queen's Bench).

6 Tom Flanagan and Christopher Alcantara, "Individual Property Rights on Canadian Indian Reserves: A Review of the Jurisprudence," *Alberta Law Review* 42 (2005), 1026–30.

7 See Christopher Alcantara, "Indian Women and the Division of Matrimonial Real Property on Canadian Indian Reserves" *Canadian Journal of Women and the Law* 18 (2006), 513–33.

8 Carmen Place, *An Historical Review of the Reserve Allotment System* (Ottawa: Department of Justice, 1981), 11.

9   Interview with Cindy Smyth, Financial Services Officer, Bank of Montreal on Six Nations, ON, 30 June 2002.

10 [2000] F.C.J. No. 470 Fed. T.D. at paragraphs 1 and 14.

11 [1994] 3 C.N.L.R. 199.

12 See also *Pronovost v. Minister of Indian and Northern Affairs* (1986), 1 C.N.L.R. 56; *Boyer v. Canada* (1986), 4 C.N.L.R. 60; *Batchewana First Nation v. Corbiere* [2000, Docket: T-1234-98], decisions.fct-cf.ca. On the right of CP holders to transfer their CP, see *Williams v. Briggs* [2001] B.C.S.C. 78; *Simpson v. Ziprick* (1995), 126 D.L.R. (4th) 754; *Simpson v. Ryan* (1996), 106 F.T.R. 158; *Cooper v. Tsartlip Indian Band* [1997], 1 C.N.L.R. 45; *Batchewana First Nation v. Corbiere*, [2000] Docket: T-1234-98, decisions.fct-cf.ca. The courts have enforced wills involving CPs: *Johnson v. Pelkey* (1997), 36 B.C.L.R. (3d) 40; *Dale v. Paul*, [2000] AJ No. 751 (Alta. Master) and the right of a CP holder to engage in a lease: *Mintuck v. Valley River Band No. 63A*, [1977] 1 C.N.L.R. 12 (Man. C.A.); *Boyer v. Canada*, [1986] 4 C.N.L.R. 53; *Tsartlip Indian Band v. Canada* (1999), 181 D.L.R. (4th) 730.

13 Six Nations, *Outstanding Financial and Land Issues & Summary of Six Nations Claims*, Six Nations, ON, January 2002; interview with Janice Martin, Six Nations lands/membership manager, and Toni Martin, Six Nations GIS technician, ON, 27 May 2002.

14 Interview with Janice Martin, Six Nations lands/membership manager, and Toni Martin, Six Nations GIS technician, ON, 27 May 2002.

15 Six Nations, "Six Nations of the Grand River Band Membership Statistics" May 2008, www.sixnations.ca, accessed 12 August 2008.

16 Interview with Shelda Johnson, Six Nations housing manager, ON, 5 June 2002.

17 Interview with Janice Martin, Six Nations lands/membership manager, and Toni Martin, Six Nations GIS technician, ON, 27 May 2002.

18 Interview with Department of Indian Affairs District Office Lands Officer Sherry Martin, Brantford, ON, 4 June 2004.

19 Interview with Janice Martin, Six Nations lands/membership manager, and Toni Martin, Six Nations GIS technician, ON, 27 May 2002.

20 Interview with Glenda Porter, Six Nations Band councillor and chair of the Lands/Membership Committee, ON, 17 June 2002.

21 Interview with David General, Six Nations Band councillor, ON, 4 June 2002.

22 Interview with Adam Carney, DIAND senior lands examiner for the east, QC, 15 July 2002.

23 Interview with Janice Martin, Six Nations lands/membership manager, and Toni Martin, Six Nations GIS technician, ON, 27 May 2002.

24 Interview with Glenda Porter, Six Nations Band councillor and chair of the Lands/Membership Committee, ON, 17 June 2002.

25 Interview with Janice Martin, Six Nations lands/membership manager, and Toni Martin, Six Nations GIS technician, ON, 27 May 2002.

26 Reynolds, *Acting for the "Purchaser" in a Conveyance of Reserve Lands*, www.cle.bc.ca.

27 Such as the Six Nations and the Mohawks of the Bay of Quinte.

28 The Mohawks of Kahnawake.

29 Westbank First Nation and Cowichan Tribes.

30 Email correspondence with Shelda Johnson, director of the Six Nations Housing Department, Six Nations, ON, 13 August 2008.

31 Christopher Alcantara, *Certificates of Possession: A Solution to the Aboriginal Housing Crisis on Canadian Indian Reserves* (MA thesis, University of Calgary, 2002), 90–102; interview with Janice Martin, Six Nations lands/membership manager and Toni Martin, Six Nations lands/membership GIS technician, 27 May 2002.

32 Interview with Elaine Lickers, community manager at the Royal Bank in Ohsweken, 26 June 2002; interview with Cindy Smyth, financial services officer at the Bank of Montreal in Ohsweken, 30 June 2002.

33 The reasons for low default and nonpayment rates at Six Nations are discussed in Christopher Alcantara, "Certificates of Possession and First Nation Housing: A Case Study of the Six Nations Housing Program," *Canadian Journal of Law and Society* 20 (2005), 183–205.

34 Email correspondence with Shelda Johnson, director of the Six Nations Housing Department, Six Nations, ON, 13 August 2008.

35 The Six Nations, Westbank First Nation, the Mohawks of the Bay of Quinte, and the Mohawks of Kahnawake.

36 Institutions include the Bank of Montreal, Royal Bank, and Caisse Populaire.

37 Cowichan Tribes.

38 The Six Nations, Westbank First Nation, and the Mohawks of Kahnawake.

39 Cowichan Tribes.

40 Interview with Westbank Land Manager Lynn Vanderburg and Westbank Housing Administrative Officer Bobbi Watts, 18 April 2002; interview with Jeneen Roberts, housing manager at Cowichan Tribes, 16 April 2002; interview with Shelda Johnson, Six Nations housing manager, 5 June 2002; Auditor General of Canada, *Chapter 6: Federal Government Support to First Nations – Housing on Reserves* (Report of the Auditor General of Canada to the House of Commons) (Ottawa: Office of the Auditor General of Canada, 2003), 5; Canadian Mortgage and Hous-

ing Corporation, *Revolving Loan Program Creates Model First Nations Community* (Ottawa: Canadian Mortgage and Housing Corporation, 2003), www.cmhc.ca.

41 According to Michael Rice, founder and past manager of the Caisse Populaire Kahnawake, "How it is different [from the Six Nations program] is that a section 24 transfer (of Indian Act) is not made to the Band Council but to a group of trustees (three out of a pool of five) for every transaction. These trustees are *pillars of the community* with no political affiliation. So no government body is involved and no band funds are encumbered. Also there are no limitations on the amounts as in Six Nations. The caisse uses Desjardins guidelines for both housing and commercial mortgage loans (25% and 40% down respectively)." Email correspondence, 30 November 2007.

42 Again, according to Michael Rice: "The trustees were recruited by myself (in my capacity as manager of the credit union) and the community economic development officer from the Band Council. We made a profile (and amongst things ensured there were absolutely no political affiliations), went out and approached persons who were acceptable to the board of the caisse. Given that these trustees act in the interest of both the caisse and community members, we informed the community what we were doing, posted their names in public places and asked if there were any objections and concerns to the names and process – there were none ... The trustees are not paid any remuneration (maybe taken out to supper once a year by the caisse). They truly act for the interests of both the members and the caisse. There have been no issues since the system has been used." Email correspondence, 30 November 2007.

43 L. Hammond-Ketilson and I. MacPherson, *A Report on Aboriginal Co-operatives in Canada: Current Situation and Potential for Growth* (Ottawa: Research and Analysis Directorate, Indian and Northern Affairs Canada, 2001), 42. Several years ago, a band member attempted to challenge the legality of the trustee system, but the challenge never made it to trial as the member chose to settle with the band.

44 This is because Indians and Indian lands fall under federal jurisdiction under s. 91(24) of the Constitution Act; see *Easterbrook v. R.,* [1931] S.C.R. 210; *Canada v. Cowichan Agricultural Society* [1950] Ex. C.R. 448.

45 [1970] 74 W.W.R. 380 (B.C.C.A.) [*Surrey*].

46 *Opetchesaht Indian Band v. Canada,* [1998] 1 C.N.L.R 134 at paragraph 57 (S.C.C.) [*Opetchesaht*]; *R. v. Devereux,* [1965] S.C.R. 567.

47 2002 FCT 16.

48 Ibid. at paragraph 3.

49 Ibid. at paragraphs 6–7.
50 [1978] 28 N.S.R. (2d) 268 (C.A.).
51 Ibid. at paragraph 6.
52 [1998] 1 C.N.L.R. 114 (B.C.S.C.).
53 Ibid. at paragraph 6.
54 Ibid. at paragraph 30.
55 This decision was upheld on appeal in *Mannpar Enterprises v. H.M.T.Q.* 1999 B.C.C.A. 239.
56 Interview with Lands Committee, Piikani First Nation, Alberta, 26 September 2002.
57 At Blood Tribe rent ranges from $20.00 to $42.50 an acre, with the band taking a 5 percent administrative fee. The council recently passed a BCR stating that all new permits would have a set rate of $40.00 an acre with a renewable term of three years; see interview with Elliot Fox, director of land management with Blood Tribe, Alberta, 16 October 2002.
58 Darrel Crow Shoe, housing manager at Piikani First Nation, Alberta, 16 October 2002.
59 Interview with Elliot Fox, director of land management with Blood Tribe, Alberta, 16 October 2002.
60 *Opetchesaht Indian Band v. Canada,* [1998] 1 C.N.L.R 134 at paragraph 53 (S.C.C.) [*Opetchesaht*].
61 See *Cowichan Tribes v. Canada (Attorney General)* 2007 BCSC 1918, at paragraphs 3–4.
62 Interview with Rhonda Sullivan, land administrator at Cowichan Tribes, BC, 16 April 2002.
63 Randall Akee, "Checkerboards and Coase: Transactions Costs and Efficiency in Land Markets," IZA Discussion Paper No. 2438, November 2006 (Institute for the Study of Labor), forthcoming in the *Journal of Law and Economics.*
64 [2000] 2 S.C.R. 634 [*Musqueam*].
65 Ibid. at paragraphs 27–8.
66 Ibid. at paragraph 31.
67 Ibid. at paragraph 35.
68 Ibid. at paragraphs 45–9. On taxation, see Jonathan R. Kesselman, "Aboriginal Taxation of Non-Aboriginal Residents: Representation, Discrimination, and Accountability in the Context of First Nations Autonomy" *Canadian Tax Journal* 48 (2000), 1525.
69 [2000] 2 S.C.R. 634 [*Musqueam*] at paragraph 53.
70 Ibid. at paragraph 28.
71 Interview of Lynn Vanderburg, Westbank First Nation land manager, BC, 18 April 2002.

72 [1998] F.C.J. No. 1032 (T.D.) (QL).
73 Ibid. at paragraph 69.
74 (2002), 226 F.T.R. 188.
75 Ibid. at paragraph 67.
76 *Morin v. Canada* 2005 F.C.A. 52.
77 Dr Tim Raybould, "Address," lecture presented to the Aboriginal Law in Canada 2001 Conference, December 2001.
78 Interview with Lynn Vanderburg, Westbank First Nation land manager, BC, 18 April 2002.
79 *Boyer v. Canada,* [1986] 4 C.N.L.R. 53 (F.C.A.).
80 Ibid., 57.
81 Ibid., 60–1.
82 (1999), 172 F.T.R. 160 [*Tsartlip*].
83 Ibid., at paragraph 7.
84 Ibid., at paragraph 56.

CHAPTER SEVEN

1 Thomas Isaac, "*First Nations Land Management Act* and Third Party Interests," *Alberta Law Review* 42 (1995), 1049–50.
2 First Nations Land Advisory Board, *Annual report 2003–2004.* (Kanata: First Nations Land Management Resource Centre), 32, www.fafnlm.com, accessed on 14 August 2008.
3 First Nations Land Advisory Board, "Signatories to the Framework Agreement," www.fafnlm.com, accessed 14 August 2008.
4 Isaac, "*First Nations Land Management Act* and Third Party Interests," 1049–50.
5 Tom Flanagan and Christopher Alcantara, "Individual Property Rights on Canadian Indian Reserves," *Queens Law Journal* 29 (2004), 514–17.
6 Tom Flanagan and Christopher Alcantara, "Customary Land Rights on Canadian Indian Reserves," in Terry Anderson, Bruce Benson, and Tom Flanagan, eds, *Self-determination: The Other Path for Native Americans* (Stanford: Stanford University Press, 2006), 152.
7 Community approval is not necessary for allocation of land to a band member. See section 13.3 of the Scugog Island Land Code.
8 Indian Affairs and Northern Canada. *Experiences in First Nations, Inuit and Northern Communities: Comprehensive Community Planning.* (Ottawa: INAC, 2004), 91.
9 Ibid., 92.
10 First Nations Land Advisory Board, *Annual Report 2006–2007* (Kanata: First Nations Land Management Resource Centre, 2007), 33–4.
11 INAC, *Experiences*, 91.

12 Ibid.
13 Ibid., 96.
14 First Nations Land Advisory Board, *Annual Report 2004–2005* (Kanata: First Nations Land Management Resource Centre, 2005), 18–19.
15 Ibid., 28–9.
16 Ibid., 29.
17 Ibid., 18.
18 Flanagan and Alcantara, "Individual Property Rights on Canadian Indian Reserves."
19 This is because customary rights, or traditional landholdings as the Muskoday First Nation calls them, are not recognized by the courts or by federal/provincial legislation. Only CPs can be registered in the Indian Land Registry.
20 INAC, *Experiences*, 97.
21 FNLAB, *Annual Report 2006–2007*, 20.
22 Ibid., 24.
23 Ibid., 30.
24 Ibid., 34.
25 Ibid., 26.

CHAPTER EIGHT

1 Arthur Mann, "The Economic Organization of the Ancient Maya," *The Americas* 30, No. 2 (1973), www.jstor.org; Charles Mann, *1491: New Revelations of the Americas before Columbus* (New York: Vintage Books, 2006); Hal Rothman, *Managing the Sacred and the Secular: An Administrative History of Pipestone National Monument* (US National Park Service, Midwest Region, 1992), www.nps.gov; Mirjam Hirch, *Trading across Time and Space: Culture along the North American "Grease Trails" from a European Perspective* (Kamloops, BC: Thompson Rivers University, Canadian Studies International Interdisciplinary Conference: Across Time & Space Visions of Canada from Abroad, 2003), www.cwis.org.
2 James Teit and Franz Boas, "The Jesup North Pacific Expedition: The Shuswap," *Memoirs of the American Museum of Natural History* (New York: Leiden, E.J. Brill Ltd, 1909), vol. 2, vii, digitallibrary.amnh.org; Edward S. Curtis, *The North American Indian,* vol. 10, 11, and 18 (2003), curtis.library.northwestern.edu.
3 Mann, *1491*.
4 Jim Holton, *Chinook Jargon: The Hidden Language of the Pacific Northwest* (California: Adisoft, 1999), www.adisoft-inc.com/chinookbook; Rena Grant, "Chinook Jargon," *International Journal of American Lin-*

guistics 11, no. 4 (1945); Jerome Offner, *Law and Politics in Aztec Tex-coco* (New York: Cambridge University Press, 1983); Richard Townsend, *The Aztecs* (London: Thames and Hudson, 1992).

5 Report of the Indian Act Consultation Meeting (Kelowna, BC, 12–16 November 1968), appendix C, 112.

6 Roger Backhouse, *The Ordinary Business of Life: A History of Economics from the Ancient World to the Twenty-First Century* (Princeton: Princeton University Press, 2002); Robert Cooter and Thomas Ulen, *Law & Economics* (New York: Addison-Wesley, 2000); Douglas Allen, "What Are Transaction Costs Anyway?" Carleton Industrial Economics Research Unit (Ottawa, Ontario: Carleton University, Department of Economics, 1988).

7 Jill Hobbs, *Markets in Metamorphosis: The Rise and Fall of Policy Institutions* (Saskatoon: University of Saskatchewan, Department of Agriculture Economics, 2004).

8 Hernando de Soto, *The Mystery of Capital: Why Capitalism Triumphs in the West and Fails Everywhere Else* (New York: Basic Books, 2000).

9 This refers to the provinces of BC (the first to implement a Torrens system), Alberta, Saskatchewan, Manitoba, Ontario, New Brunswick, and Nova Scotia.

10 Jodi Bruhn and John Graham, *In Praise of Taxation: The Link between Taxation and Good Governance in a First Nations Context* (Institute on Governance, 2008), www.iog.ca.

11 National Archives of Canada (NAC), RG10, volume 1975, reel C-11125, file: 5683; NAC, RG10, volume 2350, reel C-11206, file: 70,077.

12 NAC, RG10, volume 3144, reel C-11330, file: 341,680.

13 John Leslie and Ron Macguire, *The Historical Development of the Indian Act* (Indian and Northern Affairs Canada, Treaties and Historical Research Centre, 1979; 2nd ed.); Helen Buckley, *From Wooden Ploughs to Welfare: How Indian Policy Failed in the Prairie Provinces* (Montreal and Kingston: McGill-Queen's University Press, 1992); Royal Commission on Aboriginal Peoples, *Report of the Royal Commission on Aboriginal Peoples*, vol. 1, part 2 (1996), chapter 9, www.ainc-inac.gc.ca.

14 *Debates of the Senate of the Dominion of Canada*, Fifth Parliament, Second Session (1884); John Tobias, "Protection, Civilization, Assimilation: An Outline History of Canada's Indian Policy," in J.R. Miller, ed., *Sweet Promises: A Reader on Indian-White Relations in Canada* (Toronto: University of Toronto Press, 1991).

15 Tobias, "Protection, Civilization, Assimilation."

16 Sarah Carter, "Two Acres and a Cow: Peasant Farming for the Indians of the Northwest, 1889–1897," in Miller, *Sweet Promises*.

17 *Debates of the House of Commons*, Thirteenth Parliament, First Session (1918).

18 Ibid.

19 Bill C-115: An Act to amend the Indian Act and another Act in consequence thereof, received Royal Assent on 28 June 1988.

20 John Commons, *The Legal Foundations of Capitalism* (New York: McMillan, 1924); Nathan Rosenberg and L.E. Birdzell, *How the West Grew Rich: The Economic Transformation of the Industrial World* (New York: Basic Books, 1986); Douglass North, *Institutions, Transaction Costs and Productivity in the Long-Run* (St Louis: Washington University, 1993); Oliver Williamson, *The Economic Institutions of Capitalism* (New York: The Free Press, 1985).

21 James Womack et al., *The Machine that Changed the World* (New York: Rawson Associates, 1990).

22 The designation process is described at www.ainc-inac.gc.ca/on/nwshie_e.html.

23 Fiscal Realities Economists, *Expanding Commercial Activity on First Nation Lands: Lowering the Costs of Doing Business on Reserve* (Prepared for the Indian Taxation Advisory Board and Department of Indian Affairs Canada, 1999), www.fntc.ca.

24 Jason Calla, *An Evaluation of the Impediments to Land Use and Development on Capilano Indian Reserve Number 5* (submitted to the London School of Economics and Political Science in partial completion of the requirements for the MSC in Regional and Urban Planning Studies, 1998).

25 De Soto, *Mystery of Capital*; Harri Lorentz et al., "Emerging Distribution Systems in Central and Eastern Europe: Implications from Two Case Studies," *International Journal of Physical Distribution & Logistics Management* 37, no. 8 (2007); Emilio Bartezzaghi and Stefano Ronchi, "Internet Supporting the Procurement Process: Lessons from Four Case Studies," *Integrated Manufacturing Systems* 14, no. 8 (2003); Beverly Wagner et al., "Improving Supply Chain Relations: An Empirical Case Study," *Supply Chain Management: An International Journal* 7, no. 4 (2002).

26 Opportunity costs cannot be calculated by simply summing all the time incurred in the components of a deal that are listed above. That would assume that deals proceed in stages, with each one occurring upon completion of the previous one. In fact, many of these elements proceed concurrently or overlap substantially and do not follow a neat sequential order.

27 The other case studies were the Siksika Nation mall near Gleichen, Alberta, and a Sobeys on Uashat Mak Mak Uteman near Sept-Îles, Quebec.

28 Janna Fleming, *Walking in British Columbia: A Walking Guide* (Cicerone Press Limited, 2003); Ronald Ignace, *Oral Histories Are Our Iron Posts: Secwepemc Stories and Historical Consciousness* (Ph.D. Dissertation: Simon Fraser University, Department of Sociology and Anthropology, 2008); Teit and Boas, "The Jesup North Pacific Expedition."

29 Interview with an official from the Vancouver city planning department, February 1998.

30 In 2000, the Kamloops Indian Band purchased the Harper Ranch, which is about forty thousand acres, including associated grazing leases. They are currently in the process of adding this land to their reserve.

31 The developments at Siksika and Uashat Mak Mani Uteman took fifty-eight and fifty-seven months respectively, compared to comparable off-reserve developments that would have taken between thirteen and sixteen months based on interviews with developers and local government planning departments.

32 Charles Coffey, "The Cost of Doing Nothing: A Call to Action," *Journal of Aboriginal Economic Development* 1, no. 1 (1999); *Report of the Royal Commission on Aboriginal Peoples*, vol. 1, part 2 (1996), chapter 9; Fiscal Realities Economists, *Fiscal Costs of Poverty* (Presented to Indian and Northern Affairs Canada, 2004).

CHAPTER NINE

1 Union of British Columbia Indian Chiefs, 7th Annual General Assembly, DVD Format (1975).

2 For an excellent summary of this matter, see Robert Brown and Robert Strother, *The Taxation and Financing of Aboriginal Business in Canada* (Thomson Carswell, 1998), vol. 1, chapter 7.

3 House of Commons, Standing Committee on Aboriginal Affairs and Northern Development (AANO), Number 13, 38th Parliament, First Session (7 December 2004).

4 Department of Indian Affairs and Northern Development, Biography – Mr C.T. (Manny) Jules, (2006), www.ainc-inac.gc.ca.

5 First Nations Tax Commission, Frequently Asked Questions (2008), www.fntc.ca.

6 Interview with Tim Raybould of Westbank and Harold Calla of Squamish.

7 Interview with Ken Scopick, First Nations Tax Commission.

8 Ibid.

9 See www.tulo.ca.

10 Judgment of the Supreme Court of Canada, *Canadian Pacific Ltd. v. Matsqui Indian Band* (1995), csc.lexum.umontreal.ca/en/index.html.

11 Department of Indian Affairs and Northern Development, Fact Sheet – Taxation by First Nation Governments (2007), www.ainc-inac.gc.ca.

12 Ibid.

13 Department of Justice Canada, First Nation Goods and Services Tax Act (2003), laws.justice.gc.ca/en.

14 Department of Indian Affairs and Northern Development, Fact Sheet – Taxation by First Nation Governments (2007), www.ainc-inac.gc.ca; Canada Revenue Agency, Excise and GST/HST News (no. 67, winter 2008), www.cra-arc.gc.ca.

15 Jodi Bruhn and John Graham, *In Praise of Taxes: The Link between Taxation and Good Governance in a First Nations Context* (Institute on Governance, 2008) www.iog.ca.

16 Department of Indian Affairs and Northern Development, Frequently Asked Questions: First Nation Land Management Initiative (2004), www.ainc-inac.gc.ca.

17 Department of Justice Canada, First Nation Land Management Act (1999), laws.justice.gc.ca.

18 Paul Salembier et al., *Modern First Nations Legislation Annotated* (Ontario: LexisNexis, 2007).

19 Department of Justice Canada, First Nation Fiscal and Statistical Management Act (2005), laws.justice.gc.ca.

20 Parliament of Canada, Bill C-71: First Nations Commercial and Industrial Development Act (Legislative Summaries, 2006), www.parl.gc.ca.

21 Department of Indian Affairs and Northern Development, Fort McKay First Nation Oil Sands Project One Step Closer to Realization (2007), www.ainc-inac.gc.ca; Parliament of Canada, Debates of the Senate (Hansard) (38th Parliament, First Session, vol. 142, no. 100, November 2005), www.parl.gc.ca.

22 Department of Indian Affairs and Northern Development, First Nations Commercial and Industrial Development Act Introduced in the House of Commons (2005), www.ainc-inac.gc.cal.

23 Interview with Jason Calla, project manager, Squamish Nation FNCIDA project.

24 Martin Papillon, *Aboriginal Quality of Life under a Modern Treaty: Lessons from the Experience of the Cree Nation of Eeyou Istchee and the Inuit of Nunavik*, Institute for Research on Public Policy (2008), www.irpp.org.

25 Royal Commission on Aboriginal Peoples, *Report of the Royal Commission on Aboriginal Peoples* (1996), www.ainc-inac.gc.ca/ch/rcap.

26 Mary Hurley, *Nisga'a Final Agreement*, Parliament of Canada (1999), www.parl.gc.ca.

27 Agreements, Treaties and Negotiated Settlements Project, Westbank First Nation Self-Government Agreement 2003 (2003), www.atns.net.au.

28 Yukon First Nations Tourism Association, Land Claims and Self-Government Agreements (2008), www.yfnta.org.

29 The Council of Yukon Indians was created in 1973 to become the negotiating body for the Yukon Native Brotherhood (YNB). Subsequently in 1979 the YNB and the Yukon Association of Non-Status Indians merged and became known as the Council of Yukon Indians. In 1995, the Council of Yukon Indians transformed itself into the Council of Yukon First Nations. (Council of Yukon First Nations, Umbrella Final Agreement, 2008, www.cyfn.ca.)

30 Department of Indian Affairs and Northern Development, Council of Yukon First Nations Comprehensive Land Claim (1995), www.ainc-inac.gc.ca.

31 Ibid.

32 Department of Indian Affairs and Northern Development, Council of Yukon First Nations Comprehensive Land Claim (1995), www.ainc-inac.gc.ca.

33 Government of Yukon, *What's In a Final Agreement?* (2008), www.eco.gov.yk.ca.

34 Royal Commission on Aboriginal Peoples, Report of the Royal Commission on Aboriginal Peoples (1996), www.ainc-inac.gc.ca/ch/rcap.

35 Since the UFA, six other Yukon First Nations have completed Final Agreements. According to each individual final agreement, the six other signatories and their respective negotiation loan amounts are Kluane – $9.5m, Little Salmon/Carmacks – $7.9m, Trond'ek Hw'echin – $11.3m, Selkirk – $8.4m, Ta'an Kwach'an – $10.1m and Carcross Tagish – $14.9m. In total the loans equal $62.1m.

36 Melvin Smith, *Our Home or Native Land? What Governments' Aboriginal Policy Is Doing to Canada* (Manitoba: Friesen Printers, 1995).

37 Department of Finance Canada, A Working Paper on Indian Government Taxation (draft discussion paper, 1993), www.fin.gc.ca/fin-eng.html.

38 Report of the Auditor General of Canada to the House of Commons, Indian and Northern Affairs Canada – Transferring Federal Responsibilities to the North (2003), chapter 8, www.oag-bvg.gc.ca.

39 Gurston Dacks, "Implementing First Nations Self-Government in the Yukon: Lessons for Canada," *Canadian Journal of Political Science* 37:3 (2004), journals.cambridge.org.

40 Alaska Highway Aboriginal Pipeline Coalition, *Alaska Considers Canadian First Nations at TransCanada Hearings* (2008), www.ahapc.ca.

41 Department of Indian Affairs and Northern Development, Fact Sheet: The Nisga'a Treaty, www.ainc-inac.gc.ca.

42 Andrea McCallum, "Dispute Resolution Mechanisms in the Resolution of Comprehensive Aboriginal Claims: Power Imbalance between Aboriginal Claimants and Governments in Negotiation," *Murdoch University Electronic Journal of Law*, Australasian Legal Information Institute (1995), www.austlii.edu.au.

43 Ibid.

44 Department of Indian Affairs and Northern Development, Nisga'a Final Agreement and Background Information (1999), www.ainc-inac.gc.ca.

45 Mary Hurley, Nisga'a Final Agreement, Parliament of Canada (1999), www.parl.gc.ca; Tom Flanagan, *First Nations? Second Thoughts* (Montreal: McGill-Queen's University Press, 2008; 2nd ed.).

46 CBC News, In Depth: Aboriginal Canadians; BC Treaty Referendum (2004), www.cbc.ca.

47 Agreements, Treaties and Negotiated Settlements Project, Westbank First Nation Self-Government Agreement 2003 (2003), www.atns.net.au.

48 Bruhn and Graham, *In Praise of Taxes*.

49 Interview with Mike Rink, a developer on Westbank First Nation lands.

50 Canadian Taxpayers Federation, Westbank Self-Government Agreement (Bill C-11): Presentation to the Senate Standing Committee on Aboriginal Peoples (2004), www.taxpayer.com.

51 Interview with Tim Raybould from Westbank.

52 Randall Akee, *Checkerboard and Coase: Transaction Costs and Efficiency in Land Markets* (2006), Forschungsinstitut zur Zukunft der Arbeit, Institute for the Study of Labor.

CHAPTER TEN

1 Robert Reiter, "The Constitutional Status of Treaty Settlement Lands," Westbank First Nation Conference (Westbank, BC, 2006).

2 A lawyer with expertise in the Canadian constitution might quibble with this characterization somewhat.

3 Westbank First Nation Conference, "Making or Breaking the Treaty Process: The Constitutional Status of Treaty Settlement Land" (Westbank, BC, 2006).

4 Nisga'a Lisims Government, Nisga'a Nation Entitlement Act – Unofficial Consolidation (2008), www.nisgaalisims.ca; Nisga'a Lisims Government,

The Constitution of the Nisga'a Nation (1998), chapter 3, www.nisgaalisims.ca.

5 Diane Cragg, "Best Practices in First Nations Land Title Systems: Considerations for Improving Land Title Certainty on First Nations Lands" (First Nations Tax Commission, "Improving First Nation Land Title Certainty and Modernizing the Land Registry System," Consolidation of Research, 2007).

6 National Archives of Australia, "Documenting a Democracy: Real Property or "Torrens Title," Act 1858 (SA) (2008), www.foundingdocs.gov.au.

7 Lang Michener LLP, "Best Practices in First Nations' Land Administration Systems," in First Nations Tax Commission, "Improving First Nation Land Title Certainty and Modernizing the Land Registry System," Consolidation of Research, 2008.

8 Cragg, "Best Practices."

9 Ibid.

10 Iowa is the only US state that has all of its land under the Torrens system, and its title insurance costs are significantly less than those in the rest of the country. The Torrens system is now in use in seven Canadian provinces. Use of the Torrens system reduces the need for title insurance in these provinces.

11 Diane Cragg, "The Nisga'a Title System – Why a Torrens Title System Works for a Canadian First Nation," Speech to the 150th Anniversary of the Torrens Title System Land Administration Conference (Adelaide, Australia, 2008).

12 In addition to all three territories, British Columbia, Alberta, Saskatchewan, Manitoba, Ontario, and Nova Scotia have systems that support guaranteed title.

13 Joe Friesen, "Where they Stand: On Aboriginal Issues," *Globe and Mail*, 22 September 2008, www.theglobeandmail.com.

14 Report of the Indian Act Consultation Meeting, Department of Indian Affairs and Northern Development (Kelowna, BC, 1968).

15 The Colony of Vancouver Island adopted a Torrens system of land-title registration in 1861, the second jurisdiction in the world to do so.

16 This is economists' code for when average costs of registration are at a point where the First Nations registrar would be completely self-financing through registration and service fees like similar provincial agencies.

17 Máximo Torero and Erica Field, "Impact of Land Titles over Rural Households" (Office of Evaluation and Oversight, Inter-American Development Bank, 2005), www.iadb.org.

18 Consider the following quote taken from an interview with Hernando de Soto (Dario Fernandez-Morera, Hernando de Soto Interview, 1999, www.reason.com): "Another consequence [of no title to property] is credit worthiness. Everyone talks about creating credit systems for the less privileged. In the United States, up to 70 percent of starting businesses need credit, and they get it on the basis of some kind of real-property collateral. If you have a situation in which 90 percent of Peruvians in a particular sector of the economy do not have title to their property, they cannot get credit."

19 Alan Krueger, "Economic Scene; A study looks at squatters and land titles in Peru," *New York Times*, 9 January 2003, www.nytimes.com.

20 Ross Finnie et al., "Social Assistance Use in Canada: National and Provincial Trends in Incidence, Entry and Exit" (Statistics Canada Research Paper, Catalogue no.11F0019MIE – no. 245, 2005), www.statcan.ca.

21 Rajeev Mathur and Sanchita Chatterjee, "Encouraging Governance and Transparency for Investment" (OECD, Global Forum on Economic Investment, 2003), www.oecd.org.

22 The Canadian Press, "UN Set to Adopt Native Rights Declaration, No Thanks to Canada: Critics," 6 September 2007, CBC News, www.cbc.ca.

23 For a complete description of methods and data see Fiscal Realities Economists, *The Economic and Fiscal Impacts of Market Reforms and Land Titling for First Nations* (prepared for the First Nations Tax Commission, 2007).

24 Parliament of Canada, Standing Committee on Aboriginal Affairs, Northern Development and Natural Resources (37th Parliament, Second Session, 5 February 2003), www.parl.gc.ca.

aboriginal people, 3; as entrepreneurs, 4; and self-government,
6–7
Agua Caliente Tribal Nation (Palm
Springs, USA), 158
Aishihik First Nation (Yukon):
lawsuit on rent, 89; and UFA,
153
Alaska Highway Pipeline Project,
155
Alcantara, Chris, 8, 74
Allen, James: and DIAND, 89
American Indians: concept of
property, 30–1
Anderson, Terry, 52; and "checkerboarding" on reservations, 49;
on land allotment, 45–6
Articles of Capitulation: Article
40, 58
assets: state owned, 26
auditor general: 2003 report on
UFA, 154–5
Aztecs, xii, 180; and land
ownership, 31; and system of
commercial law, 123

Bacon, Francis: The New Atlantis,
50
Bagot, Sir Charles, 62

Bagot Commission: British
assimilation policy, 62
Band Council Resolutions (BCR):
on land allotment, 76–8
bank loans: Six Nations, 95–7
Bank of Montreal, 84, 95–6
Barclay, R.L.: on Johnstone, 73–4
Baron de La Honton: New
Voyages to North America,
(1703), 30
Bay of Quinte Indian Band
(Ontario), 83
Bear, Austin: and FNLMA, 70, 108
Bear, Ed: on FNLMA, 116
Bear, Leroy: on FNLMA, 115
Beecher Bay First Nations (BC):
and FNLMA, 117
Benson, Bruce, Comanche and
buffalo hunting tribes, 36; on
private ownership, 37
Bill C-31: eligibility for federal
funds, 82
Bill C-115 (1998), 144
Black Bear Crossing, 14–15
Blood Tribe (Alberta): and farm-
ing, 81–2; formalization of
customary rights, 76; land use
areas, 78; permits and leases,
100; tribal government, 75

Boyer v. Canada (1986), 105
Bragg Creek (Alberta), 16
British Columbia Hydro and Power Authority: deal with Squamish Nation, 133
British Columbia Land Title and Surveying Authority, 171
British Columbia Land Title Office: and Nisga'a, 165
British Columbia Ministry of Forestry: and Shxwha:y First Nations contract, 118
British Columbia Supreme Court: Calder legal action, 155
British Empire: abolition of slavery (1834), 36
British government, 62; and "Charter of Indian Rights," 59; post-1812 policy towards Indian allies, 60; Royal Proclamation (1763) on Indian property rights, 58–9
British North America Act 1867 (BNAA): passage, 65; Section 91, authority over Indians, 65
"buckshee leases,"84
buffalo: disappearance of, 38
Bureau of Indian Affairs (BIA), 49

Calla, Jason, 130
Campbell River: developable land, 176
Canada, xi–xiii, 3–4; and federal system of divided sovereignty, 27; origins of sovereignty, 26; and taxpayers, xii, 15; and Treaties of Utrecht and Paris, 27
Canadian Forestry Service: and Muskoday First Nations, 115

Canadian government: and "peasant policy," 38
Canadian Mortgage and Housing Corporation (CMHC), 83, 88, 97
Canadian Pacific Railway (CPR), 145
Carlson, Leonard, 32, 47, 52; on Dawes Act, 43–4; on US Southwest agriculture, 33
Carter, Sarah: on private property, 61
certificate of occupation (1890), 67
certificate of possession (1951), 68–9, 91–7; number issued, 91; Six Nations case study, 93–7
Champagne First Nation (Yukon): lawsuits on rent, 89, and UFA, 153; and Westbank First Nation, 157
Charlottetown Accord (1993), 161
Cherokee Nation, 33
Chichen Itza: public infrastructure, viii
Chickasaw, 33
Chief Chris Tom v. Morris (2007), 80
Chinook: trading language, 123
Choctaw Nation, 33
Churchill, Ward, 30
Coke, Richard: Coke Bill, 44–5
collective ownership: and First Nations, 5
collective title: bifurcation of, 24
Collier, John, 50–1
Columbus, Christopher, 30
communism, collapse of, 26
Communist revolutions: in China, 26; in Russia, 26
Comprehensive Land Claim Agreement: and JBNQA, 152

Conference Board of Canada, 4

Conservative Party of Canada: creation of First Nations land title system, 168

Constitution, xi, 9; national jurisdiction and Indian reserves, 27; provincial jurisdiction and natural resources, 27

Cooper v. Tsartlip Indian Band (1997), 80

Corbiere, John: section 58(3), 105

Council of Yukon First Nations: and self-government agreements, 152–3

Cowichan Tribe (BC), 74, 77; buckshee leases, 84; formalization of customary rights, 76; housing, 83; Land Investigation Committee, 79; and Walmart superstore, 100

Cragg, Diane, 35, 164–5; Nisga'a land title system, 162

Creek Nation, 33

Crowfoot, Strator: and FNLMA, 70, 108

Crown, 4–5, 7; granting leases, licenses and tenure, 28; and power of eminent domain, 28

customary rights: communal approach, 85–9; community recognition, 76–8; dispute resolution mechanisms, 78–80; and economic development, 81–4; emergence, 74–9; formalization, 74–7; treatment by Canadian Courts, 80

Dawes, Henry, 44

Dawes Act, 5–7, 11, 42–9, 72, 177; creating self-sufficient Indian farmers, 48; and heirship, 47;

implementation, 46–9; and leasing, 47; origins, 42–6

Dawkins, Richard, 17

De la Casas, Bartolomé, viii

De Soto, Hernando, 7; and individual property rights, 125; *Mystery of Capital,* 160

De Vattel, Emer, 61

Declaration of the Rights of Man and of Citizens (France), 25

Deeds registry system, 163–7

Delgamuuk: and aboriginal title, 27; and Supreme Court of Canada, 65

Deloria Jr., Vine, 30

Demsetz, Harold, 23–4, 40; property rights theory, 31; *Toward A Theory of Property Rights,* 22

Department of Finance: assisting First Nations tax frameworks, 146–7

Department of Fisheries and Oceans: and Sun Rivers proposal, 134–5

Department of Indian Affairs, viii, 4; and certificates of location, 68; Leonard and Maryanne Johnstone, 73; and Mohawk community of Tyendinaga, 126

Department of Indian Affairs and Northern Development (DIAND): advertising success of FNLMA, 118; loan fund, 83–4; and Six Nations, 94–5

Department of Justice: and Squamish Superstore negotiations, 134

Department of National Defense (DND): and Tsuu T'ina, 13–15

Derrickson v. Kennedy (2006), 80

Diamond, Jared, x

Dickason, Olive: on Bagot Commission, 62
Dominion subsidies: to Six Nations in 1908, 126
Donald, Leland, 34

Engels, Friedrich, 25
Epstein, Richard, 16, 18

Federal Court of Appeal, 104; Section 58(3), 105–6
Federal Court of Canada: *Musqueam* case, 102
fee-simple ownership, 125–6
fee-simple title, 5, 28
First Nations, xii, 3–5; and collective rights, x; and community responsibility, vii, ix; and competitive advantage, 140; creativity, xii; entrepreneurial, xii; escaping poverty, 138–51; and government, vii; and GST, 146, 150–1; and lack of private investment, 139–40; and land title system beyond Indian Act, 169–70; and market failure, 123–35; and national institutions, vii, ix; and poverty, xii; and property rights, 4, 7–8, 13; property tax system, 144–5; and restoring property rights system, 160; and standard of living, 3; and traditional methods of redistributing wealth, 126
First Nations Commercial and Industrial Development Act (2005) (FNCIDA), 146, 149–50; and Squamish, 150
First Nations Finance Authority, 149
First Nations Financial Management Board, 149

First Nations Fiscal and Statistical Management Act (2005) (FSMA), xi, 146, 148–9
First Nations Gazette, 145
First Nations Goods and Services Tax Act (2003) (FNGST), 146–7
First Nations Governance Act, 180
First Nations Land Advisory Board, 118
First Nations Land Management Act (1999) (FNLMA), 8, 70–2, 108–19, 146, 148–9; opt out of land sections of Indian Act, 108–9; Section 15, 110; Section 16(2), 110; Section 16(3), (5), and (6), 111; Section 26 (5), 111
First Nations Land Ownership Act (FNLOA): Conservative support, 169; as optional, 170–1
First Nations land registry, 115
First Nations land title system: benefits, 171–5; interest from First Nations, 177–8
First Nations Property Ownership Act (FNPOA), xi, xiii, 29, 119, 138; authors' proposal, 161; questions and answers, 177–80
First Nations property tax, 142–6
First Nations Sales Tax on Selected Products Act (1997 and 1998), 146
First Nations? Second Thoughts, 7
First Nations Statistical Institute, 149
First Nations Tax Commission, 8, 147; report on best practices, 163; "taxation without representation," 179
Fiscal Realities consulting firm, 8; seven steps for development, 128–30; study for Indian Taxation Advisory Board, 130

fishing rights, Pacific Coast Indians, 34
Five Civilized Tribes, 38
Flanagan, Tom, 7–8
Fordism, 128
Framework Agreement on First Nations Land Management, 109
French Revolution: abolition of feudalism, 24
Friesen, Joe, 168
fur trade, x, 38

General Allocation Act, 42. *See also* Dawes Act
General Council Memorandum (GCM): and Six Nations, 94
George III: Royal Proclamation and Indian property rights, 58
George v. George (1996), 80
Gonthier, Charles: ruling in *Musqueam Indian Band v Glass*, 102
Goodall, Jane, 17
Goose, Rennie, 112
Gore, Al: *Earth in the Balance*, 30
Government of Canada: apartments for Tsuu T'ina, 15; pay compensation for expropriation, 21; and property ownership, 20–1; and UFA settlements, 163
Gradual Civilization Act (1857), 63–5; enfranchisement, 64
Gradual Enfranchisement Act 1869 (GEA), 65
group ownership, 19–20

Haimila, Wayne, 160
Haldimand Grant (1784): land allotment to Six Nations, 93
Hardin, Garrett: *The Tragedy of the Commons*, 22

Harris, W.E, 68
Harvey Barracks, 13–14
Hayek, Friedrich, 16, 19, 26
Health Canada, 14–15
Hill, Elias: enfranchisement, 64
Hofer v. Canada (2002), 98
Hume, David, 16
Huron: farming, 32–3

Indian Act, vii, xii, 4–5, 74; "band lands," 134; efforts to reduce its influence, 138; first Indian-led amendment, 144; historical evolution, 57–72; and investigating real estate transaction costs, 130; and leases, 5, 81, 97–106; 1918 amendment, 127; and 1988 Kamloops amendment, 127; property rights under, 91–106; replacement by Federal legislation, 141–2; Section 18, 28; Section 21, 94; Section 24, 92, 96; Section 28 (2), "permits," 97–8; Section 38 (2), 100; Section 58 (I) (b), 104; Section 87, 92; Section 89, 92, 101
Indian Act, 1850: four main provisions, 63
Indian Act, 1876: debate and passage, 66–7; sections 5–10, 66–7
Indian Act, 1951, 68–70; section 29, 69, 92
Indian Affairs (INAC), 15; and certificates of possession, 80; minister not accountable to First Nations, 29
Indian lands: exempt from taxes and seizure, 65
Indian policy: and Bagot Commission 62–3; pre-

Confederation, 57–9; after war of 1812, 60–3

Indian Reorganization Act (IRA), 42, 50–4; passing, 47–8

Indian reservations, pressure to privatize, 43; protection, civilization and assimilation, 63–4

Indian Taxation Advisory Board (ITAB): established, 144

Indians, 4, 9; British and French policy, 57–8; concept of land ownership, 31–4; decline in US population, 43; as fishers, 34–6; as hunters, 37–40; as natural communists, 30–1; non-status, 3, 14; and property rights, 40–1; reservations, 4–5, 8; and salmon fishing, 34–6; shift to agriculture, 38; status, 14; "white man privileges," 65

Indians Land Registry, 163–4

individual ownership, 19

individual property rights: and expansion of government, 25; as a human right, 25; and UN constitution, 25

individual rights: ownership, 11; and property, 8

Inuit: concept of territorial rights, 39–40

Iroquois: allied to French, 57

Irwin, Ron, 70, 108

Joe v. Findlay (1987), 80

Johnsen, Bruce, 35

Johnstone, Leonard, 73–4

Johnstone, Mary Anne, 73–4

Joseph, Chief, vii, xi

Judicial Committee of the Privy Council, 27, 59, 143

Jules, Clarence: as "market hero," 124–5; and 1968 White Paper, 124

Jules, C.T. (Manny), 7–8, 29; on property taxes, 143

Kamloops, x, 144; and development study, 130

Kamloops Indian Band Council, x, 124; and GST, 146

Kehoe, Alice: on Locke, 60

Kitimaat Indian Band, 137

Lac la Ronge Indian Band (Saskatchewan): funding from DIAND, 83–4

Laird, David, 66

Lake Mohonk Conference of Friends of the Indian, 43

Lamer, Antonio, 145

Land Membership Committee (LMC): and Six Nations, 94

land ownership, 4

Lands Advisory Board: and FNLMA, 148, 150

Langevin, Hector, 65

Laurier, Wilfred, xiii

Le Dressay, André, 7–8, 160

leases, 97–103; long term, 100–4; property rights in Indian Act, 97; short term, 97–100

Leclerq, Chrestien: on the Attikamek, 39

Leeson, Nelson, 160

LeJeune, Paul: on the Montagnais, 39

Leonard v. Gottfriedson (1982), 80

Liberal Party of Canada: creation of First Nations land title system, 168

Linton, Ralph, 32
Locke, John, 16, 22; concept of private property, 60–1
Lone Wolf Case (1903), 53
Louie, Robert, 108; and FNLMA, 70
Lueck, Dean, 49

MacMillan v. Augustine (2004), 80
Mannpar Enterprise Ltd. v. Canada (1992), 98
Maracle v. Grant (2008), 80
Markets: failure on First Nations land, 123–35; historical accounts, 123; as social institutions, 123
Martin, Paul: and FNCIDA, 149
Marx, Karl, 25; Marxist fantasy, 41; primitive communism, 30
Master Development and Servicing Agreement: and Sun Rivers development, 135
Matsqui First Nation: and Canadian Pacific Railways, 145
Mayans, viii, ix, xii, 123, 180
McChesney, Fred: Indians as private owners, 52–3
Métis, 3
Mill, John Stuart, 16
Millbrook Indian Band v. Northern Counties Residential Tenancies Board (1978), 98
Mississaugas of Scugog Island (Ontario): case study on FNLMA and economic development, 110–13
Mistawasis First Nations (Saskatchewan): and certificates of possession, 73–4

Mitchell-Tweedie, Thomas: Indians as "wards of the state," 127
Mohawks of Kahnawake: and certificates of possession, 97
Mohawks of Tyendinaga (1875): tax system, 126
Montagnais (Quebec and Labrador): trapping rights, 38–9
Morgan, Willis, 137
Morin v. Canada (2002), 103
Moses, Don, 137
Mount Paul Industrial Park, 124
Muskoday First Nations (Saskatchewan): case study on FNLMA and economic development, 113–17
Musqueam: and developable land, 176
Musqueam Indian Band v. Glass (2000), 101–4

Nacho Nyak Dun First Nations (Yukon): and UFA, 153
natural resources, 3; and provincial jurisdiction, 27
natural rights, 16
Nipissing First Nations (Ontario): and FNLMA, 118
Nisga'a: and features of title system, 165–8; fee-simple ownership, 53; and Final Agreement Act (2000), 155; and Land Committee (1890), 155; and ownership, 34; and self-government agreement, 152–3, 155; and Torrens system, 163–8
Nisga'a Land Title Act (2000), 162
Nisga'a Nation Entitlement Act, 162

Nunavut Land Claims Agreement, 4

Opasquiak Cree Nation (Manitoba), 6
Osoyoos First Nation (BC), 158

Pacific Coast Indians: and property, 34–6; and slavery, 36
Pareto economic outcome, 21
Parliament, Canadian, 7, 21
Past civilizations: concept of zero, viii; crops, viii; downfall, x; individual property rights, ix; market structure, ix; trade language, ix
Paul v. Paul (2008), 80
Peru, viii; and First Nations home ownership, 173
Phillip Joe, x, 137
Piikani Nation: and farming, 81–2; and housing, 83; Lands Committee, 79; occupation rights and utilization privilege, 78; permits and leases, 99; tribal government, 75
Pipes, Richard, 23
Plains Indians: and property, 37
Pointe, Stephen, 168
Powell, John Wesley, 44
Prentice, Jim, 15
private property: introduction of Western concept, 42
process mapping, 128
property: duality of, 22–6
property rights: collective, 24; of First Nations, 26–9; and impact of agriculture, 24; individual, 19; private, 16–17; reform of, 6; voluntary approach, 5, 11
Proudhon, P.J.: "property is theft," 18

Real Canadian Superstore: and Squamish land development, 132–4
Redwood Meadows, 16
Report of the Royal Commission on Aboriginal Peoples: and UFA, 153–4
Richard, Greg: paper on First Nations land title systems, 172
Riel, Louis, 13
Roback, Jennifer: on allotment, 46
Roosevelt, Franklin, 51
Royal Bank of Canada, 95–6

Sack, Robert: *Human Territoriality*, 17
Sandberg, Don, 6
Sandy Lake Nation (Ontario), 74–7; formalization of customary rights, 76
Seattle, Chief, 30
Secwepemc, xiii–ix, 123; as Kamloops Shuswap people, 134; and Sun Rivers development, 134–5
Seven Years War, 58
Shuswap Memorial, xiii
Shxwha:y First Nation (BC): and FNLMA, 117–18
Siksika Nation: and buckshee leases, 84; and housing, 82–3; land dispute mechanism, 79–80; and Land Use Agreement, 78
Simcoe, John Graves: prohibition of slavery, 36
Siska First Nation: and Canadian Pacific Railway, 145
Six Nations (Ontario): certificate of possession system, 91–7; Lands Membership Committee, 94; Lands Membership

Department, 93–5; reserve lands register, 94

Squamish First Nations (BC): and developable land, 176; and development, 132–3; Stitsma Holding Ltd., 133; and tax jurisdiction, 144

Squamish Nation Council, 133

Smith, Bud, viii

St Catherine's Milling Case (1888), 59, 143; land reverts to Crown, 27

St Martin v. Canada (1998), 103

Standard of living: and access to natural resources, 140

Sun Rivers Golf Course: and land development, 134–5

Supreme Court of Canada: and Canadian Pacific Railway, 145–6; *Musqueam* case, 102; *Opetchesaht* case, 100, and precedent on 38 (2), 102

Surrey v. Peace Arch Ent Ltd. (1970), 97

Taylorism, 128

Teller, Henry: on Dawes Act, 44

Teslin Tlingit Council (Yukon): and UFA, 153

The Pas, Manitoba, 6

Thompson, Jill, 113

Torrens, Sir Robert, 163

Torrens Land Title System (1858), 163

Torrens registry system, 160–1, 163–8; contrasted with deeds system, 163

Torrens title system, xi, 25; land registry, 53; registry system, 29, 125

Transaction cost analysis: and development process on Indian reserves, 128

Treaty of Paris (1763), 27, 58

Treaty of Utrecht (1773), 27

Treaty 7 First Nations, 89

Trigger, Bruce, 32

Trudeau, Pierre: and White Paper, 155

Tsartlip doctrine, 106

Tsartlip Indian Band v. Canada (1999), 100

Tsawwassen First Nation: and FNLMA, 118

Tsuu T'ina Indian Band Council, 15

Tsuu T'ina Nation (Sarcee), 13–15; leadership, 16

Tulo Centre of Indigenous Economics, 145, 171

Umbrella Final Agreement (UFA): and Yukon First Nations, 153

Union of BC Indian Chiefs: 1975 Chilliwack meeting, 137

United Nations: criticism of Canada, 175

United States: allotment legislation, 44–6; civil war and slavery, 33; and Dawes Act, 7–9; government allotments under treaties, 42–3; and Indian nations farming, 33–4; ranchers, 20; and tribal courts, 87

Usher, Peter, 39

Walkem, Forrest, x, 137

Watts v. Doolen (2000), 92

Weight, Edmond, 160

Westbank First Nation Constitution, 156

Westbank First Nations (WFN), 102–5; and developable land, 176; and GST, 146; largest First Nation tax base, 156; local legal framework, 129; and self-government agreement, 152, 155–8; and tax jurisdiction, 144; use of Section 58 (3), 105

Westbank First Nation Self-Government Act, 156

Westbank Indian Band v. Normand (1994), 92

Wheeler-Howard Act, 51

White Paper, x; Trudeau era, 177

Whitecap Dakota First Nation (Saskatchewan), 158; and FNLMA, 118

Williams et al v. Briggs (2001), 80

World War II, 13

Yukon Agreement, 154

Yukon Association of Non-Status Indians, 153

Yukon Native Brotherhood, 153

Yukon Territorial Government, 153

Yurok (Northern California): conception of property, 36